Exploring United States History

A READER

Volume I • From Discovery Through Reconstruction

Edited by

Thomas M. Camfield

Joseph M. Rowe, Jr.

Sam Houston State University

KENDALL/HUNT PUBLISHING COMPANY
2460 Kerper Boulevard   P.O. Box 539   Dubuque, Iowa 52004-0539

• The following articles are reprinted from *American Heritage* magazine by special permission of American Heritage, a division of Forbes Inc.:

Alberts, Robert C., "Business of the Highest Magnitude, or Don't Put Off Until Tomorrow What You Can Ram Through Today," © 1971 by American Heritage, a division of Forbes Inc., February, 1971, pp. 48–53 & 101–103.

Billington, Ray Allen, "The Know-Nothing Uproar," © 1959 by American Heritage, a division of Forbes Inc., February, 1959, pp. 58–61 & 94–97.

Brant, Irving, "Timid President? Futile War?" © 1959 by American Heritage, a division of Forbes Inc., October, 1959, pp. 46–47 & 85–89.

Burwell, Basil, "A Man for All Souls," © 1971 by American Heritage, a division of Forbes Inc., December, 1971, pp. 13–16.

Carson, Gerald, "A Tax on Whiskey? Never!", © 1963 by American Heritage, a division of Forbes Inc., August, 1963, pp. 62–64 & 101–105.

Catton, Bruce, "Hayfoot, Strawfoot!" © 1957 by American Heritage, a division of Forbes Inc., April, 1957, pp. 30–37.

Donald, David, "Why They Impeached Andrew Johnson," © 1956 by American Heritage, a division of Forbes Inc., December, 1956, pp. 21–25 & 102–103.

Fleming, Thomas J., "A Scandalous, Malicious and Seditious Libel," © 1957 by American Heritage, a division of Forbes Inc., December, 1967, pp. 22–27 & 100–106.

Froncek, Thomas, "Winterkill, 1846: The Tragic Journey of the Donner Party," © 1976 by American Heritage, a division of Forbes Inc., December, 1976, pp. 29–41.

Ketchum, Richard, "England's Vietnam: The American Revolution," © 1971 by American Heritage, a division of Forbes Inc., June, 1971, pp. 6–11 & 81–83.

Ketchum, Richard, "The Thankless Task of Nicholas Trist," © 1970 by American Heritage, a division of Forbes Inc., August, 1970, pp. 12–15 & 86–90.

McGann, Thomas F., "The Ordeal of Cabeza de Vaca," © 1960 by American Heritage, a division of Forbes Inc., December, 1960, pp. 32–37 & 78–82.

Nevins, Allan, "The Needless Conflict," © 1956 by American Heritage, a division of Forbes Inc., August, 1956, pp. 4–9 & 88–90.

Oates, Stephen B., "Children of Darkness," © 1973 by American Heritage, a division of Forbes Inc., October, 1973, pp. 42–47 & 89–91.

Oates, Stephen B., "The Slaves Freed," © 1980 by American Heritage, a division of Forbes Inc., December, 1980, pp. 74–83.

Plumb, J. H., "America—Illusion and Reality," © 1976 by American Heritage, a division of Forbes Inc., August, 1976, pp. 14–25.

Robbins, Peggy, "God, Man, Woman, and the Wesleys," © 1984 by American Heritage, a division of Forbes Inc., April/May, 1984, pp. 96–103.

Welles, Arnold, "Father of Our Factory System," © 1958 by American Heritage, a division of Forbes Inc., April, 1958, pp. 34–39 & 90–92.

Wensyel, James W., "The Newburgh Conspiracy," © 1981 by American Heritage, a division of Forbes Inc., April/May, 1981, pp. 40–47.

Winston, Alexander, "Firebrand of the Revolution," © 1967 by American Heritage, a division of Forbes Inc., April, 1967, pp. 61–64 & 105–108.

Graphics by permission of Metro Creative Graphics, Inc., 33 West 34th Street, New York, New York 10001.

Contents

Preface

Although largely an acquired taste, interest in history is also an inherent trait of human beings, developing with self-consciousness and out of curiosity about one's self and others, about time and events. For those of us enamored with the study of the past, it seems a natural, meaningful, and important human activity.

For human history to be fully appreciated, it needs to be studied in its grand sweep over the centuries and, at the same time, in its minute detail. History survey courses at the university level are primarily intended to introduce students to the major themes, trends, and developments of peoples and nations. Such courses, and the textbooks used in them, necessarily focus on the sweep of events at the expense of detailed examinations of particular persons, topics, or events.

This volume is intended to supplement a survey course textbook for the early period of United States history. It has been prepared in an effort to assure that our survey course students are exposed to detailed treatments of selected people and events, thereby perhaps acquiring an appreciation of this aspect of historical study. The articles we have chosen come from among the many superb pieces of scholarship which have appeared over the past forty-odd years in *American Heritage,* one of the nation's finest popular history journals. We think they offer the student an excellent sampling of the varied, rich and exciting history of the United States and its people.

Thomas M. Camfield
Joseph M. Rowe, Jr.

Part One • The Colonial Period

In the long span of human history, few events have equalled in importance the discovery of the Western Hemisphere by Christopher Columbus. That discovery set loose a three hundred year competition among all the vigorous nations of Western Europe for control of the territories and exploitation of the resources of the New World. And nothing before in history had so aroused the curiosity or excited the imagination of man. America soon represented all things to all men, and as J. H. Plumb points out in his article, ''America: Illusion and Reality,'' the image was often in sharp contrast with the reality. However, compared with the reality of life in the Old World, the New World with all its warts not only attracted a steady stream of settlers, but also influenced many aspects of life in the Old World.

By the middle of the 16th century, Spain had established her control over the Caribbean, Mexico, Central America, and most of South America. Although she claimed North America as well, she had little more than a weak hold on the Gulf Coast, the Southwest, and the West Coast. In the rest of her American empire, Spain's success in extracting the wealth of her colonies made her the envy of the civilized world.

Spain's conquests were the result of strenuous and heroic efforts by conquistadors and clerics, seeking the harvest of riches and the harvest of souls. But not all such ventures were successful. In his article, ''The Ordeal of Cabeza de Vaca,'' Thomas F. McGann tells the tale of hardship and survival among Spanish Adventurers who explored the Gulf Coast of North America.

As other European nations tried to emulate the success of Spain, their quest was confined necessarily to those areas which had not fallen completely under Spanish control, namely, North America. During the 17th century, the French established themselves in Canada; the British spread along the eastern seaboard; the Dutch and Swedes managed nothing better than a weak toehold along the Hudson and Delaware Rivers respectively. In the period which followed, a period which might be described as competitive co-existence, the Dutch and Swedes were swallowed up by the British, the French extended their activity beyond the Great Lakes and into the Mississippi River valley, and the Spanish empire entered into a period of gradual decline. When the final showdown for control of North America came in the middle of the 18th century, the French lost out to England, leaving the British with the dominant position in that part of the hemisphere.

Our attention, as students of United States history, centers on the English colonies in North America, those colonies which would eventually form the United States of America. Here we find a pattern of colonization that was somewhat unique. The thirteen colonies planted between 1607 and 1732 were mostly corporate or proprietary enterprises. Since there was little or no mineral wealth in the region, colonists came to seek what was beyond their reach in England or Europe, land and opportunity. Or they fled from religious, political, or economic oppression. As Peggy Robbins reveals in her article, "God, Man, Woman, and the Wesleys," some religious leaders came to America consumed with zeal to work among settlers and Indians, often with unfortunate results. In the case of the Wesleys, they left their congregations wishing for freedom from religion rather than freedom of religion. All too frequently, religious convictions were compromised by the hard conditions of life in America. Obligations of Christian charity often failed, especially toward the Indians. But in his inspiring story of John Woolman, "A Man for All Souls," Basil Burwell tells about a man who remained true to his convictions only to pay the price of scorn and rejection by his neighbors.

America: Illusion and Reality

J. H. Plumb

America was an experience man could only have once. Knowledge of China, knowledge of Africa, festooned as it was with the Spanish moss of myth and legend, had penetrated Europe from the days of Imperial Rome and beyond. When discovered, the animals of Australasia were stranger by far than America's, and the aborigines and the bushmen of Tasmania were more primitive, even more uniformly naked than the Caribs whose appearance was so startling to Columbus. By then the strangeness of the Americas had destroyed the sense of novelty. There could only be one New World.

When confronted by novelty, men try to domesticate what is strange and alien; they attempt to fit the exotic into their cherished intellectual schemes and to absorb it into their interpretation of the world and its past. They retain, as it were, a husk of strangeness in which to take delight, or to weave fantasies, or worse still to construct rationalizations of their own evil intentions. The discovery of America had all of these effects and more, for no event in the history of Western man provided so profound a shock to the imagination or to the mind. And yet one might argue that the most important results of this discovery were far more mundane—maize, tobacco, gold, fur—the never-ending abundance of the land that led to the rape of a continent which became a golden pasture for human locusts.

Columbus, amazed, unsure, reluctant to accept that he was *not* in the Indies, found it easier to fit the Caribs into the legend of the Golden Age. As Peter Martyr, the friend of Columbus, wrote in the early 1500's, they ''seem to live in that golden world of which old writers speak so much, wherein men lived simply and innocently without enforcement of laws, without quarrelling, judges and libels, content only to satisfy nature.'' This was the beginning of that ever-lengthening legend of the innocence of America which shifts from island to the mainland, from Caribs to noble Indian chiefs. It took many centuries to die; indeed, it is hardly dead yet, for nowadays the innocence has been transferred to the wilderness, to the desert, to the primitive land still unscarred in the West.

The theory that the naked Caribs lived in innocent bliss was soon dispelled. The Spaniards learned with horror that the Caribs hung up the hams of men and women to cure in the sun like sides of bacon. They relished the taste of human flesh; for them it was a gourmet's revenge on an enemy. When the Spaniards began to root themselves inefficiently in Hispaniola, the denizens of the Golden Age rapidly became subhuman. The Spaniards stressed their cannibalism, their nakedness, their fornication, and their frequently deviant and public sexuality. This savage paganism made their salvation imperative and their servitude justifiable.

The Caribs wanted neither salvation nor servitude. Killed, hunted, tortured, beaten, and worked to death, they soon began to vanish, until genocide was virtually accomplished. Today scarcely any remain, but before they almost totally disappeared they had woven themselves into the imagination of Europe, as Hugh Honour has shown us in his recent book *The New Golden Land,* which is a brilliant discussion of the way the discovery of America haunted the European artistic imagination.

These Caribs, however, did more than stimulate the imagination. The brutal treatment accorded to them unleashed the passion of Bartolomé de Las Casas, whose bitter pen damned Spanish cruelty to a believing world of French, British, Germans, and Dutch—who, however, behaved no better themselves once they got a foothold in the New World. But Las Casas' fiery words and the undeniable truth of his tale of the brutalities, the killing, the torturing, and the wholesale destruction of primitive peoples started an enduring theme in America's history that still resonates in our own day. It is a long, bloody, bitter, and sad road that leads from Hispaniola to the slaughter at Wounded Knee or the atrocities in the forests of Brazil. Innocence and betrayal, fascination and disgust, illusion and reality, these have so often been the dual response of Europeans to the primitive peoples of America.

The discovery of America led to an appalling destruction of human life—probably over twenty million died in a half century—a fact all too rarely depicted in the artistic vision of America. It was the strangeness, the exotic nature of the people, the ornaments, their color that entranced the artist. They might pose them like classical heroes, but they dressed them in their own feather headdresses and feathered skirts or left them stark naked. For the first two decades these natives remained amorphous, exotic yet somewhat unreal, like strange Europeans. Many artists who painted them had never seen an Indian, although from Columbus' first voyage a few men and women had been ripped from their homes to be displayed as curiosities in the courts of Europe.

It was only quite late in the sixteenth century that Indians were depicted more accurately, placed in more exact settings, and their customs, dances, and villages shown with some appreciation of reality. John White's water colors of the Indians of Virginia, among whom he lived briefly in 1585–6, show greater precision and accuracy, even though he refrained from depicting the more primitive and savage of their customs. A Frenchman, Jacques Le Moyne, had been far more candid in his sketches of Florida Indians, but true realism had to wait until the seventeenth century, when two fine Dutch painters—Frans Post and Albert Eckhout—painted Brazilian landscapes and people ex-

actly and vividly. And yet the art of fantasy in European paintings of Indians was not
eradicated for centuries; even Delacroix in the early nineteenth century could paint Indians who looked like well-bred Europeans in fancy dress. The tradition of realism
started by John White developed more slowly and only reached its apogee with Catlin,
Bodmer, and Rosa Bonheur, just before the genocide of the Indians had begun in
earnest.

It was not only the exoticism of the people that both entranced and horrified
Europeans. Columbus had gone in search of riches, of the fabulous Cathay. The
Spaniards wanted gold. And they found it, bountifully in Mexico and beyond their
wildest hopes in Peru; and the gold in the end led to the mountains of silver in Potosi
and Taxco. This success in the search for riches came slowly. There were very barren
decades, so that every object that was rich and exotic to look at was valuable as
propaganda in the courts of Europe, which had to finance the early voyages of exploration and colonization. So the splendors of Central and South American civilizations
were soon on their way to Europe—the great golden disks, the brilliant featherwork
cloaks, the terrifying death masks in jade and greenstone, works that when Albrecht
Dürer saw them in Brussels made him marvel at "the subtle *ingenia* of men in foreign
lands."

To the emperors they were indicators of riches to come, not works of art, and the
golden vases, fountains, and animals that passed into the course of Charles V were
quickly melted down for the money he always lacked. The feather cloaks were thrown
away or left to rot in the attics of his palaces. Only a few men of taste or of obsessive
curiosity found a home for them in their cabinets, and today only a handful of objects
survive from the first century of European discovery.

Among the earliest collectors to appreciate the singularity and beauty of Mexican
art were the emperor Ferdinand I (who died in 1564) and his two sons; the extraordinary Rudolph II, a patron of everything exotic; and not surprisingly, perhaps, the
greatest family of art patrons in Italy—the Medici, who as early as 1539 had brought
together, as Hugh Honour reminds us, forty-four pieces of featherwork as well as carved
masks and animals in semiprecious stone. Perhaps the strangest fate of any American
object in the sixteenth century was that of a Mexican obsidian disk that fell into the
hands of John Dee, Queen Elizabeth I's astrologer and magician, who used it to conjure
up spirits. It was, however, the common objects, novel to Europe yet totally adaptable,
that were most quickly diffused—the first being the hammock, unknown to European
gardens and ships until discovered in the West Indies; equally adaptable but later in
time came the canoe of the American Indians and the kayak of the Eskimos.

Just as amazing to Columbus as the inhabitants of the West Indies were the flora
and fauna of the New World. Some, of course, were easy to assimilate. The rather sub-
dued colored parrots of Africa had been greatly prized possessions of the Europeans in
the late Middle Ages, but the brilliant colored parrots of Brazil rapidly replaced them.
These were represented as early as 1502 in Europe and appeared in a painting by Car-
paccio, the Venetian artist, as early as 1507. Along with hummingbirds and Mexican

quail, they were used as brilliant decorative motifs in the Loggetta of Raphael at the Vatican.

Hugh Honour has demonstrated the astonishing speed with which the artists of the Renaissance seized upon American birds and animals as well as Indians to use as dramatic motifs in their painting and sculpture. The turkey—now the all-pervasive Christmas dish of English families—reached Europe almost as quickly as the parrot. It was bred in Spain shortly after 1500, and the bird had reached Britain by 1525. Ironically, a hundred years after its discovery by Columbus the turkey had reached the East Indies. But it was the odder birds and animals that excited the most curiosity—the iguana, which was thought to be a dragon, discovered at last; the armadillo, whose true nature baffled scholars for decades; the opossum, which was the first marsupial known to Europeans; and the tapir and the llama, both of which defied description.

More important than the attempt to describe and to draw the birds, animals, and plants was the impact of their variety on the development of European botany and zoology. Knowledge of the new animals had reached Europe, along with specimens, from time to time. The rhinoceros had made a vivid impression on Europe, but Europeans had never been subjected to such a flood of wholly new birds, animals, fruits, vegetables, trees, and flowers as they were from the New World between 1500 and 1550. And it was this variety, its strangeness, and, at times, its marvelous adaptability and usefulness that led to the beginning of a scientifically precise observation—indeed, the beginning of botany and zoology as we know them.

The flora had a far greater impact than the birds and animals, so few of which could be domesticated. Maize, which could easily be grown in Europe, was exploited at once; within ten years of its discovery it was being cultivated in Italy, where it transformed Italian agriculture. Similarly, cassava, which reached West Africa very shortly after the Portuguese discovery of Brazil, had a like dramatic effect. The potato, which took far longer to establish itself as a crop rather than as a curiosity, ultimately had a more profound effect on European history than maize. The high nutritious quality of the potato enabled the European, particularly the Irish peasant, to maintain himself and his family on tinier and tinier garden plots. Millions of men and women depended on a single crop, and the disastrous potato blight of the nineteenth century destroyed the population in a monstrous famine in 1845 and, in an ironic twist of history, sent tens of thousands of starving Irish to find a new life and a new hope in America.

The contributions of the flora of the Americas to the enrichment of Europe is nearly endless; foods such as tomatoes, tapioca, chocolate, pineapples, avocados, runner beans, Jerusalem artichokes, passion fruit, and many more; flowers now common in Europe, such as morning-glory, nasturtium, dahlia, and the tobacco plant, the most dangerous and deadly of all the plants to reach not only Europe but the entire globe, certainly one of the greatest of all hazards to human health. It was thought oddly enough to be deadly and dangerous when first discovered, and no one damned it with greater vehemence than James I of England. But the habit of smoking proved contagious and the profit impossible to resist. The land of America was quickly ravaged by

Europe's addiction to tobacco—and not only America but also Africa, whence came the slave labor needed for its intensive cultivation. What in 1570 was depicted as a delicately beautiful flower decoration of Albrecht V of Bavaria's prayer book became in less than fifty years a major export for America and a sweeping addiction with traumatic economic and social effects on Africa and Europe.

The potato and tobacco, along with maize, are perhaps the best known of the vegetables that changed the eating and social habits of Europe. What, perhaps, is not such common knowledge is that the great movement in landscape gardening that changed the face of the English countryside in the eighteenth century also owed a great deal to America, above all to Virginia. The Virginian oak was planted by the hundreds of thousands; so were a large number of American pines; and the *Magnolia grandiflora* became the prize possession of even small gardens. Without the influence of America the English landscape would look quite different today.

However, the mental image of America remained more powerful than the influence upon European artistic expression of its exotic people, plants, and animals, and surely matched even the influence of such exceptional material agents as maize, the potato, or tobacco. America remained for centuries the only New World. When the northern colonies established the first federal republic, at whose birth the liberties and rights of men were proclaimed as inalienable, another New World was born, as potent as that discovered by Columbus. A new political world had come into being, utterly distinct from anything Europe had known before—and one that created as entrancing an illusion as the civilizations the conquistadors had discovered.

To the poor and downtrodden peasants and workers of Europe it held out a new hope, a glittering image of riches and freedom. It is easy to forget the bitterness and brutalities of the ghettos of Europe or the starvation and deprivation that the wretched villagers of Greece and Italy suffered. It was their despair that eventually drove them to the coffin ships in which thousands died as they made the Atlantic crossing. The reality they found in America was harsher: hunger stalked on the Lower East Side; once more deprivation for many became part of their lot in life. And yet there *was* a reality in the illusion. There was more liberty, more social hope in America than in the lands they had quitted. There still is, in spite of the black ghettos and the long-enduring memory of slavery. The destruction of primitive peoples and slavery are the harsh realities of the American experience, for whose nakedness the Constitution, with its proud declaration of liberty, proved so pathetic a rag. So often illusion provided hope, reality the fate. And yet whatever the American experience might be, it remained for most Europeans an exotic continent.

After Buffalo Bill's fabulous success small boys in Riga, in Manchester, in Lyon, in Milan, played for generation after generation at cowboys and Indians; in the twentieth century Hollywood provided the dreams for the masses, and Disney captured the imagination of the child. No longer a fairyland of exotic peoples, animals, and plants, America has created a new world of fantasy.

In the lives of children, in the dream time of adolescents, even in the sexual expectations of the adult world, America still feeds Europe with its illusions. As with the illusions of the past, a harsher reality is always breaking in: the drugs, the dropouts, the divorces. Perhaps the tobacco plant with its vivid flowers, intoxicating scent, and deadly leaves should be the enduring symbol of that strange combination of illusion and reality with which America has continued to haunt Europe since its discovery.

The Ordeal of Cabeza de Vaca

Thomas F. McGann

A crude boat carrying forty exhausted Spaniards drifted close to the long Texas beach. "Near dawn it seemed to me that the tumbling roar of the sea could be heard. Surprised, I called the boatswain and he replied that we were near the coast. We sounded and found ourselves in seven fathoms. It seemed to the boatswain that we ought to keep to sea until sunrise and I took an oar and pulled on the land side until we were a league offshore. Then we turned the stern to the sea. Near the land a breaker took and threw the boat the cast of a horseshoe out of the water. With the violent blow almost all the men, who were like dead, came to themselves and seeing the beach near they began to climb from the boat and crawl on hands and knees to some ravines where we made fire and toasted some corn that we had brought and drank some rain water that we found. The heat of the fire restored the men and they began somewhat to exert themselves. The day that we arrived here was the sixth of the month of November." The year was 1528.

Thus Álvar Núñez Cabeza de Vaca* of Jerez, treasurer of the ill-fated Narváez expedition, which had set out from Spain in June, 1527, with five ships and six hundred men to explore and settle the lands between Florida and Mexico, tells how he came with his few remaining companions to the unknown land of Texas. Years before De Soto and Coronado entered what would become the United States, he was to make one of man's great land journeys, crossing Texas and Mexico from the Gulf to the Pacific Ocean with two other white men and a Negro slave.

The Narváez expedition had bad luck from the beginning: bad luck in its commander, the rash Pánfilo de Narváez, who in 1520 had lost an eye in a fight that occurred when, at the behest of the governor of Cuba, he had attempted to halt Cortés' march to the interior of Mexico; bad luck at Santo Domingo, the first New World port

---

*The name Cabeza de Vaca means, literally, "head of a cow." The King of Spain bestowed it upon an ancestor after the battle of Las Navas de Tolosa in 1212. This man was a shepherd who had marked with a cow's skull a trail by which the Spanish were enabled to outflank and defeat a Moorish army.

of call, where 140 men quit the expedition; bad luck in Cuba, where the ships were scattered by a hurricane and sixty men and twenty horses were lost.

The expedition spent the winter of 1527–28 in Cuba, took on fresh recruits and horses, and sailed in the spring for the little-known shores of Florida. On April 14—Holy Thursday—the five vessels anchored at the mouth of what was probably Tampa Bay. Here Governor Narváez—the title was one often granted by the crown to would-be conquerors—made his most important decision, and so insured the destruction of his expedition. He divided his force. The bulk of his men he took ashore and with them set out northward toward the place which the Indians called Apalache; there, they said, the Spaniards would find much gold. The ships were ordered to run along the coast, and were supposed to meet the men marching by land at a vague rendezvous. That rendezvous was never kept. After a year of fruitless searching along the coast, the ships returned to Cuba.

The three hundred men making up the land party, each with two pounds of hardtack and half a pound of bacon, struggled along the coast of Florida, battling Indians all the while. When, late in June, they reached Apalache (perhaps near Tallahassee), the Spaniards found a few huts, corn, and hostile natives, but no gold. The invaders pushed inland, but hunger, sickness, and frequent attacks by the Indians made their march a nightmare.

In desperation Narváez turned back to the coast and called a council. Cabeza writes:

> We agreed on a remedy most difficult to execute, which was to make boats in which to depart. This appeared an impossibility to all, for we knew not how to do this work, nor were there tools, nor iron, nor a forge, nor oakum, nor resin, nor rigging. . . . But God willed it that one of the company should say that he could make some wooden tubes which, with deerskins, would serve as bellows . . . and we agreed thus to make from our stirrups, spurs and crossbows and the other things of iron that we had, the nails, saws, axes and other tools of which there was such need. . . . We agreed that every third day we would slaughter a horse to be divided among those working on the boats and the sick.

On September 20, five boats were ready, each thirty-three feet long, calked with palmetto fiber and pitched with pine resin. From palmetto fiber and the horses' tails and manes the men made rope and rigging, and from their shirts, sails. They flayed the horses' legs entire and tanned the skin to make water bottles.

Two days later, they ate the last horse. Leaving behind more than fifty companions who had died of disease or wounds, some two hundred and fifty survivors crowded into the five frail vessels and sailed from the place they called the Bay of Horses. They followed the shore line to the west, confident, in their ignorance of geography, that before long they would find safety among their countrymen in Mexico.

But the sea was as perilous as the land. The gunwales of the boats almost awash, their corn supply almost exhausted, the horsehide water carriers rotten and useless, the

Spaniards groped along the coast, stopping to beg or to fight the Indians for fish and water. Maddened by thirst, some men drank salt water and died. One day the voyagers came to the mouth of a broad river whose current drove the boats away from the shore, but repaid the men with fresh water. It was the Mississippi.

The five boats were blown out to sea by a howling north wind and became separated. At vespers, Cabeza saw two of the boats. His men drew near to one of them, that of Governor Narvaáez, who told Cabeza that he was going to try to reach the shore, and that the treasurer could do the same if he wished. Cabeza replied that in his opinion they should first try to join the third boat, which was farther at sea. But Narváez's boat began to pull toward the distant land. Cabeza writes:

> I, seeing his will, took my oar, as did all those in my boat who were able to do so, and we rowed until almost sunset. But the Governor had the strongest and healthiest of all the men in his boat and we could not by any means follow or keep up with him. Seeing this, I asked him to give me a line from his boat so that we could follow him, but he replied that it would be no small thing if they themselves were able to reach land that night. I told him that since he saw the small chance that we had of following him and of doing what he had ordered, he should tell me what it was that he would have me do. He answered that now was not the time for one man to command another, and that each one should do what seemed best to save his own life, and that that was what he intended to do, and saying this, he drew away in his boat.

Cabeza and his men joined the other boat. They sailed together for four days until another storm separated them. Of the crew, only Cabeza and the boatswain had enough strength to work the boat; only they heard the roaring breakers which hurled them upon the Texas shore that day early in November, 1528.

After the castaways had eaten what little corn they had salvaged, Cabeza ordered one of the men, Lope de Oviedo, to climb a tree to survey the country. Oviedo reported that they were on an island. Cabeza sent him off to look around, and Oviedo found some empty Indian huts not far away and took from them a dog, some fish, and a pot and started back to his companions. Cabeza meanwhile had sent two men to search for him.

> They came upon him nearby, and they saw that three Indians with bows and arrows were following him and calling to him and he likewise was beckoning them on. Thus he arrived where we were, the Indians remaining a way back, seated on the shore. Within half an hour, some one hundred Indian bowmen joined the first three, who now, whether they were large or not, our fears caused to seem like giants.

Thus, probably a few miles below the present city of Galveston, on a desolate island now joined to the mainland by the sea's powerful action and called Velasco Peninsula, Indians and white men met. This first meeting of Europeans and natives in the southwest of the United States was peaceful. The Indians brought fish and roots to the starving strangers, receiving trinkets in return. After resting a few days the Spaniards decided to try to re-embark. They dug their boat out of the sand, stripped off their clothes and put them in it, and with much exertion launched the vessel. Two crossbow shots from shore they shipped a wave that soaked and chilled them. Another wave struck the boat, and it capsized, drowning three men who clung to it; the others were tossed again by the breakers upon the beach.

Naked, the Spaniards huddled among the dunes, chilled by the north wind—the norther that carries the cold of the Great Plains across Texas and deep into Mexico. Here the Indians found them once more, and so sad was the plight of the white men (with two of their dead lying among them) that the Indians sat down upon the sand and howled their ritual lamentation. The natives brought the castaways to their huts and warmed and fed them and then danced all night, to the terror of the Europeans, who feared that they were being prepared for sacrifice.

The next day some fifty more Spaniards came into camp. Led by Andrés Dorantes and Alonso de Castillo, and including Dorantes' slave, the Negro-Moor Estevanico, these survivors of the expedition had been wrecked a few miles up the beach the day before Cabeza's boat had gone ashore.

Together the Spaniards agreed to launch the boat of Dorantes and Castillo. The men who had the strength and will might go in it; the others would make their way along the shore; and all would seek the land of Christians.

This attempt to flee the island also failed. The boat was launched, but it sank immediately. Marooned without provisions and with cold weather coming, the Spaniards decided to winter on the island. But they picked four men from the ranks—all four strong swimmers who might be more successful than some of their companions in crossing the wide bays, lagoons, and rivers—and sent them on down the coast in an effort to reach the Spanish settlements in Mexico.

Cold and stormy weather swept the island; the Indians could catch no fish and dig no roots; the flimsy huts gave no shelter; death came. Five Spaniards living apart in one hut became cannibals, ''until only one remained who, being alone, there was no one who might eat him.'' Of the more than eighty Spaniards who had come to the island, soon only fifteen remained alive. Then half the Indians died of a stomach sickness.

The Spaniards named this place Malhado—Bad Luck Island. But with the help of the Indians, the fifteen Europeans survived. These Indians were naked, except for ''the women, who covered their bodies somewhat with a wool that grows in the trees.'' The men were large and well-formed; they pierced their lower lips and sometimes their nipples with pieces of cane. They treated their children mildly, engaged in prolonged, lachrymose funeral rites, and had taboos against in-laws. Their beliefs involved the foreigners in a practice which in the end was to save the lives of some of the hapless group. ''They wished to make us physicians, without our taking examinations nor asking us for our diplomas,'' Cabeza wrote.

They cure illness by blowing on the sick, and with that breath and the placing on of hands they cast out the sickness, and they ordered us to do the same and to be useful to them in some way. We laughed at that, telling them that it was a farce and that we did not know how to cure. For this they took away our food until we did as they told us. . . . The manner in which we cured was by blessing them and breathing on them and by praying a Pater Noster and an Ave Maria and by supplicating as best we could God our Lord that he might give them health. . . . God our Lord willed in His clemency that all those for whom we had prayed (and after we had blessed them) told the others that they were sound and healthy. Because of this they treated us well, and they did without food in order to give it to us, and they gave us skins and trinkets.

In the spring of 1529, the Spaniards separated. Two, Lope de Oviedo and Alaniz, remained on Malhado because they were too weak to travel. Cabeza had earlier been isolated from his fellows, for he had been taken to the mainland by some of the Indians during the winter and there had become desperately ill. Thirteen (one more Spaniard had appeared during the winter) started off toward Mexico. Cabeza's illness prevented him from joining his companions in their journey; he was left behind, the lone white man, so far as he knew, on the vast and unexplored mainland of North America above Mexico.

For Cabeza de Vaca this was the beginning of four years of prolonged hardship, a period that called on all the castaway's courage and vitality. He suffered bad treatment from the Indians and from nature. "Among many other tasks, I had to get out roots to eat from under the water and from among the reeds where they grew in the ground and from this my fingers were so worn that they bled if a straw touched them, and the reeds, many of which were broken, tore my flesh in many places." Hunger and cold beset him. Sometimes he was alone, without even Indian companionship; at other times he was no more than a slave.

To free himself from dependence upon his Indian masters and to learn more about the surrounding country, Cabeza gradually set himself up as a trader between his tribe and others of the region, traveling among the often hostile Indians to exchange the shells, sea beans, and goods from the coast for the skins, ocher, and flints of the interior.

Each year Cabeza returned to Malhado to visit Lope de Oviedo, hoping to persuade his comrade, who was now the only white man on the island, to depart with him in search of Christians. Not until 1533 did Oviedo agree. He could not swim, but Cabeza managed to get him to the mainland and across the first four rivers which they encountered. Down the coast near a great bay the two Europeans came upon other Indians who told them that farther on there were three men, two of whom looked like the Spaniards. These Indians also knew of the fate of other members of the expedition who had come that way more than four years earlier. All had died of cold or hunger or had been killed by the natives—for sport or in obedience to omens which had come to the Indians in dreams.

Cabeza and Oviedo waited there by a river (probably the Guadalupe) because these natives told them that the strangers who looked like themselves would soon be brought by their Indian captors to the river, where the tribes gathered to eat the nuts which grew plentifully on the trees lining the banks. While Cabeza and Oviedo waited, the natives abused them, slapping them and holding drawn arrows against their chests and telling them that they were going to be killed. Oviedo's courage failed him, and he decided to return to Malhado. Cabezo implored him to remain but he would not; he turned and went back with some Indian women who had come with him from Malhado, and disappeared from history.

Two days later Alonso de Castillo and Andrés Dorantes, and Estevanico, his slave, were brought by their Indian masters to the "place of the nuts," and the four men rejoiced much at finding each other alive.

The Spaniards agreed that they must conceal from their captors their desire to escape. They plotted to stay with these Indians, and to wait until the coming of summer when the tribe that held them prisoners would move to the prickly-pear grounds to feast on tunas, the purple fruit which grows from the edges of the flat-leaved, spiny cactus. To the tuna grounds came natives from distant places; with them the Spaniards might continue their flight to the south and west. Cabeza and the others were taken as slaves by various Indian families; but before being separated from his comrades he heard from Dorantes the story of the fate of the eleven men who had left Malhado for Mexico with Dorantes and Castillo four years before, when Cabeza had been too ill to accompany them. Cabeza also learned what had become of others of the expedition who had come ashore in their rickety boats.

Thirteen had left Malhado in 1529. Six died (four by drowning) during their march along the coast. During this journey of approximately 180 miles, the survivors had come upon another Spaniard, Figueroa. He was one of the four men who had been sent ahead from Malhado in the first weeks after the wreck of Cabeza'a and Dorantes' boats to try to reach Mexico and bring assistance to the castaways wintering on the desolate island. Figuero told Dorantes that two of his companions had died of starvation and exposure; the Indians had killed the third.

But there had been yet another Spanish survivor in the land, one Esquivel, to whom the Indians had brought Figueroa. Esquivel had described to him how his boat had been wrecked far back along the coast and how he had been found by Narváez, who had employed his own boat in ferrying the men from Esquivel's boat over difficult stretches of coast. But, "one night the Governor did not wish to go ashore and a coxswain and a sick page remained with him. In the boat there was neither water nor anything to eat and only a stone for an anchor. In the middle of the night the norther came up so strongly that it took the boat out to sea without anyone observing it and they never learned anything of him again." The survivors of the boats of Narváez and Esquivel had struggled for life along the shore as their comrades were doing elsewhere on the coast, but these castaways too began to die during winter; the living dried the flesh of the dead and ate it, until only Esquivel remained.

Dorantes later learned from the Indians what had become of Esquivel. He "had wished to run away because a woman had dreamed that her son had to kill him and the Indians went after him and killed him and they showed Andrés Dorantes the sword and beads and book and the other things he had." Figueroa, who had encountered Esquivel, himself became separated "farther down the coast" from Dorantes and the survivors of the group of thirteen, and no more was ever heard of him. All the others, after the journey from Malhado, were enslaved by the Indians and then killed, except Dorantes and Castillo and Estevanico.

For more than a year the three Spaniards and the Negro lived as slaves of their Indian masters. These Indians fed mainly on the roots, but also ate spiders, worms, caterpillars, lizards, snakes, and ant eggs. ("I believe," Cabeza writes, "that were there stones in the land they would eat them.") Though Cabeza describes them as thieves, liars, and drunkards, they were at the same time "a merry people, considering the hunger they suffer." The women did the camp labor. The men were tireless runners and could follow a deer from morning to night. Sometimes the Indians set afire the grass of the plains to aid in capturing game and to drive away the intolerable hordes of mosquitoes that swarmed in the summer.

> Cattle came here, [Cabeza states] and I have seen them three times, and partaken of them. It seems to me that they are the size of those of Spain. They have small horns . . . and very long hair, flocky, like a merino's. Some are tawny, others black, and it seems to me that they have better and fatter meat than those of [Spain]. From the smaller ones the Indians make blankets to cover themselves, and from the larger ones they make shoes and shields. They come from the North over the land to the coast, spreading out over all the country more than four hundred leagues, and along their route and the valleys by which they come, the people who live nearby descend upon them and live off them.

Thus, the first description left by a white man of the American buffalo.

When the summer of 1533 came, the Spaniards and the Negro were brought by the Indians to the prickly-pear fields (most likely south of San Antonio). Before the prisoners had a chance to escape, the Indians fell to quarreling and took up their lodges and left. The four Christians (for Estevanico was a Christian) were denied by this dispute an opportunity to escape, and were separated once again, to spend another year in captivity.

After the passage of these hard months, the Indians reassembled to gorge on the tunas. The strangers gladly joined in feasting on the juicy, pear-shaped fruit. "There are many kinds of tunas," Cabeza tells, "among them some which are very good, although all of them seemed so to me, for hunger never game me time to choose." By no means all the land was covered by cactus: "Throughout the countryside are very large and fine pastures of very good grass for cattle and it seems to me that it would be a fruitful land if it were worked and inhabited by civilized people." Here the four men learned that they were indeed the last survivors of the Narváez expedition, for "the Indians told us that there were other Indians farther on, called Camones, who lived near the coast. They had killed all the men who had come in the [fifth boat from Florida], who had arrived so enfeebled that they could not defend themselves even when being killed."

As the moon grew full in September, 1534, the Spaniards and the Moor slipped away from their masters. Not far off they came upon another tribe, the Avavares, who received them well. "That same night of our arrival some Indians came to Castillo and told him that they had great pains in their heads, and begged him to cure them. After he had blessed them and commended them to God, instantly the Indians said that the evil had left them and they went to their houses and brought many tunas and a piece of venison."

Winter was not far off, and the natives told the Spaniards that the country ahead was poor in game and abandoned by the Indians in the cold months. The travelers decided to remain where they were. They stayed with the Avavares for eight months; during most of that time they were in great want.

> We went naked in that land, and since we were unaccustomed to that, in the manner of serpents we cast our skins two times each year. The sun and the air made great sores on our chests and backs, which pained us much because of the large, heavy loads which we carried. Often, after we brought wood from the thickets, blood ran from our bodies in many places. . . . Sometimes, when it was my turn to get wood, and after it had cost me much blood, I was not able to bring it out, either by carrying or dragging. When I found myself in such labors I had no other remedy or consolation but to think of the Passion of Our Redeemer, Jesus Christ, and of the blood that He shed for me, and to consider how much more serious was the torment from the thorns which He suffered than that which I was suffering. Sometimes the Indians would order me to scrape and soften hides, and the greatest good fortune that I had there was the day in which they gave me something to scrape, because I scraped very much and I used to eat those scrapings and they would sustain me for two or three days.

Castillo and, increasingly, Cabeza were obliged to attempt cures upon the Indians. The white men did so fearfully, and with many prayers that God might indeed make their ministrations effective. The Indians, at least, always responded favorably, including one man whom Cabeza restored to health, although he had "all the appearances of death."

Cabeza describes many of the customs of the tribes with whom he and his companions lived and among whom they traveled (probably between the Colorado River and the Rio Grande in southern Texas) when they resumed their journey in 1535. Children were suckled until they were twelve years old; this was often the only nourishment they could be given. Quarrels in the tribe were settled with fists and clubs, not bows and arrows, and were followed by a period during which the contestants went to live apart from the tribe. In enemy territory at night the Indians dug trenches around their camp; thus concealed, they were ready to fight surprise with surprise. Emerging from their huts in the dark, they crouched down to escape detection; this also gave them a chance to observe any unfamiliar object that might stand out against the sky. In battle they bent low and leaped about to escape enemy arrows.

He who would fight the Indians, Cabeza warned,

> should be advised that they show no weakness nor covetousness for their goods. While war lasts they have to be treated rigorously, for if they discover fear or covetousness in others they are men who know how to take the opportunity for vengeance and they take strength in the fear of their adversaries. . . . They see and hear better and have keener senses than any men I know of in the world. They are great in withstanding hunger and thirst and cold, as though they were more accustomed to these and made for them more than other men.

In the last spring or early summer of 1535 the wanderers started again on their quest for Mexico. Now the pattern of their lives changed. They had acquired a reputation as medicine men, and as they moved from tribe to tribe those whom they visited met them with rejoicing; those left behind wept. Their diet also changed, although not for the better: now they ate beans of the mesquite tree, mashed and mixed with water and earth.

Perhaps at this stage of their journey they crossed the lower Rio Grande and entered Mexico. They were still lost, and still hundreds of miles from the nearest Spanish settlements to the south at Pánuco. But their march took on the character of a triumphal procession, or at least that of a successful traveling medicine show. At each village the Indians crowded around them, brought children and the sick to be touched and cured, and then escorted the travelers to the next settlement.

> [So] began another novel custom: those who accompanied us began to act badly, taking the goods and looting the houses of those who received us so well, without leaving anything. It worried us greatly to see those who received us well badly treated, and also we feared that this would cause dispute . . . but the Indians who lost their goods, knowing our sadness, consoled us, telling us that the matter should not grieve us but that they were so content to see us that they considered their goods well bestowed, and that farther on they would be repaid by others who were very rich.

When the wanderers came in sight of the mountains of northeastern Mexico, they made what seems a strange decision. They turned from the coastal plain and headed inland, away from the direct route to the Spanish settlements. Cabeza gives the reason for this change: fear of the evil disposition of the coastal Indians, in contrast to the good treatment received from the inland tribes. Cabeza also hints that these indomitable men swung away to the west and north in search of that discovery of untold riches, that conquest of fabled cities, which had eluded them since they had sailed from Spain eight years earlier.

Perhaps also they took pleasure in their prosperity and power. Laden with gifts, which they distributed as fast as they were received, and exercising such authority over the awed and superstitious Indians that none dared to take a drink of water without permission from the strangers, the four wandered on. Their followers engaged in chain-reaction plundering while extolling to the plundered their own example and the magical powers of the Children of the Sun.

Along river valleys and across mountain ridges they went west and northwest through northern Mexico. The land was rugged and dry, except in the verdant valleys. The natives continued their attentions, presenting the strangers with ceremonial rattles and a bell of copper, and introducing them to piñon tree. In this country the travelers were given corn flour. And Cabeza worked a true cure (of his other ''cures'' he was always careful to point out that the Indians *believed* that they had been cured). He operated on an Indian who had been shot by an arrow, removed the arrowhead from deep in the man's chest, and with a deer bone as a needle sewed up the wound.

Now they had roast quail and venison to eat and rabbits killed by throwing-sticks, and they blessed the food of the crowds of natives who frequently accompanied them. On they went, crossing ''a great river,'' probably the Rio Grande again, near the Big Bend; then, after journeying 250 miles through dry, rough country, they again forded ''a very large river,'' having come back once more to the Rio Grande, farther north. Here they saw the first habitations that looked like houses rather than huts, and the Indians gave them corn, pumpkins, and beans.

The Indians' superstitious fear grew as the journey went on, until the Spaniards themselves began to pray that the terrorized natives would not flee, abandoning their new-found alien gods in the wilderness. Despite their fear, the Indians continued to care for the strangers and to hand them on from tribe to tribe as they moved westward toward a land reported to be rich in maize.

The years had hardened the four men physically and confirmed them in their faith.

We used to walk all day without eating until night, and we ate so little that the Indians were astonished to see it. . . . We possessed much authority and influence with the Indians, and in order to preserve these we seldom spoke to them. The Negro always spoke to them, keeping himself informed of the routes we wished to follow. . . . We passed through a great many [peoples of] diverse tongues; with all of them Our Lord God favored us, for they always understood us, and we them. We asked and answered questions by signs as well as though they spoke our language and we theirs, because, although we knew six languages, we were not able to use them everywhere, there being a thousand variations. In all those lands those who were at war made peace so as to come and to receive us and to bring us all they possessed. In this manner we left the land in peace, and we told them by signs which they understood that in Heaven there was a man Whom we called God, He Who had created Heaven and Earth, and we adored Him and held Him as Our Lord, and that we did as He commanded us and that all good things come from His hand and that if they did thus all would go well with them. Their comprehension was so great that had we had a language by which we could have made ourselves perfectly understood we would have left them all Christians.

Week after week they walked westward from the Rio Grande, across northwestern Mexico, over the passes of the Sierra Madre, down the western mountain valleys toward the coast, into a land of relative plenty where there were corn and beans, fixed habitations, and cotton cloth. The Indians brought the Spaniards corals from the Gulf of California and turquoises that came from a land of lofty mountains and large buildings far to the north—the Pueblo country of Arizona and New Mexico. In one town Dorantes was presented with six hundred open deer hearts; this place they named Corazónes. It was near what is now Ures, in Sonora, "the entrance into many provinces on the South Sea."

It was the spring of 1536. There were no other Christians, nor rumors of them, here in the unexplored far northwest of Mexico.

To the south the wanderers made their way, threading the valleys between the mountains and the ocean. One day, while waiting for a rain-swollen river to subside,

> Castillo saw at the neck of an Indian the buckle of a sword belt and stitched to it a horseshoe nail. We took them and we asked the native what they were: he told us that they had come from the sky. We questioned him further as to who had brought them thence. They all replied that some men who wore beards like us had come from the sky and arrived at that river, bringing horses and lances and swords, and that they had lanced two [Indians]. With as much dissimulation as we could attain we asked them what these men had then done. They replied to us that they had gone to the sea and put their lances beneath the water and that they themselves had gone beneath the water and that afterward they saw them go on the surface toward the sunset. We gave many thanks to God, Our Lord, for what we heard, for we were despairing of ever hearing of Christians.

The four hurried on with their retinue. News about the other Christians became frequent, but it was bad news, at least for the Indians. The fertile countryside deserted, the villages burned, and the remaining inhabitants hidden in the mountains—all told of a Spanish slaving expedition from across the frontier of European settlement to the south. Still the four travelers were joined by awed Indians bearing gifts; still the Indians who had come with the four men from as far as three hundred miles back along the trail continued to journey on, assured by Cabeza of his protection.

Signs of Christians became numerous. Only the day before, some Indians reported to Cabeza, they had seen them. On the morning of the next day, near the Petatlán River (now the Sinaloa), Cabeza

> came upon Christians on horseback, who received a great shock to see me, so strangely dressed and accompanied by Indians. They stared at me a long time, so astonished that they neither spoke to me nor drew near to question me. I told them to bring me to where their captain was . . . and I asked him to give me a certificate of the year and the month and the day on which I had arrived there and the manner in which I came, and thus it was done.

By the Sinaloa River, not far from the Pacific Ocean and about one hundred miles north of the border settlement of San Miguel, the odyssey of Cabeza, Dorantes, Castillo, and Estevanico ended. The Indians accompanying the gods did not wish to abandon them until they had been conveyed into the safekeeping of other Indians; nor did these Indians wish to lose their protectors, for fear of the other white men.

Cabeza relates that the slave-hunting Christians

took offense at this and made their interpreter tell [the Indians] that we were like themselves, and that we had been lost a long time, and that we were people of no account, and that they were the lords of that land, who had to be obeyed and served. But all this that was said to them the Indians reckoned as little or nothing, and conversing among themselves they said that the Christians lied, because we came from where the sun rises, and they whence it sets; that we healed the sick, while they killed the sound; that we came naked and barefooted, while they came clothed and on horses and with lances; and that we were not covetous of anything, but at once all that was given to us we gave away and we remained with nothing, while the others had no aim but to rob everything they found and never gave anything to anyone.

Cabeza finally persuaded the Indians to return to their homes and fields, and he thanked them and dismissed them in peace. With an escort the four travelers started on their way to Mexico City. But their efforts to protect the natives from the slave-hunters had endangered their own lives. Only the arrival of a well-disposed higher official saved Cabeza and the others from possible death at the hands of their own countrymen. At the request of this official, Cabeza and his companions pacified the frightened and rebellious Indians of the country through which they passed.

From the border settlement of San Miguel they pushed on three hundred miles to Compostela, where the cruel governor of the province resided; then another five hundred miles to Mexico City. There they were joyfully received and honored by the viceroy, Mendoza, and by the conqueror Cortés. The harsh imprint of their journey was still upon them, for Cabeza tells that it was some time after returning to the land of Christians before he could stand the touch of clothes upon his body, or sleep anywhere but upon the ground.

Cabeza reached Spain the following summer, but by 1540 he was again in the New World, now as governor of Paraguay. Political difficulties led to his recall and imprisonment; he returned to Spain and obscurity until his death, perhaps in the 1550's.

Castillo and Dorantes settled in Mexico.

It was the Negro Christian from North Africa, Estevanico, who died like the conquistador he was. Incited by the rumors of civilizations and treasures in the unknown lands to the north of the regions crossed by Cabeza and his companions, Viceroy Mendoza sent out an expedition led by Fray Marcos de Niza. Its guide was Estevanico. Carrying the medicine rattle which he had picked up on his journey from the Atlantic to the Pacific, the Negro-Moor from Azamor, on the coast of Morocco, was killed in 1539 by Indians in the Pueblo country of New Mexico. He had blazed the trail that would be followed, a year later, by Coronado.

An associate professor at the University of Texas, Thomas F. McGann specializes in the history of Latin America. He is the author of Argentina, the United States and the Inter-American System, 1880–1914, *and many articles, including "Prescott's Conquests"* (AMERICAN HERITAGE, *October, 1957).*

For further reading: The Journey and Route of Alvar Núñez, Cabeza de Vaca, *by Cleve Hallenbeck (Arthur H. Clark Co., 1939);* The Narrative of Álvar Núñez Cabeca de Vaca, *edited by Frederick W. Hodge (Scribner's, 1907);* The Odyssey of Cabeza de Vaca, *by Morris Bishop (Century, 1933).*

God, Man, Woman, and the Wesleys

Peggy Robbins

The success of John and Charles Wesley in founding Methodism is well documented, but what is seldom mentioned is that they started their ecclesiastical careers with a period of unrelieved bungling. It all took place in colonial Georgia in the early eighteenth century when the Wesley brothers, as the colony's founder, Gen. James Oglethorpe, said, attempted to "unroll their rolled-up rules for England" in this struggling young settlement. John and Charles' adventure, Oglethorpe concluded disgustedly, should be made "a play or tale of."

Yet it was with Oglethorpe and at his insistence that the Wesleys went to Georgia. On December 10, 1735, the general's flagship, *Simmonds,* and a second ship, *London Merchant,* escorted by the sloop of war HMS *Hawk,* left the shores of England with settlers bound for Georgia, a colony that had been chartered in 1732. Oglethorpe had established a settlement there to provide a home for persecuted religious sects, imprisoned debtors, and other unfortunates. Aboard the *Simmonds* were thirty-two-year-old John Wesley and his brother Charles, four years younger. At the time Oglethorpe thought the two clergymen were the most important passengers. On his return to England from Georgia the year before, he had told his fellow colonial trustees that the settlement's most urgent needs were spiritual guidance for its inhabitants and missionary service for the Indians.

Oglethorpe was an old friend of the Wesley family: Samuel Wesley, rector of Epworth, and the rector's eldest son, another Reverend Samuel, had helped to promote his original colonization plan and to select candidates for emigration—but neither had suggested that the younger sons, John and Charles, go along. Indeed, the younger Samuel, who had paid for Charles's education, bitterly opposed his brother's agreeing to go on Oglethorpe's second trip. The father had died in April 1735, before Oglethorpe had approached John and Charles about the mission. Their mother, Susanna, did not side with her son Samuel in the family argument. When John, her fifteenth and favorite child, hesitated, she told him, "Had I twenty sons, I should rejoice that they were all so employed, though I should never see them more." Charles, her eighteenth and last child, got the same maternal prod, but it was John's persuasion that most influenced Charles's decision.

Oglethorpe's selection of John and Charles Wesley, "progeny of a Race of Preachers," was widely approved in England. Four months before his sixth birthday John had been miraculously saved from a fire that destroyed the family rectory—"a brand plucked out of the burning." His father saw the rescue as God's sign that John was "intended for a Great Purpose," and the boy was educated to fulfill whatever the purpose might be. At Christ Church College at Oxford a friend described him as "a very sensible, active collegian, baffling every man by the subtleties of his logic . . . a young fellow of the finest classical tastes, of the most liberal and manly sentiments, gay and sprightly, with a turn to wit and humor." John was ordained a deacon of the Church of England in September 1725 and began preaching; a few months later he was elected a fellow of Lincoln College, and in September 1728 he was ordained a priest.

Charles Wesley, "a bright, rollicking young fellow with more genius than grace," had entered Christ Church College in 1726. At first he had preferred writing poetry and attending the theater to religion: he "objected to becoming a saint all at once." But many years later, looking back on his undergraduate days, he declared that his "diversions" had kept him "dead to God, and asleep in the arms of Satan." John dismissed such statements by Charles as "unpardonable exaggerations."

When, in 1729, John was recalled to Oxford to teach, he found his brother had lost his eagerness for Satanic diversion. Now a bachelor of arts and a college tutor, Charles had gathered around him a small circle of students so serious-minded that local wits referred to the group as the "Holy Club." When Garrett Wesley, a wealthy, childless relative in Ireland, offered to adopt Charles so that the young man could inherit his estates, Charles refused. This didn't much surprise anybody: as a friend remarked, "All the Wesley men are eccentric—devout, learned, superior, but eccentric."

Charles immediately and eagerly turned leadership of the Holy Club over to John, who promptly organized the members into a "Society" and drew up rules and regulations for their living "in a manner more regular and systematic" as they "promoted each other's intellectual, moral and spiritual improvement." The new movement stressed intense Bible study. Charles Wesley recorded that the "harmless nickname of Methodists" was bestowed upon the society by the university community "because of the members' strict conformity to a prescribed method of study." The term had been used before to denigrate dissension, but John Wesley liked it; he defined a Methodist as "one that lives according to the *method* laid down in the Bible."

In 1735, after John had bound himself to go to America with Oglethorpe as "Minister to Savannah and Missionary to the Indians" at a salary of fifty pounds a year, his younger brother agreed to go as secretary to the governor. The Reverend Dr. John Burton, one of the Georgia trustees, insisted that Charles take his religious orders before leaving so that Oglethorpe would have two "full clergymen." Charles was reluctant. "I took my degree, and only thought of spending all my days in Oxford," he recalled years later. "But my brother, who always had the ascendant over me, persuaded me to accompany him and Mr. Oglethorpe to Georgia. I exceedingly dreaded entering into Holy Orders but he over-ruled me here also, and I was ordained deacon by the Bishop of Oxford, and the next Sunday, priest by the Bishop of London."

How poorly fitted Charles was to his secretarial post is indicated by his diary entry after his first day of writing letters for Oglethorpe: "I would not spend six days more in the same manner for all of Georgia."

In a letter to Dr. Burton, John explained why *he* was going: "My chief motive is the hope of saving my own soul. I hope to learn the true sense of the Gospel of Christ by preaching it to the heathen." The prospect of the venture was distasteful to him— which was precisely why he had to go. He was convinced that the self-denial and discomforts, sacrifices, and dangers involved would be mighty factors in the soul-saving process.

John and Charles Wesley were both short and slight, but they were handsome young men. John, according to one account, was "a prince charming . . . his countenance was singularly impressive and arresting." Charles was "fair-haired, with sunny blue eyes and fresh Saxon complexion." He was "softer" than his older brother, and he "had a musical mind and a voice of true beauty."

From the beginning the brothers found the stormy Atlantic forbidding, but they "unrolled their Holy Club rules" and determinedly organized their days. They rose at four each morning, prayed privately for an hour, then read from the Bible for two hours with two friends who had sailed with them: twenty-three-year-old Benjamin Ingham, the youngest member of the Oxford Holy Club, and twenty-one-year-old Charles Delamotte, son of a London sugar merchant, who was a great admirer of John. At seven each morning the Wesleys ate breakfast, after which they conducted public prayers; all the eighty English passengers were urged to be present, but usually only thirty or forty turned out. The entire day until nine each night was meticulously segmented, with duties, all related in some way to soul-saving, assigned to each segment.

During one daily period Charles wrote sermons and John studied German. John felt it was necessary that he learn the language of the twenty-six Moravians, German emigrants whom the Georgia trustees had given free passage aboard the *Simmonds* as religious refugees. He also attended the German's public service each night at seven.

The Wesleys ate dinner at one o'clock and from then until four read to and instructed the passengers. At four there were evening prayers, after which "the children were catechized and instructed before the congregation." Then there was another period of private prayer, another period of public reading, this one with attention to individual passenger needs—as the clergymen saw those needs—and on and on until bedtime. The Wesleys were determined to "improve every soul on board"—including themselves. They consumed no meat or wine and limited their diet to rice, vegetables, and biscuits. John made a minor step up the ladder to Heaven by learning to "sleep well on the hard floor."

Oglethorpe was soon faced with complaints that the preachers were overzealous. Many passengers strongly objected to the public cabin being taken over for religious services so much of the time. An uneducated servant woman complained that John read to her for nearly two hours from books she did not understand and that he refused to believe she did not like it. Several young married women who John said were "giddy" fussed about "being exhorted to night and day." Charles Wesley, the passengers said, "flounced and bounced" too much as he "pursued sinners," and he was too sure he knew what was good for everybody.

John Wesley wrote in his diary, "All the people are angry at my expounding so often"; he added that he would continue to expound until all were "convinced and affected." One passenger was so angry at the Wesleys' interference with his life that he decided to interfere with theirs: he danced on the deck above their cabin between twelve and one o'clock for several nights, keeping them awake.

Oglethorpe soothed the complainers as best he could, partially by providing a place between decks for some of the prayer and reading sessions that had previously monopolized the public cabin. He gave the *Simmonds* passengers short respites from the Wesleys by taking the two with him when he was rowed over to the *London Merchant* to check on the welfare of its passengers. The busy preachers did as much soul-saving on the second ship as time and circumstances allowed.

Oglethorpe did not interfere with the Wesleys' "methods of salvation"—except when John dared to reprove *him* for "talking too much to the women." The handsome, gallant soldier at first took the admonition good-naturedly—and continued his attentions to certain of the ladies aboard. But when John rebuked him again, Oglethorpe told him in no uncertain terms to confine his shipboard efforts to the colonists. The preacher noted in his diary that he had begun most earnestly praying for the founder of Georgia.

To the Wesley brothers, one experience of the voyage stood out as the most wonderful. They were very frightened during the storms at sea, and their fear puzzled them. John, after being terrified when a wave rolled over part of the ship and nearly drowned him, asked himself, "How is it that thou hast no faith, being still afraid to die?" A few days later the ships were caught in a hurricane. While the English screamed and whimpered in terror, the Moravians calmly sang songs of praise. When the gale died down, John exclaimed to one of them, "Were you not afraid, and were your women and children not afraid?" "I thank God, no," came the answer. "None among us is afraid to die." John talked at length to the English passengers of the "Germans' calm born of great faith." That night he wrote wistfully in his diary of discovering people who had overcome fear.

The Wesleys, bachelors who had had no experience women of questionable character, felt they had a duty to save the souls of several "women of the world" aboard the *Simmonds*. John concentrated his efforts on Mrs. Hawkins and Mrs. Welch. Lively, daring, young Mrs. Hawkins was the wife of the doctor being sent to the colony; she had such a shady reputation that the lenient Georgia trustees had almost rejected the couple as colonists, finally accepting them only because of the need for a doctor. Mrs.

Welch, a friend of Dr. and Mrs. Hawkins, was crude in speech and manner; she was pregnant, sick, and quarrelsome.

The two women eased the boredom of the voyage by pretending John Wesley was leading them from their sinful paths. His diary, page after page, tells of his progress in saving their souls. Mrs. Hawkins in particular put on a good show; she wept aloud and proclaimed that she knew, from her "close conversations" with John Wesley, that God had sent him to her.

Ingham and Delamotte recognized that the women were playing an ugly game; they knew from experience that Mrs. Hawkins was actually flirting with John Wesley. Charles, too, soon caught on, but none of them could convince John that his two penitents were actually amusing themselves at his expense. He was surprised when the women, resentful because he had remained blind to their charms, became hostile toward the end of the voyage. They had several times fought over the preacher during the journey; now they resolved together to have revenge upon the "holy Wesleys" once Georgia was reached.

On February 6, 1736, the travelers arrived at Savannah, a village of some two hundred houses and over five hundred inhabitants. Oglethorpe, the Wesleys, and the Moravians, on going ashore, gave thanks to God for a safe voyage, but not many of the other newcomers bothered. The Wesleys were very conscious of being strangers in a strange land, but they got busy with their job. When John Wesley returned to the *Simmonds* on an errand, he found that some of the crew and passengers who were on board waiting for temporary camps to be prepared were celebrating the end of the voyage by getting drunk—illegally so, as the statutes of the colony forbade the consumption of alcoholic beverage. He promptly staved in the casks of rum—which may have been the first incidence of the enforcement of prohibition in America.

In spite of the animosity shown him by Mrs. Hawkins and Mrs. Welch on the voyage, the gullible preacher did not give up. Soon after arriving in Savannah, he read to Mrs. Hawkins from *The Life of God in the Soul of Man*. He was disappointed because the "serious effect" it had on her "quickly vanished in light company." The Moravian minister with whom he lodged until his parsonage was prepared counseled him to let Mrs. Hawkins alone and quietly "commend her to God," advice that he did not heed. Charles Wesley decided to apply himself to the salvation of Mrs. Welch, whose ribald manner he attributed largely to the evil influence of Mrs. Hawkins. Mrs. Welch remained "all storm and tempest."

After a week, Oglethorpe, Charles Wesley, Ingham, and the majority of the new colonists—four small boatfuls—including the Hawkinses and the Welches, went to Frederica, a new settlement on St. Simons Island, about one hundred miles south of Savannah. John Wesley and Delamotte remained at Savannah.

John began his ministry to the town with a sermon on charity delivered to a noisy crowd in the courthouse, which served as church. He soon had his schedule for "regular and proper living" worked out—Sunday, for instance, was divided into morning service at five, sermon and Holy Communion at eleven, children's catechism session at two, another service at three, and then a meeting for "reading, prayer, and praise." He attended the Moravian service at six and then studied.

John even studied Spanish so he could converse with a few Spanish Jews. He later worked special services for the Italian and French into the schedule, and from the beginning he conducted prayer services in two neighboring settlements on Saturdays in French and German. He and Delamotte also established day schools. When some of the boys who wore shoes and stockings laughed at the ones who had to go barefoot, John went barefoot himself until he had "cured the lads of their vanity."

John Wesley expected all in his parish—saints and sinners—to adjust to his schedule. He had either forgotten or he ignored the advice Dr. Burton had given him before he left Oxford: to "consider the settlers as babes in their progress, and feed them with milk." Instead, as one of his contemporaries put it, he "drenched his parishioners with the physic of an intolerant discipline." He refused Church burial to those who had not received Anglica baptism; and he refused communion to all who had not been baptized by an ordained Episcopalian minister—and that included a pastor, J. M. Bolzius, who was the leader of an industrious community of Salzburg Lutherans, and one of the most devout and respected Christians in Georgia. "Can anyone carry High Church zeal higher than that?" John asked ruefully years later. "And how well have I been beaten with mine own staff!"

Pat Tailfer, one of the colonial malcontents at Savannah, wrote of Wesley's "new kind of religious Tyranny," saying that "Mr. John Wesley, receiv'd by us as a Clergyman of the Church of England soon discovered that his Aim was to enslave our Minds, as a necessary Preparative for enslaving our Bodies. The Attendances upon Prayers, Meetings, and Sermons inculcated by him, so frequently, and at improper Hours, inconsistent with necessary Labour, especially in an infant Colony . . . tended to propagate a Spirit of Indolence and of Hypocrisy . . . it being easier by an effected Shew of Religion and Adherence to Mr. Wesley's Novelties, to be provided by his Procurement from the publick Stores. . . . Nor could the Reverend Gentleman conceal the Design he was so full of, Having frequently declar'd, That he never desired to see Georgia a Rich, but a Religious, Colony."

Charles Wesley faced even more resentment in Frederica than his brother did in Savannah. He "held constant services, calling his tired, sweating parishioners to assembly by beat of drum." The settlers complained that he meddled in everyone's business and kept the village "in a state of confusion." He got so involved in petty jealousies among the female colonists that they finally banded together in hatred of him.

Oglethorpe had ordered that there be no shooting on Sundays, but the first Sunday he was away from Frederica, Dr. Hawkins, who regarded himself "above petty regulations," fired off a gun in the middle of Charle's best sermon. The constable put the doctor in jail for the rest of the day—at the preacher's urging, the constable said later. That afternoon a woman miscarried, which, everyone agreed, would not have happened if the doctor had been available. The furious colonists threatened Charles's life, scaring him "into a frenzy." Oglethorpe, already displeased by Charles's poor performance as a secretary, heard about the prison episode on his return to Frederica, and "flailed the little priest with harsh words for his blind zeal." Charles wrote in his diary after a funeral service that he "envied the corpse his quiet grave."

But it was Mrs. Hawkins and Mrs. Welch who finally brought about Charles Wesley's downfall. They "confessed" to him that they both had committed adultery with Oglethorpe, then told the governor that the "gossipy reverend" had made up the tale and was spreading it. They further confided to Oglethorpe that Mrs. Welch had been intimate with the priest—at his insistence, of course. That was not hard for Oglethorpe to believe: Charles was known to have stayed frequently until midnight with Mrs. Welch. He said that the time was spent simply praying, reading, and talking—which undoubtedly was true—but many colonists preferred to believe that his attentions had gone beyond pastoral duties. Frederica seethed with confusion and malice.

Charles found himself suddenly out of favor with Oglethorpe, with whom he resided. The governor gave orders that his secretary was not to have use of anything in his house, leaving Charles without even a bed to sleep on. The servant who had washed his linen now sent it back dirty. When he asked to borrow one of Oglethorpe's teakettles, he was told there would be "no issue" for him. He wrote in his diary, "I was enabled to pray earnestly for my enemies, particularly Mr. Oglethorpe, whom I now look upon as the chief of them." Bewildered, crushed, sick in body as well as mind, he lay on the dirt floor in the corner of a shack belonging to one of very few friendly colonists, rising only to hold Anglican services for a congregation numbering three. Fearing he was going to die, either from sickness or violence—a bullet had barely missed him— he wrote a long letter to John detailing the whole situation and induced Ingham to take it to Savannah.

John Wesley made the difficult trip to Frederica as fast as he could. He was able to convince Oglethorpe of Charles's innocence. The governor said he had intended to have Charles "tried and imprisoned for spreading false rumors to hide his own sin" but had delayed, "considering the effect it would have on religion"; now he was glad he had hesitated. John improved the situation further by spending a week on the secretarial work that had piled up during his brother's trouble and illness.

One day, when John stopped by Dr. Hawkin's house to get some medicine, Mrs. Hawkins threatened him with a pistol in one hand and a pair of scissors in the other; she was going to cut off all his curls, she said—and she nearly succeeded. Rescued by a sergeant who happened to be in the house, the priest had hardly regained his composure before Mrs. Hawkins pushed him down and tore his cassock with her teeth. This time it took both the officer and Dr. Hawkins to save him. He hurried to tell Oglethorpe what had happened. The governor reprimanded Mrs. Hawkins, and he privately lamented that "wild women and prying priests" were about to "wreck" his colony.

Oglethorpe did forgive Charles his "errors in judgment," but he was also quite sure the colony would be better off without the young man. As a sop to the preacher's dignity, the governor suggested that he return to England with "important dispatches" for the trustees. Charles, more than ready to go, offered his resignation, which was promptly accepted. Just before he sailed in August 1736, he got this advice from Governor Oglethorpe: "On many accounts I should recommend to you marriage, rather than celibacy. You are of a social temper, and would find in a married state the difficulties of working out your salvation exceedingly lessened. . . ."

Thirteen years would pass before Charles Wesley took Oglethorpe's advice. He would live to become a remarkably powerful preacher and "the great hymn-writer of all ages," according to Canon Overton; "Hark! The Herald Angels Sing" and "Jesus, Lover of My Soul" are two of his best-loved hymns. Long before his death in his eightieth year, Wesley would declare, "Whatsoever I do prospers."

John Wesley, a pastor of Christ Church in Savannah in 1737, continued to labor devoutly and devotedly—and largely to fail because he "estranged his people by his malapropos zeal." He simply would not let go of his "rubrical rigor." Nor was he successful as a missionary to the Indians, but that was partly due to the fact that major Indian missions were forbidden because of the danger of French attacks.

However, it was mainly an *affaire de coeur* that completely doomed John Wesley's ministry in Georgia. He fell in love with pretty, intelligent Sophia Hopkey, the eighteen-year-old niece and ward of Thomas Causton, the chief magistrate of Georgia and the trustees' storekeeper. A regular attendant at his services, she often visited the parsonage to receive "spiritual guidance and comfort." Then "Miss Sophy," as John called her, nursed him through an attack of fever, and he began giving her daily French lessons. Both Causton and Oglethorpe promoted the attraction between the two, with Causton going so far as to tell Wesley that Sophia was quite well off, so that the poor financial status of the minister would in no way hinder a marriage between the two. Oglethorpe strongly advised John to get married, and then, playing cupid, directed him to escort Sophia to Frederica and back to Savannah.

John Wesley was deeply in love but feared that marriage "would probably obstruct the design" of his endeavors; he was "not strong enough to bear the complicated temptations of a married state."

He fled Savannah for a few days, leaving his surprised love a note: "I find, Miss Sophy, I can't take fire into my bosom without being burnt. I am therefore retiring for a while to desire the direction of God. Join with me, my friend, in fervent prayer, that He would shew me what is best to be done."

He returned to inform the anxious young woman that he had decided against marriage until he had "accomplished a mission to the Indians"—which was about as indefinite as he could get. Sophia, at Mrs. Causton's urging and to the preacher's shock, married William Williamson, Causton's clerk. Wesley in his old age recalled, "I was pierced through as with a sword." His stark diary entry reads: "Could not pray. Tried to pray—lost—sunk."

A few months later Rev. John Wesley felt it his duty to rebuke Sophia Williamson for neglect of her religious duties and for "falseness and inconsistency of life." He refused her the Communion. His diary entry that night was also short: "Eucharist, Miss Sophy repelled."

The next day, August 8, 1737, a warrant was issued for the arrest of John Wesley "on the complaint of William Williamson and Sophia, his wife, for defaming the said Sophia in a public congregation without cause. . . ." All Savannah buzzed. A week later Sophia swore to an affidavit accusing John Wesley of attempting to seduce her, vowing she would be made holier by living with him.

By August 22, when the court acted upon the complaint, nine other articles had been added to the indictment. These complaints had to do with autocratic procedures in Wesley's church ritual—procedures that, as Wesley proclaimed, were "none of the court's business." After hearing an address by the chief magistrate, Causton, the forty-four-man grand jury found a true bill against the preacher on all charges.

Wesley demanded, but did not get, a quick trial on the complaints. Toward the end of November, with the trial date still not named, but with animosity against Wesley flaring up, he posted a notice in the public square telling the community he intended to leave. The court promptly warned him not to quit the province until the charges had been resolved, and another notice went up in the square, this one forbidding any man to help him get away.

"I now saw clearly," wrote Wesley, "the hour was come for me to fly for my life, leaving this place, and as soon as evening prayers were over, about eight o'clock, the tide then serving, I shook off the dust of my feet, and left Georgia, having preached the Gospel there with much weakness indeed and many infirmities, not as I ought but as I was able."

In getting away he had little help except from the faithful Delamotte, who wanted to accompany him but lacked the passage money. (Ingham had returned to England earlier.) Wesley set out in a small boat with a three-man crew—"a barber, a constable and a tithing-man, all fugitives from their creditors or their families"—and after a difficult and dangerous trip, arrived cold and hungry in Charles Town, South Carolina, on December 13, 1737. He sailed for England on Christmas Eve.

On shipboard John Wesley immediately resumed his sermons, prayer meetings, and reading and instruction sessions. But his diary entries reveal that he was profoundly troubled. "I went to America," he wrote, "to convert the Indians, but oh! who shall convert me? This have I learned in the ends of the earth, that I am fallen short of the glory of God, that my whole heart is altogether corrupt and abominable, and consequently my whole life. Alienated as I am from the life of God, I am a child of wrath, an heir of hell."

The thirty-four-year-old priest struggled out of his despair after he reached England. By 1739 he had drawn together several religious groups into the United Society of Methodists. (In America the Methodist Church was formally organized in 1784.) In addition to launching Methodism, John Wesley revitalized Christianity in England. During more than half a century of itinerant preaching, he delivered forty thousand sermons, the last only a week before he died in March 1791 as he neared his eighty-seventh birthday.

Peggy Robbins is a free-lance writer who lives in Mississippi.

A Man for All Souls

Basil Burwell

On October 19, 1720, was born one of the few saints and prophets this country has produced. John Woolman, the Quaker, of Mount Holly, New Jersey, is still relatively unknown in his own land though his *Journal* is extensively read in England, Germany, and France. That he lacks fame in his own land is not surprising. Too many of his ideas ran counter to those held by a majority of the population in his own time. His greatness lay in his compassionate humanity, a quality that is only rarely in fashion.

It was compassionate humanity that led Woolman to make journey after journey south through Virginia and the Carolinas and north to Providence, Rhode Island, and Massachusetts to plead with slaveowners to set free the fellow humans they held captive. It was compassionate humanity that led him to journey westward to regions where he was in danger of losing his scalp: he wished to bring a message of peace and brotherhood to the Indians.

He began his adult life as a shopkeeper's assistant, and he proved to have such a talent for business that he might well have become a colonial merchant prince. His success when he went into business for himself was so great that it alarmed him. He saw that the increasing burden of success would be more than his spirit could bear. It would be a chain, and he wanted to be free. "Truth required me to live more free from outward Cumbers," he said. "I saw that a humble Man, with the blessing of the Lord, might live on a little; and that where the Heart was set on Greatness, Success in Business did not satisfy the craving; but that commonly, with an Increase of Wealth, the Desire of Wealth increased."

He took up tailoring and set up a little shop along with it to sell buttons and notions, thinking that a plain man would so have more time for his inward life. He kept the little shop and his tailoring until he was thirty-six and during that time showed real concern for the welfare of his customers. He refused to deal in luxuries because they enticed people to go into debt, and he made every effort to dissuade his poorer customers from buying goods they could not afford. Despite these scruples, or possibly because of them, his trade increased year by year. The man who had rejected business success found that a partial rejection was no rejection at all. It had to be complete. "I lessened my outward Business and . . . told my Customers of my Intention, that they might consider what Shop to turn to: And in a while, wholly laid down Merchandize, following my Trade, as a Taylor myself only, having no apprentice."

In addition he kept a nursery of apple trees in which he employed some of his time in "hoeing, grafting, trimming and inoculating." He believed that man should live in harmony with nature—bird, beast, plant, and soil. "To impoverish the Earth now to support outward Greatness," he said, "appears to be an injury to the succeeding Age." The deforestation of Nantucket and its infertile soil distressed him, for example, as did the stench arising from the filth of the thickly settled towns he visited in England and the spoiling he saw there of good earth "where much of their die stuffs have drained away." He believed in conservation long before that term came into use, and among the resources he wished to see preserved and nurtured was the child.

Woolman, of whom no certain likeness exists, taught school at various intervals during his life, wrote a primer that went into three editions, and developed certain ideas about education. He favored, for example, smaller classes. Individual attention produced better results. So did teachers who were not bowed down by poverty. Here, too, his feeling for his fellow humans reveals itself; but the truth is that he felt a "Tenderness . . . towards all Creatures" and thought that we should take every care "not [to] lessen that Sweetness of Life, in the animal Creation, which the great Creator intends for them under our Government."

Woolman's reverence for all life stemmed from a childhood experience, when he threw a stone and killed a mother robin that had been trying to distract him from molesting the little ones in her nest. Pleased at first by his exploit, he was soon overcome by horror and remorse. The mother had been so careful of her young, and now, without her to nourish them, they would perish. Rather than let them endure the suffering of slow starvation, he climbed up to the nest and killed the nestlings one by one. The cruelties he had committed weighed upon him, and he came to the conclusion that "true Religion consisted in an inward Life, wherein the Heart doth love and reverence God the Creator, and learns to exercise true Justice and Goodness, not only toward all Men, but also toward the brute Creatures."

During his travels in England prior to his death in York from smallpox at the age of fifty-one, Woolman demonstrated that this tender concern for animal as well as human life was still with him. He refused to send letters or be conveyed himself by a post system that encouraged stagecoaches to travel a hundred miles in twenty-four hours so that, as he said, it is "common for horses to be killed with hard driving, and many others are driven till they grow blind. . . . So great is the hurry in the Spirit of this world, that in aiming to do business quick, and to gain wealth, the Creation at this day doth loudly groan!"

The gaining of wealth at the expense of one's fellow creatures was the major source of trouble to what he called the "great family" of man. "Where men give way to a desire after wealth, and to obtain their ends proceed in that wisdom which is from beneath, how often does discord arise between different branches of the great family?" The answer was: too often. Over and over again great numbers of men were torn away from useful employment, such as tilling the earth, and forced to defend what the contending parties claimed as their interest but what was actually an interest of the few. Wars, he believed, came about because some people had too much and wanted more, while some other persons had not even the decencies of life. "Feeling an increasing desire to live in the Spirit of Peace, I have often been sorrowfully affected with thinking on the unquiet Spirit in which Wars are generally carried on, and with the Miseries of many of my Fellow Creatures engaged therein; some suddenly Destroyed, some Wounded, and after much Pain remaining Cripples; some Deprived of all their outward Substance and reduced to Want; and some carried into Captivity." Woolman was much troubled by the advent of the French and Indian War in 1754 and met with some young men in relation to the draft, counselling them that they should hold fast to their stand "that they could not bear Arms for Conscience sake; nor could they hire any to go in their Places, being resigned as to the Event." If the only true objective was to create the one world-family, then it was necessary "to keep to right Means in labouring to attain a right End."

A portion of that world-family were the original owners of the land where Woolman's orchard stood, of the woods through which he journeyed on horseback and the streams that he forded or followed. Having for many years felt love in his heart for the Indians who dwelt far back in the wilderness, he conceived an increasing desire to make a personal demonstration of that love. "I thought," he said, "that the Affectionate care of a good man for his only Brother in Affliction, does not exceed what I then felt for that people." He said farewell to wife and friends in 1763 and set forth.

Some years before he had seen a scalped corpse being hauled through the streets of Philadelphia, and Woolman had been repeatedly warned that the Indians were freshly stirred up and had taken to the warpath. "The Thoughts of falling into the Hands of *Indian* Warriours were, in Times of Weakness, afflicting to me; and being of a tender Constitution of Body, the Thoughts of Captivity amongst them were, at times grievous . . . but the Lord alone was my Keeper; and I believed, if I went into Captivity, it would for some good End."

He had one encounter that gave him at least a moment of real uneasiness. As he approached an Indian to speak to him, the brave whipped out a concealed tomahawk. Woolman did not retreat. Speaking in a friendly fashion, he continued toward the Indian with outstretched hand. As Woolman put it, "Though his taking [his] hatchet in his hand at the instant I drew near him, had a disagreeable appearance, I believed he had no other intent than to be in readiness in case any violence was offered to him."

Having travelled two hundred miles into the forest, he reached the Indian village of Wyalusing, which he had selected as his destination. There he remained for several days, frequently meeting and talking to the Indians. At first making use of an interpreter, he soon dispensed with translation, explaining that he believed if he prayed rightly, God would hear him and the Indians would understand. It was on this occasion that Papunehang, the great and peaceful chief of the Delawares, summed up his feelings by saying, "I Love to Feel where words come from." It was an eloquent response to the love of mankind that inspired this strange missionary.

But if Woolman was concerned for the well-being of the red man, he was even more deeply affected by the oppression suffered by the black. Racial injustice, he was among the first to see, not only debases the victim but corrupts the victimizer as well. Over and over again, as he journeyed north or south, reasoning quietly with slaveowners, he listened to the kind of argument used even to this day to defend the system of slavery. That the system rescued the Negro from savagery. That the Good Book ordained that he should be a slave. That he was naturally lazy and needed a strong master. "Men are wont to take hold of weak Arguments," said Woolman, "to support a Cause which is unreasonable." The true motives for keeping slaves and trading in them, he believed, were ease and gain. "I saw in these southern Provinces so many Vices and Corruptions, increased by this Trade and this Way of Life, that it appeared to me as a Gloom over the Land; and though now many willingly run into it, yet, in future, the Consequence will be grievous to Posterity."

These observations came to him in 1746. Some few years later he published two essays entitled *Considerations on Keeping Negroes,* in the second of which he said, "Placing on Men the ignominious Title SLAVE, dressing them in uncomely Garments, keeping them to servile Labour, in which they are often dirty, tends gradually to fix a Notion in the Mind, that they are a Sort of People below us in Nature, and leads us to consider them as such in all our Conclusions about them." It needs but little change to give that statement application more than two centuries later. "If we bring this Matter home, and as Job proposed to his Friends, *Put our Soul in their Souls' stead.* If we consider ourselves and our Children as exposed to the Hardships which these People lie under in supporting an imaginary Greatness. Did we in such Case behold an Increase of Luxury and Superfluity amongst our Oppressors, and therewith felt an Increase of the Weight of our Burdens, and expected our Posterity to groan under oppression after us. Under all this Misery, had we none to plead our Cause, nor any Hope of Relief from Man, how would our Cries ascend to the God of the Spirits of all Flesh who judgeth the World in Righteousness, and in his own Time is a Refuge for the Oppressed!''

To ''put our soul in their souls' stead.'' This is what John Woolman was always able to do, whether it was for the soldier drafted into war, the Indian encouraged to trade whiskey for the furs that would have purchased food, the slave whipped by the overseer, or, by some Saint Francis-like reach of the imagination, the animal or the bird or even the very earth that man despoiled for his own enrichment. The little boy who had felt such remorse when he killed the mother robin became the man moved to love and identify with all mankind and all creation. Put your soul in their souls' stead, he said, but only a few listened, a very few. As the historian George Macaulay Trevelyan said, ''Close your ears to John Woolman one century and you will get John Brown the next, with Grant to follow.''

A Quaker himself, Basil Burwell is consultant to the proposed John Woolman Room of the Burlington College Library in Pemberton, New Jersey. He is dean of faculty at the Cherry Lawn School in Darien, Connecticut. His text for this article is based chiefly on the Everyman's Library edition of the Journal, *edited by Vida D. Scudder (Dutton, 1910).*

FREEDOM

Part Two • The American Revolution and the Founding of the Nation

During the colonial period, the relationship between colonies and the mother country made revolution almost inevitable. The relationship was one of exploitation. The interests of the colonies and the colonists were subordinated to the interest of the mother country. If such a connection was understandable and tolerable during the early period of colonial development, it became less understandable and more intolerable with the passage of time. By the middle of the 18th century, the American colonists began to strain against the limitations of the British imperial system.

Ironically, in the aftermath of England's greatest colonial triumph—the elimination of the French from North America in the Seven Years' War, the seeds of colonial discontent began to germinate. In the quest for greater efficiency, England attempted to reinforce the unitary structure of her empire. She tried to transform what had been essentially a commercial empire into a territorial empire. But every proposed change in policy aroused colonial opposition and protest. In successive crises, the colonial attachment to England was weakened, the relationship strained to the final breaking point— revolution and the demand of independence.

How had this happened? In his excellent account of these events, ''Firebrand of the Revolution,'' Alexander Winston traces the progression of colonial disenchantment and the evolution of colonial attitudes in the period of Samuel Adams, one of the most remarkable men of that crucial period of American history. After a decade of recurring crises, American refusal to be subordinated to British policy and British failure to redress American grievances led to revolution. From the very beginning of the conflict, some thoughtful men in England questioned the ability of the government to reestablish control over the colonies. The problems were too insurmountable. In his well-conceived analogy, "England's Vietnam: The American Revolution," Richard M. Ketchum discusses those problems and makes a brief comparison with the more recent United States involvement in Vietnam.

Victory in the war for American independence may have resolved the conflict over home-rule, but it did not insure that the Americans could rule themselves successfully. Indeed, during the crucial last months of the war, George Washington was forced to contend with the threat of mutiny, a mutiny which challenged the principle of civilian rule. James W. Wensyel explains the circumstances in his article, "The Newburgh Conspiracy."

If the principle of civilian rule survived that challenge, among many who had been in the forefront of the fight for independence, the Confederation set up in 1781 seemed unequal to the task of governing in the United States. With each successive crisis in the 1780s, the movement to create "a more perfect Union" gained momentum, culminating in the Philadelphia Convention of 1787 and a new constitution. Robert C. Alberts traced these events in his article, "Business of the Highest Magnitude." With the completion of the ratification process, "We the People of the United States" ordained and established our present form of government, that of the Constitution.

Firebrand of the Revolution

Alexander Winston

Members of the British Parliament who voted approval of the Stamp Act late one night in 1765 and went yawning off to bed had never heard, it would seem, of Boston's "Man of the Town Meeting," Samuel Adams. It was a fatal lapse. From that moment until the Declaration of Independence, Sam Adams pounced on Britain every time she moved to impose her will on the colonies. He made politics his only profession and rebellion his only business. He drove two royal governors out of Massachusetts and goaded the British government into open war. New England Tories branded him the "grand Incendiary," the "all-in-all" of colonial turmoil, and neatly capsuled Boston resistance as "Adams' conspiracy." In the opinion of his astute cousin John Adams, Sam was "born and tempered a wedge of steel to split the knot of *lignum vitae* that tied America to England."

"Born and tempered," as Cousin John put it, was more than rhetorical flourish. Sam's father—also named Samuel—made an avocation of politics, and was suspected of republican leanings. The boy got a taste for public affairs almost with his milk; while he was but a toddler his father was deep in the Caucus Club, the same radical brotherhood that Sam was to use with such adroitness. Sam senior clashed with the royal governors, and in 1741 saw his Land Bank venture—an effort to aid debtors by putting negotiable paper money into circulation—outlawed by Parliament. Father and son shared the bitter conviction that Britain's colonial policy was both arbitrary and unjust.

From his parents Sam also inherited a strenuous Calvinism that was to make his vision of the conflict with Britain resemble a huge and murky illustration for *Paradise Lost*. The American patriots, Sam was sure, were children of light who fought England's sons of Belial in a struggle decisive for the future of mankind. Everyone knew where God stood on that. Sam saw England through a glass, darkly; her government venal, her manners effeminate and corrupt, her religion popish. In saving the colonies from her tyranny Sam hoped to save their manly virtues as well, and make of Boston a "Christian Sparta"—chaste, austere, godly. By 1765 three dominant strains were firmly fixed in his character: puritanism, political acumen, and hatred of British rule. He laced them together tight as a bull whip and, as Parliament was to discover, twice as deadly.

Any calm appraisal of his life up to that point, however, would surely have rated him among those least likely to succeed. After Harvard (M.A., 1743) he had dabbled at the study of law and later spent a few fruitless months as apprentice in a countinghouse. His father loaned him a thousand pounds to make a try at business—any business. The money ran through his fingers like water. Appointed Boston's tax collector in 1756, he combined softheartedness and negligence so ably that he ended at least four thousand pounds in arrears and faced court action. The prosperous little malt works that his father had left the family fell to ruins. The sheriff threatened to sell his house for debts. When the Stamp Act was passed in 1765, Sam was forty-two; he looked prematurely old, his hands trembled, his head shook with a palsied tremor.

But while his private affairs were in a perpetual state of collapse, Sam was making himself the gray eminence of Boston politics. The base of his power was the Caucus Club, a judicious mixture of shipyard laborers ("mechanics") and uptown intellectuals. They met in a garret to drink punch, turn the air blue with pipe smoke, and plot the next political move. Their decisions were passed quietly along to other radical cells— the Merchants' Club (which met in the more genteel Boston Coffee House), the contentious Monday Night Club, the Masons, the Sons of Liberty. With tactics mapped out and support solidified, the action was rammed—or finessed, if need be—through town meeting. Nothing was left to chance; Sam and his tight coterie of patriots simply outworked, outmaneuvered, and, on occasion, outlasted the opposition.

At first rumor of the Stamp Act, Sam cried that "a deep-laid and desperate plan of imperial despotism has been laid, and partly executed, for the extinction of all civil liberty." But Parliament considered its act perfectly just. England's recent conquest of Canada, which had removed an armed threat to the colonies from the French, had also run up a burdensome debt. Obviously the colonies, who had benefited most from the costly Canadian expedition, should not mind paying part of the bill. Passed in the spring of 1765, the Stamp Act required that after November 1 of that year validating stamps be bought from government offices and affixed to all legal documents, customs papers, newssheets, and pamphlets. To enforce the act Parliament decreed that offenders be tried in admiralty courts, where there were no juries, and pay their fines in silver coin, which was hard to get.

Sam rolled out his artillery months before the act went into effect. The instructions from the Boston town meeting to its representatives in the Massachusetts House constituted one of the first formal protests made in the colonies against the act, and one of the first appeals for united resistance. Sam declared that since the act imposed taxation by a body in which the taxed were not represented it flouted the Massachusetts charter, violated the established rights of British subjects, and was therefore null and void.

On the morning of August 14, 1765, the effigy of old Andrew Oliver, Boston distributor of stamps, hung from the Liberty Tree, a great oak in Hanover Square. Sam inspected the stuffed figure with care and wondered aloud how it got there. That night a mob knocked down the frame of the stamp office and built a fire of the debris in front of Oliver's house. After burning the decapitated effigy, they made the real Oliver swear to resign at the Liberty Tree—which he did, finally, under the added humiliation of a driving December rainstorm.

Sam was pleased. The event, he announced, "ought to be for ever remembered in America," for on that day "the People shouted; and their shout was heard to the distant end of this Continent." Two weeks later rioters sacked and gutted the mansion of Lieutenant Governor Thomas Hutchinson, emptying his wine cellar and scattering his papers in the street.

On November 1, 1765, the day the Stamp Act went into effect, church bells tolled as for the dead. Flags hung at half-mast; from the harbor rolled the dull boom of minute guns. For the next six weeks the people of Boston refused to buy stamps. Port business came to a halt, law courts tried no cases. Sam had warned the farmers: "If our Trade may be taxed why not our Lands? Why not the Produce of our Lands and in short everything we possess or make use of?" He doubly damned the stamp revenue by prophesying that it would be used to fasten an episcopacy on puritan New England. In the provincial House, to which he had been elected in September, Sam had a gallery installed to bring waverers under the accusing eye of his patriots. He and his colleague James Otis published a black list of those House members whose antagonism to the act lacked proper vigor. Frightened stamp officials fled for protection to Castle William in the harbor. Enforcement collapsed, and early in the next year Parliament repealed the act. But Sam did not join in Boston's celebration. Why rejoice, he grimly demanded, when Parliament has only granted us our just due?

The defeat of the Stamp Act suggested that no one in the colonies could hatch and execute a scheme with half Sam's cunning. His strategy was to let Britain make all the moves and then give her a bloody nose. "It is a good maxim in Politicks as well as War," he counselled, "to put and keep the enemy in the wrong." Britain soon obliged again. In May, 1767, Parliament launched a series of colonial bills named for their sponsor, Charles Townshend, Chancellor of the Exchequer. The Townshend Acts placed import duties on painters' colors, glass, lead, paper, and tea. At the same time they set up Commissioners of Customs with broad powers, authorized search warrants, and specified that the revenue would be used to pay Crown officials previously salaried (and therefore in part controlled) by the colonies.

Sam worked hard at nonimportation as the chief weapon against the Townshend Acts. By 1769 all the colonies had joined in the boycott. Sam revelled in their unity: "The *tighter* the cord of unconstitutional power is drawn round this bundle of arrows, the *firmer* it will be."

To enforce the boycott in Boston, gangs ranged outside the homes of Tory merchants by night, and small boys pelted their customers with dirt and dung by day. One shopkeeper, more obstinate than the rest, was ridden out of town to the gallows and loosed only when he swore never to return. Tories slept with loaded pistols by their beds. Governor Francis Bernard pleaded for military protection, and in September of

1768 two regiments of soldiers sailed in from Halifax. They set up guardposts, and levelled a pair of cannon at the town hall.

Overnight Governor Bernard became the most hated man in Massachusetts. The House demanded his removal; at Harvard, students slashed his portrait. Sam denounced him as a "Scourge to this Province, a curse to North America, and a Plague on the whole Empire." Recalled to England, Bernard sailed at the end of July, 1769, leaving Hutchinson to act as governor in his place. Despite Sam's outraged cry that Boston was now an occupied town, the troops remained, and he began sending a periodic *Journal of Events* to other colonies, accusing the redcoats of beating defenseless boys and raping women.

Early in March, 1770, a soldier was injured in a scuffle with dockmen. One morning soon after, the town was plastered with forged notices, allegedly signed by redcoats, promising a broad-scale attack on the townspeople. That night, March 5, as a bright moon shone on the late snow, a crowd gathered in front of the Custom House. It began to taunt the nine-man guard; snowballs and brickbats flew, the guard fired, and five citizens were left dead or dying.

The town was in a frenzy of anger. On the following afternoon an immense rally of excited citizens massed in and around Old South Church. Hutchinson told a committee of protest that he was willing to send the one offending regiment to the fort at Castle William but that he had no military authority to send the other as well. At dusk Sam came to the State House to deliver his ultimatum: "If you . . . have the power to remove *one* regiment you have the power to remove *both*. It is at your peril if you refuse. The meeting is composed of three thousand people. They are become impatient. A thousand men are already arrived from the neighborhood, and the whole country is in motion. Night is approaching. An immediate answer is expected. Both regiments or none!" Hutchinson caved in and ordered the two regiments out of town.

Sam relished his moment of triumph. "If Fancy deceive me not," he reported, "I observ'd his Knees to tremble. I thought I saw his face grow pale (and I enjoy'd the Sight)." Copley's fine portrait catches Sam at the moment of confrontation: broad forehead, heavy eyebrows, steady blue-gray eyes, nose like the prow of a ship, stubborn mouth, a chin you could plow with.

Sam wanted the soldiers who had fired the fatal shots to be tried immediately, while indignation still flamed white-hot, but the judges put it off for six months. He acquiesced when two patriots, his cousin John and Josiah Quincy, volunteered to be defense attorneys, sure that they would not press too hard on prosecution witnesses. The two proved more honorable than he had counted on; they argued their case ably and the sentence was light—a pair of soldiers were branded on the thumb. Sam was disgusted. He retired the case in the Boston *Gazette,* over the signature "Vindex," the avenger. (For a full count of the Boston Massacre trial, see AMERICAN HERITAGE, December, 1966.)

After that, to Sam's chagrin, things quieted down. The blood of the "massacre" had washed away with the melting snow. In England a liberal government had assumed power and in April it repealed the Townshend Acts, except for the duty on tea. A majority of the colonists were tired of agitation, and the radical patriots temporarily lost control of the Massachusetts House. John Hancock courted the royalists; John Adams shook the dust of politics from his shoes and went back to pastoral Braintree. James Otis, who had been bludgeoned in a brawl, sank into recurrent fits of dementia.

Only Sam never let up. "Where there is a Spark of patriotick fire," he vowed, "we will enkindle it." Between August, 1770, and December, 1772, he wrote more than forty articles for the *Gazette*. Night after night, a lamp burned late in the study off his bedroom. Friends, passing in the small hours, could look up at the yellow square of window light and comfort themselves that Sam Adams was busily at work against the Tories. Sam alternately stated the fundamentals of colonial liberty (based on the charter, British law, and, finally, natural right) and whiplashed the British for transgressing it. His style in this period was at times severely reasoned, more often impassioned; the content was unfailingly polemical, partisan, and, on occasion, willfully inaccurate. As the conflict with Britain deepened, his accusations became more violent. "Every dip of his pen," Governor Bernard had once said, "stung like a horned snake." As clerk of the House (to which office he had been elected in 1765) Sam poured out a stream of remonstrances, resolves, and letters to the colony's London agent; but beyond their effect as propaganda he expected them to do little good. When his daughter expressed awe that a petition to the King might be touched by the royal hand, he growled that it would more likely be spurned by the royal foot.

In November, 1772, Sam managed to set up a Boston Committee of Correspondence to link the Massachusetts towns. Within a few months other towns had followed suit, and he had a taut organization poised to act at his command. A discerning Tory declared it the "foulest, subtlest, and most venomous serpent ever issued from the egg of sedition."

In fact, everything Sam did for a decade smacked of sedition. As early as 1768 Hutchinson had secretly sent depositions to England to see if there might be grounds for his arrest. Parliament dusted off a neglected statute of Henry VIII that would bring all treasonable cases to London for trial. Tories were sure that Sam would now end on the gibbet, where he belonged. They gloated that he "shuddered at the sight of hemp." A Londoner wrote jubilantly to Hutchinson: "The talk is strong of bringing them over and trying them by impeachment. Do you write me word of their being seized, and I will send you an account of their being hanged." But the British solicitor general took a long look at the evidence and decided that it was not sufficient—yet.

Meanwhile Sam was out to ruin Hutchinson, and didn't care how he did it. To beat the devil any stick would do. The chance came in 1772 when Ben Franklin, then in London as an agent for the Massachusetts House, laid hands on a bundle of letters written by Hutchinson and Andrew Oliver to correspondents in England. Franklin sent them to Boston with instructions to share them among the trusted inner circle of patriots and return them uncopied and unpublished. Whether he meant these instructions to be strictly obeyed, or issued them for his self-protection, we do not know. The patriots brooded over the letters for several months; then Sam announced that "a most shocking scene would soon open," and that a vicious plot against American liberties would be disclosed.

Expectation of horrifying news was raised to a fever pitch. In June, 1773, Sam ordered the House galleries cleared. He told the members in grave tones that he had letters vital to their concern, but that they must first swear neither to copy them nor make them public. At this Hancock rose to say that someone unknown to him had thrust copies of letters into his hand on the street. Might they be the same as those held by Mr. Adams? If so, were the letters not already abroad? Yes, to be sure, they were the same; obviously they were abroad. The House decided that the letters should no longer be concealed.

Hutchinson's correspondence was really fairly mild, and said little that he had not already stated openly, but Sam managed to put it in the worst possible light. When the letters were published, passages had been slyly snipped from their context, and an outraged commentary had been so mixed with the text that the unwary reader was easily led to see an evil purpose when none was intended. Other letters in the packet were more damaging than Hutchinson's, but he was neatly smeared with their brush. He suffered great discredit even in the rural villages, where most of his conservative support lay. The House petitioned the King, asking that Hutchinson be removed from office.

Now the storm was gathering. Alone of the revenue acts, the duty on tea remained. For years Boston matrons had boycotted the rich English brew, and instead had concocted somewhat unsavory beverages of catnip and mint. Prompted by the desperate straits of the East India Company, Parliament tried in 1773 to help the company unload its embarrassing stockpile of tea on the colonies. Boston patriots decided that the flesh should not be so tempted. While ships bearing 342 chests of tea lay at the wharfs, Sam gave the signal and a band of his mechanics disguised as Mohawk Indians whooped off toward the harbor. As every schoolboy knows, they dumped the whole cargo into Massachusetts Bay. "Sam Adams is in his glory," said Hutchinson; and he was.

Parliament retaliated in a rage. In March, 1774, it ordered the port of Boston clamped shut. It decreed that after August 1 the Provincial Council, which formerly had been elected by the House, would be named by the governor, as would the higher judges. The royal sheriff would select all juries; town meetings throughout the province would assemble only with the governor's consent, and discuss only what he authorized. General Thomas Gage, commander in chief of His Majesty's forces in America, supplanted Hutchinson as governor. By June, four regiments of redcoats were encamped on the Common. This was the showdown; it was knuckle under or risk war.

Sam knew that to pit Boston (population 17,000) against British power was to place the mouse beneath the lion's paw. "I wish we could arouse the continent," he had written to a fellow patriot the year before. Now, in the spring of 1774, the continent was awakening: a Continental Congress was in the making. How could this matter be discussed and delegates elected before Gage got wind of it and prorogued the Massachusetts legislature? He already had moved the House temporarily from troublesome Boston to the Tory stronghold of Salem; the town swarmed with redcoats.

For ten days the House dispatched routine business with disarming amiability while Sam lined up votes behind the scenes. On June 17, when all was ready, he suddenly ordered the doors of the meeting hall locked. Sensing a plot, one Troy member slipped past the doorkeeper and hurried away to alert Gage. Sam put the key in his pocket and presented a slate of delegates (of which he was one) to attend the Congress, set for Philadelphia in September. Gage scratched off a hurried order to dissolve the House, but the messenger beat on the door in vain. Inside, the House leisurely elected the delegates and assessed the towns for their expenses.

For the first time in his life Sam Adams was to leave the shores of Massachusetts Bay. He still lived in the crumbling ancestral home on Purchase Street, with land running down to the harbor, where he had a small dock. The household consisted of his second wife, Elizabeth Wells Adams (his first wife had died in 1757), a son and a daughter by his earlier marriage, a servant girl, and a shaggy dog famed for biting redcoats. Elizabeth Adams was devoted and above all frugal, for since their marriage his only earnings had been the meager allowance granted him as clerk of the House of Representatives. Fortunately he had few personal wants, and would live on bread and milk and dress in threadbare clothes, if the cause of liberty were thereby served. "He says he never looked forward in his Life," recorded Cousin John, with Yankee amazement at such carelessness, "never planned, laid a scheme, or formed a design of laying up any Thing for himself or others after him."

Friends put together the money to outfit him for the journey to Philadelphia. He was resplendent in new suit, wig, hose, shoes, and cocked hat; he swung a gold-topped cane, and in his pocket there was a much-needed purse of money. On August 10, 1774, the delegation—John Adams, Sam Adams, Thomas Cushing, and Robert Treat Paine—rolled out of Boston in full array—coach, coachmen, and mounted servants.

They were received with great honor along the route, but friendly patriots in Philadelphia advised them that the other colonies were suspicious of Boston's hotheaded radicals. John Adams summed up their warning: "You must not utter the word independence, nor give the least hint or insinuation of the idea, either in Congress, or any private conversation; if you do, you are undone, for independence is as unpopular in all the Middle and South as the Stamp Act itself. No man dares speak of it. . . ."

During the seven-week session the Massachusetts delegation stayed discreetly in the background. When Sam urged that an Anglican clergyman be permitted to open the sessions with prayer, southerners decided that the dour Calvinist might have some good in him after all. But he was bold in opposing any concessions to Britain: "I should advise persisting in our struggle for liberty, though it was revealed from heaven that nine hundred and ninety-nine should perish, and only one of a thousand survive and retain his liberty. One such freeman must possess more virtue and enjoy more happiness than a thousand slaves; and let him propagate his like, and transmit to them what he hath so nobly preserved."

From 1774 to 1781 Sam Adams' public life was bound up with successive Congresses. He brought to them the same stubborn energy and forehandedness that had worked so well in Boston. "He was constantly holding caucuses of distinguished men," Jefferson recalled, ". . . at which the generality of the measures pursued were previously determined on, and at which the parts were assigned to the different actors who afterwards appeared in them." His name bobs up almost daily in the congressional journal. Joseph Galloway, leader of the conciliatory wing in the Congress, recognized him as one to keep a wary eye on, "a man who, though by no means remarkable for brilliant abilities, yet is equal to most men in popular intrigue and the management of a faction. He eats little, drinks little, sleeps little, thinks much, and is most decisive and indefatigable in the pursuit of his objects. It was this man, who, by his superior application, managed at once the faction in Congress at Philadelphia and the factions in New England."

Sam was ready for independence when most Congress members still clung to compromise. Philadelphia Quakers were for leaving the issue to Providence; he tartly replied that Providence had already decided for liberty. To James Warren in Plymouth he wrote during the spring of 1776: "The Child Independence is now struggling for Birth. I trust that in a short time it will be brought forth, and, in Spite of Pharaoh, all America will hail the dignified Stranger."

In July he signed the Declaration of Independence, and with that stroke of the pen signed away his real vocation. Success put him out of business. America no longer needed an agitator; now it had to defeat an army in the field and build a new nation.

Sam admitted that he was unfit for "founding Empires," and in various ways he proved it. In Congress he favored a citizen militia until forced to concede that the war could be fought only with a more permanent army and a unified command. Frankly critical of Washington's Fabian tactics, Sam was widely accused of involvement in a cabal to replace him, but there is no evidence to support the charge. He disapproved of any social gaiety in so grave an hour, and had Congress pass rules forbidding members to attend balls or entertainments. They voted the rules, and diligently ignored them. His weakness for government by committee led the French minister to lament over the man "whose obstinate, resolute character was so useful to the Revolution at its origin, but who shows himself so ill-suited to the conduct of affairs in an organized government."

Yet Sam worked with his old doggedness through the dark years of war. Jefferson considered him "more than any other member, the *fountain* of our more important measures." At the low ebb of American fortunes in October, 1777, he was one of only twenty members who stuck with Congress. "Though the smallest," Sam remarked, "it was the truest Congress we ever had." He was on the committee that framed the Articles of Confederation in 1777. Four years later, when Congress celebrated their ratification with a keg of wine and some biscuits, Sam alone remained of the original drafters. In April, 1781, he went home and never crossed the borders of Massachusetts again.

He returned, like Ulysses, to find his hall full of strangers—the young, the new postwar merchants: unfamiliar faces, other times. John Hancock, who had been elected the first governor of independent Massachusetts, led Boston a merry romp of feasts and revels; it was far from the "Christian Sparta" of which Sam still dreamed. The old radical was elected to the state Senate and became its president, but he was no longer invincible. In 1783 and again in 1787 he lost the race for the rather empty and unsalaried office of lieutenant governor; in 1788 a youngster defeated him for the first Congress under the federal Constitution. But in 1789, when he teamed with Hancock to become lieutenant governor, some enthusiasts wrote his name on their ballots in gold. At Hancock's death in 1793 he succeeded to the governor's chair, and was re-elected by solid majorities for three more one-year terms.

Changing times even forced the revolutionary into the camp of reaction. As president of the Senate, which under the state constitution required its members to have an estate of four hundred pounds, he headed a body designed to check the democratic excesses of the House. Some Bostonians thought the town's growth warranted a change to representative government; Sam reported for his committee that the town-meeting system had no defects in it. Debtors in the western counties who in 1786, under a Revolutionary War veteran named Daniel Shays, resorted to mob violence discovered in the former rebel an implacable foe. He branded them "banditti" and urged the execution of their leaders. Popular opinion was more merciful; Hancock commuted the death penalty. As governor, Sam vetoed a bill to permit stage performances, and Bostonians howled that he was robbing them of their natural rights. Toward the dispossessed Tories, others softened, but Sam's hatred burned with its old fierceness. He would not have a British subject left on American soil nor, indeed, admitted by naturalization.

But Sam had not really changed at all, and that was his misfortune. He earned the lasting enmity of Federalists by his opposition to the new federal Constitution proposed in 1787. Shocked to discover that it would set up "a National Government instead of a Federal Union of Sovereign States," he declared himself "open & decided" against it. But he also insisted that the state convention called in 1788 to ratify the federal Constitution give the document the careful paragraph-by-paragraph discussion that it deserved. Antifederalists who wanted a quick vote while their hostile majority was intact pleaded financial inability to stay for a long session. Sam dryly remarked that if they were so pressed he would dig up funds for their living expenses.

Very likely some of the fight went out of him with the death of his doctor-son while the convention was going on. According to one story, the Federalists finally swung him around by a shrewd move. They staged a meeting of Sam's beloved mechanics at the Green Dragon Inn, where resolutions were passed urging ratification. Daniel Webster wrote a dramatized account of how Paul Revere brought Sam the news:

" 'How many mechanics,' said Mr. Adams, 'were at the Green Dragon when the resolutions were passed?'

" 'More, sir,' was the reply, 'than the Green Dragon could hold.'

" 'And where were the rest, Mr. Revere?'

" 'In the streets, sir.'
" 'And how many were in the streets?'
" 'More, sir, than there are stars in the sky.' "

Sam, Webster tells us, thought that over for a while. To him, the voice of the common man was as close to the voice of God as one could get. "Well," he mused, "if they must have it, they must have it."

He retired from public life in 1797, and lived six years more in a yellow frame house on Winter Street. Its parlor was hung with engravings of the great champions of liberty. He liked to sit on the doorstep or wander in the little garden, talking about old times. Death came on October 2, 1803, when he was 81 years of age.

The Federalist regime in Massachusetts was embarrassed about full burial honors for its political foe. The governor was absent; no subordinate dared risk a misstep, and the first suggestion was a modest cortege of school children. Aroused at this, friends rallied a fitting processional of state and town officials, dressed out with a muster of cadets. But eulogies delivered in the Massachusetts House were whittled down for public consumption. In Congress no member from Sam's state rose to memorialize him. It fell to Virginia's John Randolph of Roanoke to remind the House that a great patriot had died. With these small honors "The Father of the Revolution" went to his last sleep in the soil of a free and independent America.

Alexander Winston specializes in Revolutionary and pre-Revolutionary history. Currently, he is working on a book about three famous seventeenth-century pirates: William Dampier, Henry Morgan, and William Kidd.

For further reading: Samuel Adams, by James K. Hosmer (Houghton, Mifflin, 1898); Sam Adams, Pioneer in Propaganda, by John C. Miller (Little, Brown, 1936).

England's Vietnam: The American Revolution

Richard M. Ketchum

If it is true that those who cannot remember the past are condemned to repeat it, America's last three Presidents might have profited by examining the ghostly footsteps of America's last king before pursuing their adventure in Vietnam. As the United States concludes a decade of war in Southeast Asia, it is worth recalling the time, two centuries ago, when Britain faced the same agonizing problems in America that we have met in Vietnam. History seldom repeats itself exactly, and it would be a mistake to try to equate the ideologies or the motivating factors involved; but enough disturbing parallels may be drawn between those two distant events to make one wonder if the Messrs. Kennedy, Johnson, and Nixon had their ears closed while the class was studying the American Revolution.

Britain, on the eve of that war, was the greatest empire since Rome. Never before had she known such wealth and power; never had the future seemed so bright, the prospects so glowing. All, that is, except the spreading sore of discontent in the American colonies that, after festering for a decade and more, finally erupted in violence at Lexington and Concord on April 19, 1775. When news of the subsequent battle for Bunker Hill reached England that summer, George III and his ministers concluded that there was no alternative to using force to put down the insurrection. In the King's mind, at least, there was no longer any hope of reconciliation—nor did the idea appeal to him. He was determined to teach the rebellious colonials a lesson, and no doubts troubled him as to the righteousness of the course he had chosen. "I am not sorry that the line of conduct seems now chalked out," he had said even before fighting began; later he told his prime minister, Lord North, "I know I am doing my Duty and I can never wish to retract." And then, making acceptance of the war a matter of personal loyalty, "I wish nothing but good," he said, "therefore anyone who does not agree with me is a traitor and a scoundrel." Filled with high moral purpose and confidence, he was certain that "when once these rebels have felt a smart blow, they will submit. . . ."

In British political and military circles there was general agreement that the war would be quickly and easily won. "Shall we be told," asked one of the King's men in Commons, "that [the Americans] can resist the powerful efforts of this nation?" Major John Pitcairn, writing home from Boston in March, 1775, said, "I am satisfied that one active campaign, a smart action, and burning two or three of their towns, will set everything to rights." The man who would direct the British navy during seven years of war, the unprincipled, inefficient Earl of Sandwich, rose in the House of Lords to express his opinion of the provincial fighting man. "Suppose the Colonies do abound in men," the First Lord of the Admiralty asked, "what does that signify? They are raw, undisciplined, cowardly men. I wish instead of forty or fifty thousand of these *brave* fellows they would produce in the field at least two hundred thousand; the more the better, the easier would be the conquest; if they did not run away, they would starve themselves into compliance with our measures. . . ." And General James Murray, who had succeeded the great Wolfe in 1749 as commander in North America, called the native American "a very effeminate thing, very unfit for and very impatient of war." Between these estimates of the colonial militiaman and a belief that the might of Great Britain was invincible, there was a king of arrogant optimism in official quarters when the conflict began. "As there is not common sense in protracting a war of this sort," wrote Lord George Germain, the secretary for the American colonies, in September, 1775, "I should be for exerting the utmost force of this Kingdom to finish the rebellion in one campaign."

Optimism bred more optimism, arrogance more arrogance. One armchair strategist in the House of Commons, William Innes, outlined for the other members an elaborate scheme he had devised for the conduct of the war. First, he would remove the British troops from Boston, since that place was poorly situated for defense. Then, while the people of the Massachusetts Bay Colony were treated like the madmen they were and shut up by the navy, the army would move to one of the southern colonies, fortify itself in an impregnable position, and let the provincials attack if they pleased. The British could sally forth from this and other defensive enclaves at will, and eventually "success against one-half of America will pave the way to the conquest of the whole. . . ." What was more, Innes went on, it was "more than probable you may find men to recruit your army in America." There was a good possibility, in other words, that the British regulars would be replaced after a while by Americans who were loyal to their king, so that the army fighting the rebels would be Americanized, so to speak, and the Irish and English lads sent home. General James Robertson also believed that success lay in this scheme of Americanizing the combat force: "I never had an idea of subduing the Americans," he said, "I meant to assist the good Americans to subdue the bad."

This notion was important not only from the standpoint of the fighting, but in terms of administering the colonies once they were beaten; loyalists would take over the reins of government when the British pulled out, and loyalist militiamen would preserve order in the pacified colonies. No one knew, of course, how many "good" Americans there were; some thought they might make up half or more of the population. Shortly after arriving in the colonies in 1775, General William Howe, for one, was convinced that "the insurgents are very few, in comparison with the whole of the people."

Before taking the final steps into full-scale war, however, the King and his ministers had to be certain about one vitally important matter: they had to be able to count on the support of the English people. On several occasions in 1775 they were able to read the public pulse (that part of it, at least, that mattered) by observing certain important votes in Parliament. The King's address to both Houses on October 26, in which he announced plans to suppress the uprising in America, was followed by weeks of angry debate; but when the votes were counted, the North ministry's majority was overwhelming. Each vote indicated the full tide of anger that influenced the independent members, the country gentlemen who agreed that the colonials must be put in their place and taught a lesson. A bit out of touch with the news, highly principled, and content in the belief that the King and the ministry must be right, none of them seem to have asked what would be best for the empire; they simply went along with the vindictive measures that were being set in motion. Eloquent voices—those of Edmund Burke, Charles James Fox, the Earl of Chatham, John Wilkes, among others—were raised in opposition to the policies of the Crown, but as Burke said, ". . . it was almost in vain to contend, for the country gentlemen had abandoned their duty, and placed an implicit confidence in the Minister."

The words of sanity and moderation went unheeded because the men who spoke them were out of power and out of public favor; and each time the votes were tallied, the strong, silent, unquestioning majority prevailed. No one in any position of power in the government proposed, after the Battle of Bunker Hill, to halt the fighting in order to settle the differences; no one seriously contemplated conversations that might have led to peace. Instead the government—like so many governments before and since—took what appeared to be the easy way out and settled for war.

George III was determined to maintain his empire, intact and undiminished, and his greatest fear was that the loss of the American colonies would set off a reaction like a line of dominoes falling. Writing to Lord North in 1779, he called the contest with America "the most serious in which any country was ever engaged. It contains such a train of consequences that they must be examined to feel its real weight. . . . Independence is [the Americans'] object, which every man not willing to sacrifice every object to a momentary and inglorious peace must concur with me in thinking this country can never submit to. Should America succeed in that, the West Indies must follow, not in independence, but for their own interest they must become dependent on America. Ireland would soon follow, and this island reduced to itself, would be a poor island indeed."

Despite George's unalterable determination, strengthened by his domino theory; despite the wealth and might of the British empire; despite all the odds favoring a quick triumph, the problems facing the King and his ministers and the armed forces were formidable ones indeed. Surpassing all others in sheer magnitude was the immense distance between the mother country and the rebellious colonies. As Edmund Burke described the situation in his last, most eloquent appeal for conciliation, "Three thousand miles of ocean lie between you and them. No contrivance can prevent the effect of this distance in weakening government. Seas roll, and months pass, between the order and the execution; and the want of a speedy explanation of a single point is enough to defeat a whole system." Often the westerly passage took three months, and every soldier, every weapon, every button and gaiter and musket ball, every article of clothing and great quantities of food and even fuel, had to be shipped across those three thousand miles of the Atlantic. It was not only immensely costly and time consuming, but there was a terrifying wastefulness to it. Ships sank or were blown hundreds of miles off course, supplies spoiled, animals died en route. Worse yet, men died, and in substantial numbers: returns from regiments sent from the British Isles to the West Indies between 1776 and 1780 reveal that an average of 11 per cent of the troops was lost on these crossings.

Beyond the water lay the North American land mass, and it was an article of faith on the part of many a British military man that certain ruin lay in fighting an enemy on any large scale in that savage wilderness. In the House of Lords in November, 1775, the Duke of Richmond warned the peers to consult their geographies before turning their backs on a peaceful settlement. There was, he said, "one insuperable difficulty with which an army would have to struggle"—America abounded in vast rivers that provided natural barriers to the progress of troops; it was a country in which every bush might conceal an enemy, a land whose cultivated parts would be laid waste, so that "the army (if any army could march or subsist) would be obliged to draw all its provisions from Europe, and all its fresh meat from Smithfield market." The French, the mortal enemies of Great Britain, who had seen a good deal more of the North American wilds than the English had, were already laying plans to capitalize on the situation when the British army was bogged down there. In Paris, watchfully eyeing his adversary's every move, France's foreign minister, the Comte de Vergennes, predicted in July, 1775, that "it will be vain for the English to multiply their forces" in the colonies; "no longer can they bring that vast continent back to dependence by force of arms." Seven years later, as the war drew to a close, one of Rochambeau's aides told a friend of Charles James Fox: "No opinion was clearer than that though the people of America might be conquered by well disciplined European troops, the country of America was unconquerable."

Yet even in 1775 some thoughtful Englishmen doubted if the American people or their army could be defeated. Before the news of Bunker Hill arrived in London, the adjutant general declared that a plan to defeat the colonials militarily was "as wild an idea as ever controverted common sense," and the secretary-at-war, Lord Barrington, had similar reservations. As early as 1774 Barrington ventured the opinion that a war in the wilderness of North America would cost Britain far more than she could ever gain from it; that the size of the country and the colonials' familiarity with firearms would make victory questionable—or at best achievable only at the cost of enormous suffering; and finally, even if Britain should win such a contest, Barrington believed that the cost of maintaining the colonies in any state of subjection would be staggering. John Wilkes, taunting Lord North on this matter of military conquest, suggested that North—even if he rode out at the head of the entire English cavalry—would not venture ten miles into the countryside for fear of guerrilla fighters. "The Americans," Wilkes promised, "will dispute every inch of territory with you, every narrow pass, every strong defile, every Thermopylae, every Bunker's Hill."

It was left to the great William Pitt to provide the most stirring warning against fighting the Americans. Now Earl of Chatham, he was so crippled in mind and body that he rarely appeared in the House of Lords, but in May, 1777, he made the supreme effort, determined to raise his voice once again in behalf of conciliation. Supported on canes, his eyes flashing with the old fire and his beak-like face thrust forward belligerently, he warned the peers: "You cannot conquer the Americans. You talk of your numerous friends to annihilate the Congress, and of your powerful forces to disperse their army, but I might as well talk of driving them before me with this crutch. . . . You have been three years teaching them the art of war, and they are apt scholars. I will venture to tell your lordships that the American gentry will make officers enough fit to command the troops of all the European powers. What you have sent there are too many to make peace, too few to make war. You cannot make them respect you. You cannot make them wear your cloth. You will plant an invincible hatred in their breast against you. . . ."

"My lords," he went on, "you have been the aggressors from the beginning. I say again, this country has been the aggressor. You have made descents upon their coasts. You have burnt their towns, plundered their country, made war upon the inhabitants, confiscated their property, proscribed and imprisoned their persons. . . . The people of America look upon Parliament as the authors of their miseries. Their affections are estranged from their sovereign. Let, then, reparation come from the hands that inflicted the injuries. Let conciliation succeed chastisement. . . ." But there was no persuading the majority; Chatham's appeal was rejected and the war went on unabated.

It began to appear, however, that destruction of the Continental Army—even if that goal could be achieved—might not be conclusive. After the disastrous campaign around Manhattan in 1776, George Washington had determined not to risk his army in a major engagement, and he began moving away from the European battle style in which two armies confronted each other head to head. His tactical method became that of the small, outweighed prizefighter who depends on his legs to keep him out of range of his opponent and who, when the bigger man begins to tire, darts in quickly to throw a quick punch, then retreats again. It was an approach to fighting described by Nathanael Greene, writing of the campaign in the South in 1780: "We fight, get beat, rise, and fight again." In fact, between January and September of the following year, Greene, short of money, troops, and supplies, won a major campaign without ever really winning a battle. The battle at Guilford Courthouse, which was won by the British, was typical of the results. As Horace Walpole observed, "Lord Cornwallis has conquered his troops out of shoes and provisions and himself out of troops."

There was, in the colonies, no great political center like Paris or London, whose loss might have been demoralizing to the Americans; indeed, Boston, New York, and Philadelphia, the seat of government, were all held at one time or another by the British without irreparable damage to the rebel cause. The fragmented political and military structure of the colonies was often a help to the rebels, rather than a hindrance, for it meant that there was almost no chance of the enemy striking a single crushing blow. The difficulty, as General Frederick Haldimand, who succeeded Carleton in Canada, saw it, was the seemingly unending availability of colonial militiamen who rose up out of nowhere to fight in support of the nucleus of regular troops called the Continental Army. "It is not the number of troops Mr. Washington can spare from his army that is to be apprehended," Haldimand wrote, "it is the multitude of militia and men in arms ready to turn out at an hour's notice at the shew of a single regiment of Continental Troops. . . ." So long as the British were able to split up their forces and fan out over the countryside in relatively small units, they were fairly successful in putting down the irregulars' activities and cutting off their supplies; but the moment they had to concentrate again to fight the Continentals, guerrilla warfare burst out like so many small brush fires on their flank and rear. No British regular could tell if an American was friend or foe, for loyalty to King George was easy to attest; and the man who was a farmer or merchant when a British battalion marched by his home was a militiaman as soon as it had passed by, ready to shoulder his musket when an emergency or an opportunity to confound the enemy arose.

Against an unnumberable supply of irregular forces the British could bring to bear only a fixed quantity of troops—however many, that is, they happened to have on the western side of the Atlantic Ocean at any given moment. Early in the war General James Murray had foreseen the difficulties that would undoubtedly arise. Writing to Lord Barrington, he warned that military conquest was no real answer. If the war proved to be a long one, their advantage in numbers would heavily favor the rebels, who could replace their losses while the British could not. Not only did every musket and grain of powder have to be shipped across the ocean; but if a man was killed or wounded, the only way to replace him was to send another man in full kit across the Atlantic. And troop transports were slow and small: three or four were required to move a single battalion.

During the summer of 1775 recruiting went badly in England and Ireland, for the war was not popular with a lot of the people who would have to fight it, and there were jobs to be had. It was evident that the only means of assembling a force large enough to suppress the rebellion in the one massive stroke that had been determined upon was to hire foreign troops. And immediately this word was out, the rapacious petty princes of Brunswick, Hesse-Cassel, and Waldeck, and the Margrave of Anspach-Bayreuth, generously offered up a number of their subjects—at a price—fully equipped and ready for duty, to serve His Majesty George III. Frederick the Great of Prussia, seeing the plan for what it was, announced that he would "make all the Hessian troops, marching through his dominions to America, pay the usual cattle tax, because, although human beings, they had been sold as beasts." But George III and the princes regarded it as a business deal, in the manner of such dubious alliances ever since: each foot soldier and trooper supplied by the Duke of Brunswick, for instance, was to be worth seven pounds, four shillings, fourpence halfpenny in levy money to his Most Serene Highness. Three wounded men were to count as one killed in action, and it was stipulated that a soldier killed in combat would be paid for at the same rate as levy money. In other words the life of a subject was worth precisely seven pounds, four shillings, fourpence halfpenny to the Duke.

As it turned out, the large army that was assembled in 1776 to strike a quick, overpowering blow that would put a sudden end to the rebellion proved—when that decisive victory never came to pass—to be a distinct liability, a hideously expensive and at times vulnerable weapon. In the indecisive hands of men like William Howe and Henry Clinton, who never seemed absolutely certain about what they should do or how they should do it, the great army rarely had an opportunity to realize its potential; yet, it remained a ponderous and insatiable consumer of supplies, food, and money.

The loyalists, on whom many Englishmen had placed such high hopes, proved a will-o'-the-wisp. Largely ignored by the policy makers early in the war despite their pleas for assistance, the loyalists were numerous enough but were neither well organized nor evenly distributed throughout the colonies. Where the optimists in Britain went wrong in thinking that loyalist strength would be an important factor was to imagine that anything like a majority of Americans *could* remain loyal to the Crown if they were not continuously supported and sustained by the mother country. Especially as the war went on, as opinions hardened, and as the possibility increased that the new government in America might actually survive, it was a very difficult matter to retain one's loyalty to the King unless friends and neighbors were of like mind and unless there was British force nearby to safeguard such a belief. Furthermore, it proved almost impossible for the British command to satisfy the loyalists, who were bitterly angry over the persecution and physical violence and robbery they had to endure and who charged constantly that the British generals were too lax in their treatment of rebels.

While the problems of fighting the war in distant America mounted, Britain found herself unhappily confronted with the combination of circumstances the Foreign Office dreaded most: with her armies tied down, the great European maritime powers—France and Spain—vengeful and adventurous and undistracted by war in the Old World, formed a coalition against her. When the American war began, the risk of foreign intervention was regarded as minimal, and the decision to fight was made on the premise that victory would be early and complete and that the armed forces would be released before any threatening European power could take advantage of the situation. But as the war continued without any definite signs of American collapse, France and Spain seized the chance to embarrass and perhaps humiliate their old antagonist. At first they supported the rebels surreptitiously with shipments of weapons and other supplies; then, when the situation appeared more auspicious, France in particular furnished active support in the form of an army and a navy, with catastrophic results for Great Britain.

One fascinating might-have-been is what would have happened had the Opposition in Parliament been more powerful politically. It consisted, after all, of some of the most forceful and eloquent orators imaginable, men whose words still have the power to send shivers up the spine. Not simply vocal, they were highly intelligent men whose concern went beyond the injustice and inhumanity of war. They were quick to see that the personal liberty of the King's subjects was as much an issue in London as it was in the colonies, and they foresaw irreparable damage to the empire if the government followed its unthinking policy of coercion. Given a stronger power base, they might have headed off war or the ultimate disaster; had the government been in the hands of men like Chatham or Burke or their followers, some accommodation with America might conceivably have evolved from the various proposals for reconciliation. But the King and North had the votes in their pockets, and the antiwar Opposition failed because a majority that was largely indifferent to reason supported the North ministry until the bitter end came with Cornwallis' surrender. Time and again a member of the Opposition would rise to speak out against the war for one reason or another: "This country," the Earl of Shelburne protested, "already burdened much beyond its abilities, is now on the eve of groaning under new taxes, for the purpose of carrying on this cruel and destructive war." Or, from Dr. Franklin's friend David Hartley: "Every proposition for reconciliation has so constantly and uniformly been crushed by Administration, that I think they seem not even to wish for the appearance of justice. The law of force is that which they appeal to. . . ." Or, from Sir James Lowther, when he learned that the King had rejected an "Olive Branch Petition" from the provincials: "Why have we not peace with a people who, it is evident, desire peace with us?" Or this, from General Henry Seymour Conway, inviting Lord North to inform members of the House of Commons about his overall program: "I do not desire the detail; let us have general outline, to be able to judge of the probability of its success. It is indecent not to lay before the House some plan, or the outlines of a plan. . . . If [the] plan is conciliation, let us see it, that we may form some opinion of it; if it be hostility and coercion, I do repeat, that we have no cause for a minute's consideration; for I can with confidence pronounce, that the present military armament will never succeed." But all unavailing, year after year, as each appeal to reason and humanity fell on ears deafened by self-righteousness and minds hardened against change.

Although it might be said that the arguments raised by the Opposition did not change the course of the war, they nevertheless affected the manner in which it was conducted, which in turn led to the ultimate British defeat. Whether Lord North was uncertain of that silent majority's loyalty is difficult to determine, but it seems clear that he was sufficiently nervous about public support to decide that a bold policy which risked defeats was not for him. As a result the war of the American Revolution was a limited war—limited from the standpoint of its objectives and the force with which Britain waged it.

In some respects the aspect of the struggle that may have had the greatest influence on the outcome was an intangible one. Until the outbreak of hostilities in 1775 no more than a small minority of the colonials had seriously contemplated independence, but after a year of war the situation was radically different. Now the mood was reflected in words such as these—instructions prepared by the county of Buckingham, in Virginia, for its delegates to a General Convention in Williamsburg: ". . . as far as your voices are admitted, you [will] cause a free and happy Constitution to be established, with a renunciation of the old, and so much thereof as has been found inconvenient and oppressive." That simple and powerful idea—renunciation of the old and its replacement with something new, independently conceived—was destined to sweep all obstacles before it. In Boston, James Warren was writing the news of home to John Adams in Philadelphia and told him: "Your Declaration of Independence came on Saturday and diffused a general joy. Every one of us feels more important than ever; we now congratulate each other as Freemen." Such winds of change were strong, and by contrast all Britain had to offer was a return to the status quo. Indeed, it was difficult for the average Englishman to comprehend the appeal that personal freedom and independence held for a growing number of Americans. As William Innes put it in a debate in Commons, all the government had to do to put an end to the nonsense in the colonies was to "convince the lower class of those infatuated people that the imaginary liberty they are so eagerly pursuing is not by any means to be compared to that which the Constitution of this happy country already permits them to enjoy."

With everything to gain from victory and everything to lose by defeat, the Americans could follow Livy's advice, that "in desperate matters the boldest counsels are the safest." Frequently beaten and disheartened, inadequately trained and fed and clothed, they fought on against unreasonably long odds because of that slim hope of attaining a distant goal. And as they fought on, increasing with each passing year the possibility that independence might be achieved, the people of Britain finally lost the will to keep going.

In England the goal had not been high enough, while the cost was too high. There was nothing compelling about the limited objective of bringing the colonies back into the empire, nothing inspiring about punishing the rebels, nothing noble in proving that retribution awaited those who would change the nature of things.

After the war had been lost and the treaty of peace signed, Lord North looked back on the whole affair and sadly informed the members of the House of Commons where, in his opinion, the fault lay. With a few minor changes, it was a message as appropriate to America in 1971 as to Britain in 1783: "The American war," he said, "has been suggested to have been the war of the Crown, contrary to the wishes of the people. I deny it. It was the war of Parliament. There was not a step taken in it that had not the sanction of Parliament. It was the war of the people, for it was undertaken for the express purpose of maintaining the just rights of Parliament, or, in other words, of the people of Great Britain, over the dependencies of the empire. For this reason, it was popular at its commencement, and eagerly embraced by the people and Parliament. . . .

Nor did it ever cease to be popular until a series of unparalleled disasters and calamities caused the people, wearied out with almost uninterrupted ill-success and misfortune, to call out as loudly for peace as they had formerly done for war.''

Mr. Ketchum, senior editor of this company, is the author of our series of vignettes called Faces from the Past (recently published in book form under the same title). He was editor of The American Heritage Book of the Revolution *and is currently writing a book about the crucial events of 1776, which he regards as the turning point of the struggle.*

For further reading: The British Empire Before the American Revolution, *Vol. 12,* The Triumphant Empire: Britain Sails into the Storm, 1770–1776, *by Lawrence Henry Gipson (Knopf, 1965);* British Politics and the American Revolution: The Path to War, 1773–75, *by Bernard Donoughue (St. Martin's Press, 1965);* The War for America, 1775–1783, *by Piers G. Mackesy (Harvard University Press, 1964);* The First Year of the American Revolution, *by Allen French (Octagon, 1967).*

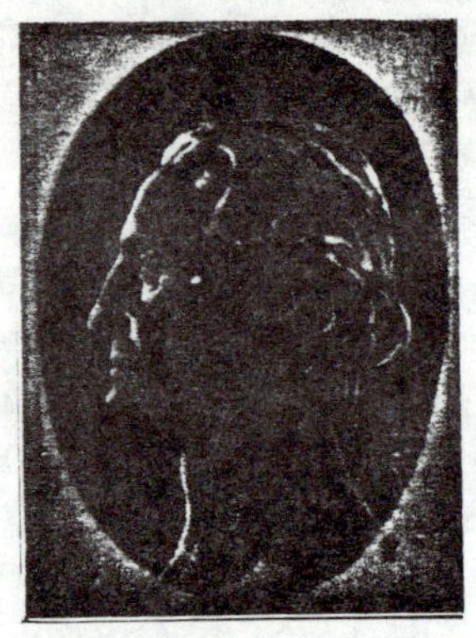

The Newburgh Conspiracy

James W. Wensyel

Sunday, October 27, 1782. Mist and intermittent sheets of cold rain shrouded the granite spine of Butter Hill as it stretched west from the Hudson River above West Point toward the distant Shawangunk mountain range. Farmers, working neat, stone-walled fields, watched the storm without noticing anything unusual along the mountain's crest. At dusk, however, the rain eased and the mist lifted to reveal something new and strange. High on the mountain hundreds of small lights flickered like fireflies. Highlanders were puzzled, then exclaimed, "They're campfires. It's the army. Back for winter."

They were right. Washington's northern wing of the Continental Army had marched from its summer camp near Peekskill, New York, to Constitution Island, ferried across the Hudson, then climbed the steep mountain. This night would be the last the army would spend on an open, rain-soaked field. In the morning it would march to nearby New Windsor to build its final winter camp.

The campsite, about four miles southwest of Washington's Newburgh headquarters, was well chosen. Butter Hill (now called Storm King Mountain) protected it from sudden attack, yet it lay within a forced march of West Point, with its crucial command of the Hudson. It also lay near main roads from New England and mid-Atlantic supply bases.

At dawn villagers watched the ragged army closing on New Windsor. The infantrymen drew a mixed response. After more than seven years fighting most Americans still opposed the war or were neutral. Others ignored political considerations to trade with the British. Even those who stood squarely for independence were not terribly happy about having hardened veterans camped nearby, destroying wood lots, fouling streams, practicing "midnight requisitions" upon nearby farm stock. So the loose-striding infantrymen and the watching civilians eyed each other warily.

The New Windsor Cantonment quickly became the most substantial American camp of the war. Its fourteen to fifteen regiments totaled some seven to eight thousand men, but throughout the winter many were furloughed, and sickness struck one out of eight of the rest. Units came from Massachusetts, New Hampshire, New York, New Jersey, and Maryland. Away from the main camp, Rhode Island, Connecticut, and Canadian regiments protected the Highlands' approaches. Others rotated two-week tours ''on the lines'' facing British outposts in Westchester.

More than seven hundred log huts, each built by soldiers from whatever material lay at hand, marked the camp's sixteen thousand acres. Washington warned that ''any hut that will be built irregularly . . . shall be demolished.'' As promised, he had several nearly completed huts torn down. But veterans learned quickly, and Washington soon felt able to take pleasure in ''the present comfortable and beautiful situation of the troops. . . .''

During the next ten months several historical firsts occurred at the camp's central building. On a hill overlooking the regimental areas, solider-artisans erected a large building to be used for administrative and social functions, and for brigade-size chapel services on Sundays. Chaplains called it the ''Temple''; adjutants referred to it as the ''Public Building''; the riflemen simply called it the ''new building.'' By whatever name, it served the army well. It was the first chapel built by American soldiers. It sheltered an awards board, which granted three sergeants purple, heart-shaped medals of valor, the first time in any army that enlisted soldiers were so honored. From its steps Washington's adjutants announced the cease fire ending the war.

And here, on March 15, 1783, Washington's officers met for what the historian James Thomas Flexner saw as ''probably the most important single gathering ever held in the United States.'' That gathering involved mutiny. Mutiny by Washington's officers.

Some historians call the incident the ''Newburgh Addresses''; others know it as the ''Newburgh Conspiracy.'' Simply stated, it was a chain of events culminating in a meeting to decide whether the officers would trust Congress to redeem overdue pay and pension claims or whether they would open the national treasury with the army's bayonets. In every successful armed rebellion the generals eventually must decide whether to yield to civil authority or opt for military dictatorship. The choice they make frames that country's future. For America the hour of decision fell in the last, bitter winter of the war.

Washington's concern for his camp's appearance was not for aesthetics alone. Having commanded the army for more than seven years—outlasting three British counterparts—he knew his regiments well. And he sensed that the army's morale, particularly that of its officers, was as low now as it had been at any other time during the war—even the dark winter days of Valley Forge. He expected trouble. Keeping everyone busy might help.

Although the Yorktown victory a year before seemed decisive, the British fleet still owned the Atlantic. Spring reinforcements could make it a whole new war. Washington had to hold his army together. The army, however, believed that the Paris negotiations soon would end the fighting. That happy prospect also brought concerns. Pay was as much as six years overdue. Pensions had not been settled. Appeals to the various states went unanswered or were referred to the Congress. And Congress could not afford a wintering army, let alone consider back pay or postwar benefits.

Washington's officers were particularly concerned. In 1781 they had agreed to a pension of half-pay for life. The promise, however, seemed, like the national currency, "not worth a Continental." So long as the army lived, officers saw hope for their claims. Once it disbanded, however, their scattered voices would be politically inaudible. All felt that congressional action had to come before spring, before peace.

Washington repeatedly urged Congress and the states to redeem their pledges. Meanwhile he furloughed hundreds of officers and men and tried to keep the others busy. Baron von Steuben pushed training and inspections. Washington considered raids on Long Island and Manhattan, against Fort Oswego and other lake forts, against the British at Penobscot. He decided against a short visit to Mount Vernon. In seven years he'd been there only briefly during the Yorktown campaign, but now instinct told him to stay close to camp.

As snow covered the Highlands, his problems worsened. Washington reported that his hard-worked horses had been four days without feed of any kind. Senior officers could not visit their scattered units, and express riders had to carry dispatches on foot.

Bone-chilling winds blew in from the Atlantic, reddening the cheeks of British grenadiers on Manhattan's ramparts. They swept upriver, freezing the Hudson. The bitter gusts divided the West Point; some leaped the mountain's crest to race downhill and make miserable Washington's Life Guards shivering outside the stone house on Newburgh's river bluff.

Uniforms were ragged and scant. Promised trousers never arrived. Philadelphia shipped less than half the shirts promised. Soldiers with none were issued one; lots were drawn for the rest. Outposts shared on winter coat among six men.

Food was adequate for veterans but there was little to spare and little variety. Hospitals were full. Shortages affected discipline. Riflemen at cantonment markets squabbled with farmers and merchants. Despite guards, repeated fist fights frightened away civilians. The infantrymen complained bitterly that civilians profited while they suffered. Enterprising soldiers swapped firewood, stolen from woodcutting details. If they were caught, punishment was swift and painful.

On Christmas Day, 1782, ten light infantrymen of the 1 Massachusetts Regiment feasted on eleven stolen geese. The court sentenced each man to receive one hundred lashes and ordered stoppages of pay until fifteen dollars were returned to the farmer. Light infantrymen, the toughest of Washington's soldiers, could not have relished standing stripped to the waist in the biting wind to receive one hundred lashes but probably laughed at the idea of forfeiting pay they had never received and probably never would.

Desertions increased. Silas Rodgers of the 3rd Massachusetts Regiment, and John Murrow and Benjamin Fisk of the 9th Massachusetts Regiment, caught outside the camp without passes, received one hundred lashes on the spot.

Officers' morale continued to fall, too. Congress ordered that regiments be reorganized with five hundred officers and men for each regiment. Smaller states had to recruit or lose their regiments. And states refused to recruit. The war was winding down: why pay enlistment bonuses for an army that might not be needed or wanted? Tested leaders, many of them in the field since Bunker Hill, faced loss of their appointments, their pay, their promised pensions and land grants.

The more knowledgeable realized that neither Washington nor the Congress could do much. No one could give what he didn't have. Under the loose Confederation, Congress could not demand money from the states or collect taxes itself. A national impost duty requested in 1781 by the superintendent of finance, Robert Morris, and his assistant, Gouverneur Morris, and supported by such strong nationalists as Alexander Hamilton and James Madison, still had not been ratified. Realizing all that, however, eased no one's anger.

Even if money existed, the officers knew that their countrymen, many of whom had grown rich while the soldiers fought the war, would never approve continuing veterans' pensions. So in December, 1782, led by General Henry Knox, the officers drew up another petition to the Congress. It demanded long-overdue pay and suggested that the half-pay-for-life provision be commuted to a one-time lump-sum payment.

From Philadelphia, General Arthur St. Clair had warned Knox to make it very clear that, unless Congress acted quickly, it could expect "a convulsion of the most dreadful nature and fatal consequences." Following that suggestion, Knox wrote: "We have borne all that men can bear . . . our property is expended . . . our private resources are at an end . . . our friends are wearied . . . with our incessant applications." Knox ended the petition with the obvious threat that "any further experiments on their [the army's] patience may have fatal effects."

In a private letter, Washington confided to his friend Congressman Joseph Jones of Virginia: "The temper of the Army is much soured, and has become more irritable than at any period since the commencement of the War.

"The dissatisfactions of the Army had arisen to a great and alarming height. . . . No part of the community has undergone . . . hardships, and borne them with the . . . patience and fortitude, as the Army has done."

He added: "Hitherto the Officers have stood between the lower order of the Soldiery and the public and . . . have quelled very dangerous mutinies. [I]f their discontents . . . rise equally high, I know not . . . the consequences." He ended wearily: "The spirit of enthusiasm . . . is now done away."

Major General Alexander McDougall and Colonels John Brooks and Matthias Ogden carried the petition, signed by almost all the officers at the cantonment, to Philadelphia. Superintendent Morris, however, immediately dashed their hopes for a quick and satisfactory response by telling them that Virginia had repealed her earlier ratification of the 1781 impost. As Rhode Island had never ratified the tariff, Virginia's added rejection killed that legislation. The nationalists had called that impost "the only means of restoring Public Credit, of preventing a Disunion of the States, and saving the Country. . . ." Now that hope seemed dead.

If the officers smelled defeat, however, the nationalists viewed the situation differently. A customs duty remained vital to their plans for national revenue and a strong central government. Now they saw the officers' petition as their weapon to get it. Its threat of "exhausted patience" was potent. Congress had to find new revenue. Paper money was worthless. More foreign loans were unlikely. A new impost amendment was the only answer. Hamilton assured Washington that "the necessity and discontents of the army presented . . . a powerful engine"; and Gouverneur Morris predicted, "Depend on it, good will arise from the situation to which we are hastening."

The "good" had to be reached by a dangerous route. Even now historians cannot agree on the nationalists' exact plan or the specific roles individuals played in it. Their basic idea, however, was extortion, pure and simple. Let the states yield power to raise funds and satisfy the army, or face mutiny. And, with mutiny, loss of the war. Morris and his associates played a dangerous game. Without risking it, they saw no impost, only continuing erosion of the Confederation. If they tried it, they risked anarchy, civil war, a violent end to the Confederation. They decided to chance it. Let the army threaten, even act. Then the nationalists could force an acceptable impost. What is not clear (and never has been) is how far they were willing to let the army go before stopping it—and how they expected the mutiny genie, once uncorked, to be forced back into its bottle.

Morris had General McDougall open the campaign. The general easily convinced Congress that Washington was sitting on a powder keg, that only a satisfactory response to the army's petition could prevent an explosion at Newburgh.

While Hamilton drafted a report supporting the army's claims, Morris offered a new impost proposal. Then, as Congress debated, Morris upped the ante by threatening his own resignation unless "permanent provision for the public debt of every kind" be established. Congress took the bait, but Morris could not win the whole pot. The legislators accepted only the back-pay claims and urged Morris to "make every effort to obtain from the respective states substantial funds, adequate to the object of funding the whole debt of the United States." Morris had won the responsibility but no authority to carry it out. Our federal bureaucracy worked in strange ways, then as now. As January, ended, Congress again rejected Morris' efforts for commutation and impost.

If his campaign moved slowly in Philadelphia, Morris also had problems in Newburgh. Washington was the best choice to handle the army's role. Most of the officers genuinely respected and admired him; only he and Henry Knox had the broad support needed. The conspirators agreed, however, that Washington never would sanction their plan. They turned to Knox. By letters and through several briefings by General McDougall, Morris urged Knox to use the army to force congressional action. He even suggested that a limited mutiny might be necessary but added that if it happened, Knox had to be ready to snuff it out. To Morris' dismay, Knox remained silent. Knox knew Washington would never use the army as a political weapon, and it seemed he would not oppose Washington. Morris and Hamilton decided to look further.

They approached General Horatio Gates, Washington's second-in-command. Politically minded and ambitious, Gates felt that he had never received proper credit for his victory at Saratoga. He disliked Washington and earlier had worked behind the scenes to replace him. His plan had failed, and the sourness between the two generals never sweetened. Gates's staff included young, ambitious officers. They would support him. And Gates, known to the army as "Granny," could be manipulated by skilled politicians. The plotters were dubious about Gates, but they had no one else on whom to gamble.

The game began quickly. Congress again rejected commutation. On February 21 Knox finally wrote McDougall, "I consider the reputation of the American Army as one of the most immaculate things on earth. . . . [W]e should even suffer wrongs and injuries to the utmost verge of toleration rather than sully it in the least degree." To Morris he added the warning that the army would exert no pressure except when directed by the "proper authority." And about the same time, Washington answered a cautious, testing letter from Hamilton.

The general had been only too aware of his army's discontent. And friends had alerted him to rumors in Philadelphia. Congressman Jones reported hearing of "dangerous combinations in the Army" made up of "those who are abandoned enough to use their arts to lessen your popularity . . . in hopes . . . [you] will prove no obstacle to their ambitious design."

Hamilton's letter had come hard on the heels of Jones's warnings. He stressed the injustice to the army and his fear that peace, surely coming soon, would end hope of a settlement. He reported suggestions "by others" that the army force its claim by bayonet. The problem there was to "keep a *complaining* and *suffering army* within the bounds of moderation." Again a well-controlled little mutiny. Hamilton concluded by warning his former commander "*to take the direction* of the Army's anger" as many officers felt Washington's past efforts lacked "sufficient warmth."

This is a particularly interesting letter. It clearly suggested Washington use the army to pressure Congress but warned of the danger of a mutiny pressed too far and of Washington's losing his own influence unless he took a stronger hand in the game. Why did Hamilton alert Washington to the challenge to his leadership? Perhaps he hoped to cover his bet on the weaker Gates. If Gates had to lead the army to mutiny, then could not call a halt, even a weakened Washington would be awfully nice to have around.

Washington's answer was characteristically direct. He described himself as caught between the "sufferings of a complaining Army on one hand, and the inability of Congress and tardiness of the States on the other. . . ." He would just have to "pursue the same steady line of conduct which [had] governed [him] hitherto; fully convinced that the sensible, and discerning part of the Army cannot be unacquainted . . . of the services [he had] rendered it. . . ." He reminded his former aide that the commander in chief should be kept abreast of Congress' plans as "the adoption of Military and other arrangements that might be exceedingly proper in some circumstances would be altogether improper in others." Involving the army in civil matters, he concluded, "would be productive of Civil commotions and end in Blood. . . . God forbid we should be involved in it.''

Studying Washington's and Knox's letters, the conspirators knew they had to find a more amenable general. Gates would be their man in Newburgh.

Walter Stewart, a Pennsylvania colonel who had been politicking in Philadelphia during the winter, became their emissary. On Saturday, March 8, Stewart visited Gates's headquarters. No one knows what they said to one another, but as the storm broke the following Monday and involved work by Gates's aides from the eighth on, Stewart's visit seems significant.

On Sunday, the ninth, Washington attended chapel at the cantonment. Later he corrected Lieutenant Andrew Bradford for marching the guard ''in a very irregular and unmilitary manner.'' Otherwise all seemed calm. That evening he entertained guests at his headquarters. He seemed calm and relaxed but rather reserved and preoccupied.

The dawn muster on Monday, March 10, scarcely had ended when an anonymous summons circulated among the units. Officers from every staff and company were to meet the following morning at the Public Building to consider Congress' response to their petition and to vote new measures.

Within hours a second anonymous message appeared. Written Saturday, the eighth, its author identified himself as ''Brutus,'' a ''fellow-soldier.'' Having shared their misery for long months, Brutus wrote, his own faith in Congress was gone. That's why he had called the Tuesday meeting. His words bit deeper: ''But faith has its limits as well as temper—and there are points; beyond which neither can be stretched without sinking into cowardice. . . .'' Whether its use is valid or not, soldiers react strongly to the word ''cowardice.'' Brutus' other words struck home, too. Pledges, he pointed out, didn't fill stomachs, warm camps, or provide for loved ones. The army deserved better.

''Suspect the man, who would advise to more moderation and longer forebearance,'' he said in an obvious reference to Washington, and then went on to argue that, if this was how they were to be treated while still under arms, what could they expect from peace? Once disbanded, the army would be only nine thousand feeble and separate voices.

Pointing to those who prospered at home while the army fought, he asked, ''Can you then consent to be the only sufferers by this revolution, and, retiring from the field, grow old in poverty, wretchedness and contempt?''

Finally he proposed an ultimate resolution to Congress—one written with the point of a bayonet.

Washington studied Brutus' work. The man had summoned an unauthorized general meeting to advise that, if the officers' claims were not immediately met, they settle them by force or simply march to the Ohio and let Congress end the war as it could, ''and mock when their fear cometh on.'' Brutus was skilled. His argument was appealing; its logic and its solutions hard to deny. But Washington knew those solutions could lose the war even as it was nearly won.

At camp, angry officers weighed Brutus' words. Most approved the meeting, and many leaned strongly toward Brutus' suggestions. Only the very thoughtful realized the immensity of the act already begun. The line of authority between the military establishment and the civil government was now to be tested.

Washington was caught in the middle. He could not defy Congress' jurisdiction. Nor could he ignore his officers' anger. To oppose that anger—even to counsel moderation—could destroy his own authority.

He moved quickly. His general orders referred to the anonymous summons as "disorderly" and "irregular," but as commander in chief he now authorized the meeting to be held on Saturday, the fifteenth. That left time for reflection. He charged the officers to study the latest report on congressional actions, then "devise . . . further measures." As he directed the ranking officer present to report the meeting's results, all inferred Washington would not attend.

On Tuesday a second Brutus letter to the soldiers defended the writer's actions. His sentiments were not new, Brutus argued. He had heard them muttered at many campfires. let them now be spoken aloud. "Till now," he charged, "the Commander-in-Chief has regarded the steps you have taken for redress with good wishes alone." Now Washington sanctioned their general meeting. Nevertheless, Brutus added, Washington's views "cannot possibly lessen the independency of your sentiments." The challenge was obvious.

Brutus remained anonymous. Much later, Major John Armstrong, aide-de-camp to Gates, would admit to writing the three messages; Captain Christopher Richmond and Major William Barber, also of Gates's staff, copied and distributed them. Gates's own role and the limits he had set on the action are not clear, but Washington guessed correctly when, in his letter to Hamilton, he attributed much of the army's sullenness to "the old leven," clearly referring to Gates's long-standing discontent.

On Thursday Washington circulated the report on Congress' action. Its vague assurances for redress "when funds become available" satisfied no one. Washington also wrote to Benjamin Harrison, who was the president of the Congress, to Congressman Jones, and to Alexander Hamilton. All the while, however, he knew they could do nothing in the time remaining. Knox, von Steuben, and other trusted lieutenants offered no solutions. Washington was on his own, as he had been so often during this long war.

He rode to the cantonment. All seemed calm, but a sixth sense sharpened by many crises warned him that it was not. Long-shared camaraderies seemed strained. Officers swept off their hats in salute but avoided his eyes and did not smile. This was new. An unmistakable hostility lurked near the surface. The officers seemed almost embarrassed by his presence.

He regretted their anger but understood it. Still they all had to yield to civil authority or the war had been for nothing. He would say that in open meeting, then see whether "Brutus" would debate the issue.

Just before noon, March 15, Washington rode to the Public Building. Many horses waited at the long hitching rail. Inside, hundreds of officers crowded the benches.

General Gates, on the stage, began the meeting. Washington's completely unexpected appearance, however, halted his introductory remarks.

The word quickly spread. Excited talk was replaced by the shuffling of boots, the rattling of shifted scabbards, the crash of benches accidentally overturned as the officers rose. Then there was complete silence. Gates quickly yielded the floor.

Washington faced his officers. He bade them be seated, then took papers from his tunic. His aides, mindful of his dimming vision (during the past week he had been trying a pair of bifocals in the privacy of his office), had copied his notes in large script. His strong farmer's hands flattened the sheets. The deep-set blue eyes slowly scanned the room. He knew most of the officers well. Now they disappointed him. Some seemed angry or sullen. Some welcomed him. Most just seemed embarrassed, like children caught doing something wrong yet determined to do it anyway. The estrangement remained.

Anger edged his voice. He quickly branded the anonymous summons "unmilitary" and "subversive." The officers' claims were valid, however, so he had sanctioned the meeting to discuss their mutual problem.

He turned to the anonymous letters. Their author, he said, was persuasive, but lacked "a regard to justice, and love of country." He pressed his attack: "I have never left your side one moment, but when called from you on public duty." How then, he asked, could they question his concern?

Many of Brutus' arguments, he continued, were valid; his recommendations, however, were not. They were ruinous. Washington suggested, for example, that they consider the fate of their families and property if the army left the field to the British. As for using force to win their claims, he charge, "What can this writer have in view . . . ? Can he be a friend to the Army? Can he be a friend to this Country?" Pitting the army against civil authority would, Washington continued, invite civil war—the end to all they had fought for. No, he concluded, neither of Brutus' alternatives was acceptable. They must not give up what they had earned on a hundred battlefields.

Now his voice was calm, reassuring, persuasive. The solution, he suggested, was continued patience and trust that Congress would redeem its pledges.

Washington turned to his last notes. Moderation and patience would not come easily. They never had. But, he concluded, "By thus determining and thus acting, you will pursue the plain and direct road to . . . your wishes . . . [Y]ou will give one more distinguished proof of unexampled patriotism and patient virtue, rising superior to the pressure of the most complicated sufferings; and you will, by the dignity of your conduct, afford occasion for Posterity to say . . . had this day been wanting, the World had never seen the last stage of perfection to which human nature is capable of attaining."

That ended his formal speech. He had read it all. And it had failed. He knew it had failed. They were not persuaded.

Washington shuffled his papers. He had labored over his speech. But it held long, involved, cumbersome sentences. When spoken, the muscle was lost in the flesh or ornate composition. Washington could not match Brutus as a writer.

In desperation he took a letter from a pocket of his regimentals. In it Congressman Jones praised the army and pledged his support. Perhaps this would help. As Washington opened the note, there was a murmur among his officers. Washington took that as impatience. He cleared his throat and attempted to read.

He could not. The script was too small. His eyes could not focus. The dim letters blurred. Helplessly he fumbled in another pocket for his spectacles. As he donned them, the murmur increased. Again he thought it impatience. He adjusted the spectacles. "Gentlemen," he said, "you must pardon me. I have grown gray in your service and now find myself growing blind."

It was enough. They'd not been impatient. The murmur was one of sympathy, understanding, affection. In their eight years together they had never seen Washington wear spectacles. He had seemed tired and worn before. Now he seemed older and vulnerable. He was only fifty but had aged this week. He had problems they didn't even know about. If he still trusted the Congress, they could do not less.

Few heard as Washington haltingly read from Jones's letter. No matter.

When he stopped, the officers crowded about him in reassurance and contrition. Some wept. Others simply stood, stunned and silent, as the general left the room.

If Gates hoped to regain the initiative, he had no chance. Henry Knox quickly moved to thank the commander for his speech. Then, after a quick review of McDougall's report, General Rufus Putnam moved that Knox's committee prepare new resolutions for the officers' consideration. In short order the officers resolved their "unshaken confidence" in Washington and in the Congress. The crisis was over.

News of the army's action swept the states, redounding to the credit of Washington and his officers. The public knew nothing of the political manipulations that had caused the crisis. A congressional committee recommended commuting half-pay pensions to five years' full pay, a compromise more palatable to Yankee constituents. Within another month Congress accepted a new impost amendment.

The states, however, ratified neither program in time to help the army. New Englanders once more resisted commutation and impost. Meanwhile, peace came at last. Washington ordered a cease fire for noon, April 19, 1783—eight years to the day since the war began. Congress ordered the army disbanded. To save money, Washington quickly furloughed his veterans, the furloughs to become discharges once the peace treaty was ratified. There was no back pay or pension settlement. It would be years before most soldiers saw them. By then many hard-pressed riflemen had sold their country's IOWs to speculators.

Disillusioned and angry officers and men took up their scant belongings and the weapons Congress authorized them to keep for posterity. The New Windsor Cantonment quickly became a ghost camp.

Much of the Newburgh crisis remains hidden. Those contemporaries—like Washington—who pieced together the puzzle had few facts with which to prove a conspiracy. That is probably just as well. It was better that the world did not know of politician's tinkering with the American experiment in democracy. Better yet that it never knew how nearly they succeeded.

In the end, what is important about the Newburgh crisis is what did *not* happen. There was no mutiny, no coup, no military dictatorship. Had the public even considered that imminent possibility, relations between the military and the government it served would have been permanently strained. Once trust between military and civil authorities is broken, it never can be healed. Tyranny attempted once always can be tried again. The precedent that *was* set was that the first national army of the young republic totally rejected military interference in the government and affirmed its subordination to civil authority. America stood at a real crossroads in March of 1783. That Washington, by personal leadership, persuaded his officers to civil obedience ranks as one of his greatest victories.

At the New Windsor Cantonment our army waited for the peace treaty while its soldiers' minds and wills were turned from thoughts of mutiny and military power to civilian authority. Here they received the word of peace and disbanded—but not in a victorious march with pomp and show. Like the winter snows they simply melted away—down the mountain roads back to the farms, back to the cities, back to the schools. For the succeeding two hundred years Americans have honored their soldiers and won great wars. But always they have yielded to the civil state. And General Washington left this post to become, not a king, but the President of a democracy.

James W. Wensyel, a retired Army colonel, directed the Bicentennial restoration of the New Windsor Cantonment.

Business of the Highest Magnitude or

Don't Put Off Until Tomorrow What You Can Ram Through Today

Robert C. Alberts

Dr. Benjamin Rush believed the hand of God must have been involved in the noble work. John Adams, writing from Grosvenor Square, London, called it the greatest single effort of national deliberation, and perhaps the greatest exertion of human understanding, the world had ever seen. A great many people, however, held a contrary view, and in the fall of 1787 their opposition made it seem likely that the proposed Constitution of the United States would not be forwarded to the states by the Continental Congress, or, if forwarded, would not be ratified by the American people.

Opposition was especially intense in Pennsylvania, the only state with a well-developed, statewide two-party system. The Pennsylvania Democrats (Antifederalists) were efficiently organized; they controlled the state militia and the mobs in most cities; and they were led by a group of uncompromising idealogues who were determined that their state would not ratify the new Constitution. Both the Democrats and the pro-Constitution Federalists knew that Pennsylvania was the pivotal state and that the fight there would be an influential and perhaps decisive factor in the large national contest. The struggle that ensued has not often been equalled in this country for bitterness, violence, vehemence of debate, or political high comedy.

The Constitutional Convention completed its work on September 17, after sixteen weeks of almost daily sessions. The engrossed Constitution, signed by thirty-nine delegates from twelve states, was sent forthwith to the Congress in New York City. With it went a covering letter from General George Washington, written, it is thought, by Gouverneur Morris of Pennsylvania. A resolution of the Convention asked the Congress to submit the Constitution for ratification, not, as expected, to the state legislatures, but to a convention of delegates popularly chosen in each state, and convened solely for that purpose.

The next day Benjamin Franklin led the Pennsylvania delegation to the second floor of the State House in Philadelphia to appear before the Pennsylvania House of Assembly. General Thomas Mifflin, Speaker and one of the delegates, read the Constitution aloud. When he finished, the citizens standing in the rear of the chamber broke into applause. On Wednesday the Constitution was printed in full in the *Packet,* the *Journal,* and the *Independent Gazetteer or Chronicle of Freedom,* and thereafter in others of the country's eighty-odd newspapers. It was distributed in Pennsylvania as a pamphlet, with five hundred copies in the German language for the benefit of the state's large German-speaking population.

The first public response seemed to be favorable, but the Democrats were bursting with protest. Speaking ''for the present and future ages—the cause of liberty and mankind,'' they went to work with handbills and pamphlets, with squibs and speeches, with articles and letters in the papers, in meetings and in exchanges in the boarding houses and taverns. To Democrats the new Constitution was the product of ''as deep and wicked a conspiracy as ever was invented in the darkest ages against the liberties of a free people,'' and it ''would surely result in a monarchy or a tyrannical aristocracy,'' and perhaps in civil war. They voiced these major objections:

1. Congress had instructed the Convention delegates to recommend possible amendments to the Articles of Confederation and Perpetual Union. Instead, meeting behind locked doors in a ''dark conclave,'' they had willfully written a plan for an entirely new form of government.

2. Their Constitution would annihilate the present confederation of coequal states, where the sovereign power should properly reside, and substitute for it a consolidated national government. The authority of the states would be grievously curbed if not obliterated. The ability of the new Congress to impose internal taxes and duties at its pleasure would undercut the taxing powers of the individual state legislatures.

3. Unprotected by their state governments, the citizens would be at the mercy of the central government. There was no bill of rights; liberty of the press, habeas corpus, and religious toleration were not assured; trial by jury was abolished in civil cases; and there was no prohibition of a standing army in time of peace.

4. The government of three branches, this ''triple-headed monster,'' was unworkable. The President was too powerful, the Vice President ''a needless and dangerous officer,'' the Senate too aristocractical, the House too small to represent the people, the jurisdiction of the Supreme Court too extensive. The country was too large to be ruled under the principles of liberty by a consolidated government.

5. The whole proposition was extravagant and would bankrupt the nation.

The more zealous Pennsylvania Democrats pounded hard on those objections and added several others of their own. For one thing, none of the eight Pennsylvania delegates to the Convention had been Democrats, and none had come from the six counties beyond the western mountains, where, among Scotch-Irish and German immigrant farmer-frontiersmen, the chief opposition to the Constitution lay. For another, the Democrats would lose jobs, power, and their control over the Pennsylvania militia. For a third, they would probably see the repeal of their ultrademocratic (and unworkable) state constitution. Without having bothered with the formality of a popular vote, they had imposed this constitution on the state in the turmoil of 1776, and they held it to be a model for other states and nations to follow. (Much of it was written by James Cannon, a mathematics professor at the College of Philadelphia who seems to have been somewhat ahead of his time. He tried but failed to include an article reading, "That an enormous proportion of property vested in a few individuals is dangerous to the rights, and destructive of the common happiness, of mankind; and therefore every free state hath a right by its laws to discourage the possession of such property.")

In New York, the Continental Congress had been unable to muster a quorum of seven states throughout the summer, but on Thursday, September 20, attendance picked up and the members took under consideration the new frame of government that had been placed before them. The assent of nine of the thirteen states was required for approval.

Pennsylvania's Federalist congressmen, under the leadership of William Bingham, a wealthy Philadelphia merchant and banker, pushed hard through a week-long debate to forward the Constitution with an affirmative and unanimous endorsement. Richard Henry Lee of Virginia, leading a strong minority, spoke of "essential alterations" and of the need to call another constitutional convention. He moved that a bill of rights and a long list of amendments be added, and he proposed a resolution stating that the new plan of government be submitted to the existing state legislatures rather than to state conventions assembled solely for that purpose. The minority then offered to forward the plan to the states for consideration, but with the warning that the Convention had acted improperly in producing it and with a reprimand to the delegates. The two sides worked for a suitable compromise.

Back in Philadelphia, without waiting for formal word from the Continental Congress, Democrats and Federalists prepared for a mighty struggle in the House of Assembly. The Democratic minority planned a delaying action. The House had resolved to adjourn sine die on Saturday, September 29. Delay would carry the issue over to a new Assembly to be elected five weeks later. Democrats might win a majority in that body and thus have the votes to defeat a call for a state convention—if the Congress really did send the Constitution forward. Or they might elect a majority of anti-Constitution delegates in the convention—if one had to be called. Defeat of the Constitution in Pennsylvania, or delay in calling a state convention, would strengthen the anti-Constitution forces in the twelve other states.

The Federalists not only wanted the Constitution to be ratified in Pennsylvania; they also wanted their state to be the first to act. That would strengthen the movement in the other states. It would take advantage of the early wave of sentiment in favor of the Constitution and give the western farmers less time to find fault with it. It would allow the Democratic leaders the least opportunity to return to their inland counties and organize the opposition. And early ratification would give Pennsylvania a leg up on placing the new seat of government near Philadelphia, where it obviously belonged.

The Federalists drew up a plan designed to take their opponents by surprise. They would make a motion for a state convention on Friday morning, one day before adjournment, and attempt to rush it through before the Democrats could recover. The procedure was irregular, perhaps, since the Congress had not yet *asked* for a convention, but the issue was vital and the cause was just.

William Bingham arranged to send news from New York by dispatch riders who would change horses at frequent posts along the ninety-mile route.

On Friday morning, September 28, every Federalist member was in his seat. After the House attended to some routine business, George Clymer, merchant of Philadelphia, signer of the Declaration of Independence and one of the framers of the new Federal Constitution, rose in place. The members, he said suavely, could not have forgotten a business of the highest magnitude that had been recommended to their attention by the federal Convention. He was persuaded that they would readily concur in taking the necessary measures, and therefore he had prepared a resolution to that end.

His resolution was promptly seconded by Gerardus Wynkoop, who sat for Bucks County.

Robert Whitehill, member from Cumberland County, one of the authors of the ultrademocratic Pennsylvania constitution, rose to object. The members, he said, ought to have time to consider the subject. He moved, therefore, to postpone consideration until the afternoon session.

Thomas Fitzsimons (City of Philadelphia), one of the signers of the federal Constitution, declared that the business was of the highest consequence. The only object of consideration was not the merits of the new Constitution, but solely whether the election of the delegates should be held. It was the general wish of the people that the House should go forward in the matter.

William Findley (Westmoreland County), Ulsterborn, former weaver and teacher, now a farmer and Democratic leader, agreed that the subject was important. It was so important, indeed, that the House should to into it with deliberation. It was so important that the members should not be surprised into it.

Daniel Clymer (Berks County), cousin of George, said (in extract): "I have heard, Sir, that only four or five leading party-men in this city are against it, whose names I should be glad to know, that their characters might be examined; for I am confident they will be hereafter ashamed to show their faces among the good people whose future prosperity they wish to blast in the bud. Let them be careful, lest they draw upon themselves the odium of that people who have long indulged their rioting upon public favor."

Findley: "The gentleman from Berks has spoken warmly against opposing the present measure in a manner as if intended to prevent men from speaking their minds.

He has charged some leading characters in this city with giving opposition; if he means me as one of them—"

Daniel Clymer (addressing the Speaker): "No, Sir, upon my honor, I did not mean him."

Findley: "Well, then, I don't consider that part of his speech as addressed to the House, but merely to the gallery."

Daniel Clymer: "The measure will be adopted; for it is too generally agreeable, and too highly recommended, to be assassinated by the hand of intrigue and cabal."

Whitehill: "The gentlemen that have brought forward this motion must have some design. Why not allow time to consider it? I believe if time is allowed, we shall be able to show that this is not the proper time for calling a convention; and I don't know any reason there can be for driving it down our throats without an hour's preparation."

George Clymer: "To hesitate upon this proposition will give a very unfavorable aspect to a measure on which our future happiness, nay, I may also say, our future existence, as a nation, depends."

Hugh Henry Brackenridge of Westmoreland County, Princeton graduate, former schoolteacher and chaplain in the Revolutionary Army, now a lawyer, author, and wit, was the only member from the western counties and the only Democrat to support the Constitution actively. He rose to express the view that, "from its magnitude and importance," the members surely must have reflected for some days on the matter. In his opinion they were as well prepared now to determine upon the principle as they would be after having eaten their dinner.

Whitehill: "Congress ought to send forward the plan before we do anything at all in this matter. For of what use was sending it forward to them, unless we meant to wait their determination? Now as these measures are not recommended by Congress, why should we take them up? Why should we take up a thing which does not exist? Is it not better to go safely on the business, and let it lie over till the next House? When we have adjourned, let our constituents think of it, and instruct their representatives to consider of the plan proper to be pursued. Will not the next House be able to determine as we are?"

Daniel Clymer: "The Constitution lately presented to you [was] framed by the collective wisdom of a continent, centered in a venerable band of patroits, worthies, heroes, legislators and philosophers—the admiration of a world. No longer shall thirty thousand [Philadelphians] engage all our attention—all our efforts to procure happiness. No!— The extended embrace of fraternal love shall enclose three millions, as a band of brothers!

"As this subject is now before us, let us not hesitate, but eagerly embrace the glorious opportunity of being foremost in its adoption. Let us not hesitate, because it is damping the ardor with which it should be pursued. Sir, it is throwing cold water on the flame that warms the breast of every friend of liberty, and every patriot who wishes this country to acquire that respect to which she is justly entitled."

The question was put: Would the House agree to postpone consideration of the matter? It was defeated.

George Clymer spoke to the real Federalist concern. "If this House order a convention," he said, "it may be deliberated and decided some time in November, [1787], and the Constitution may be acted under by December. But if it is left over to the next House, it will inevitably be procrastinated until December, 1788."

The Federalists began to cry, "Question! Question!" and a vote was taken on the resolution: Would the House agree to elect delegates and call a state convention? It was carried 43 to 19.

Whitehill then moved that the session adjourn until four o'clock that afternoon, at which time, he said, they might decide the lesser issues of time and place of the election of delegates and the holding of the convention.

Undoubtedly, congratulations were exchanged, and there was much joking at the Federalists' luncheon tables at how smoothly everything had been managed and how clearly the victory had been won. But when the session resumed at four o'clock, the Federalists were astounded to find not one of the nineteen Democratic members in his seat. With forty-four members present, the House was two votes short of a quorum—which meant that no business could be conducted.

Mr. Wynkopp observed that the missing members were those who had given opposition that morning, and he suspected that they had conspired to absent themselves. He moved that the sergeant at arms be ordered to fetch them. The sergeant accordingly was dispatched. When he returned, he was examined at the bar of the House.

SPEAKER: "Well, Sergeant, have you seen the absent members?"

The sergeant replied that he had seen seventeen members at Major Boyd's boarding house on Sixth Street.

SPEAKER: "What did you say to them?"

SERGEANT: I told the gentlemen that the Speaker and the House had sent for them, and says they, 'There is no House.' "

SPEAKER: "Did you let them know they were desired to attend?"

SERGEANT: "Yes, Sir, but they told me they could not attend this afternoon, for they had not made up their minds yet."

DANIEL CLYMER: "How is that?"

SERGEANT: "They had not made up their minds this afternoon to wait on you."

SPEAKER: "Who told you this?"

SERGEANT: "Mr. Whitehill told me first."

CLYMER: "Who told you afterward?"

SERGEANT: "Mr. Clarke said they must go *electioneering* now."

CLYMER: "Was there no private citizens there?"

SERGEANT: "No, Sir."

CLYMER: "There was none then, but *men in public offices?*"

SERGEANT: "No."

CLYMER: "Did you hear of any one willing to come?"

SERGEANT: "No, Sir."

The Federalists, outwitted, baffled, and angry at this breach of trust, debated what to do next. If no business could be conducted, the Assembly would be forced to adjourn the next day without naming a date for selecting delegates or for holding the convention. Mr. Wynkoop declared, "I would be glad to know, if there is no way to compel men, who deserted from the duty they owed their country, to a performance of it, when they were within reach of the House. If there is not, then *God be merciful to us!!!*"

A search of the books revealed no regulation compelling an absent member to attend, the only penalty being loss of one third of a day's pay for each absence. The Speaker declared a recess until nine thirty the following morning.

Federalist discussed the affair in homes and taverns throughout the evening, with liberal abuse for the nineteen recalcitrant members and much speculation about what the minority would do when the Assembly reconvened. The Democratic leaders worked through the night behind locked doors at Major Boyd's; they were preparing an address to their constituents in which they set forth their objections to the new plan of government.

When General Mifflin took the chair on Saturday morning, the minority members were again absent and again no quorum could be declared.

George Clymer presented to the House a packet of documents he had received from New York in the early morning. It contained, he said, a resolution of Congress, passed unanimously, requesting the legislature of each state to put the proposed Constitution to a vote of a popularly elected convention. This had been signed the day before, and Mr. William Bingham had forwarded it to him by express rider, "having chosen this mode in preference to the ordinary conveyance by post." The resolution was read aloud.

Fortified by this new evidence of regularity, the Speaker again sent the sergeant at arms to find the missing members and request their attendance, this time accompanied by the assistant clerk carrying the resolution of Congress. They returned to report that they had seen a dozen of the members in various places and had delivered the message and shown them the resolution. Mr. Findley had "mended his pace" and escaped; others had declared they would not attend; one said he would consider the matter and do what he thought just.

In the meantime word had spread around the city that the Democrats had "absconded" from their duties at the Assembly. A crowd of men gathered, and as time passed they grew impatient. They marched off in search of any two absent members, and the path led straight to Major Boyd's boarding house. There they found two Democrats: James McCalmont of Franklin County and Jacob Miley of Dauphin. Both men had been militia officers in the Revolution. McCalmont, fifty, a major, had a distinguished record as a frontier scout and Indian fighter; he had been famous for his speed in running and his ability to reload a musket or rifle while in full flight or pursuit.

Several of the crowd entered and read the congressional resolution aloud. McCalmont and Miley refused to budge. When that information was conveyed to those waiting outside, they shouted imprecations, smashed windows with stones, broke down the front door, and stormed into the house. McCalmont and Miley were collared, dragged from the premises, and pushed and pulled through the streets to the State House. General Mifflin, hearing a commotion outside and suspecting the reason, discreetly absented himself for a while from the chamber. The two men, their clothes dirtied and torn, their faces white with anger, were thrust onto the floor of the House and escorted to their seats. The clerk wrote in his minutes, in what must be considered something of an understatement, "The Speaker left the chair, and in a few minutes Mr. James McAlmont and Mr. Jacob Miley entered the House. The Speaker resumed the chair, and the roll was called." Both men answered to their names or were declared present by others. With forty-six members on the floor the Speaker declared a quorum.

McCalmont rose to protest that he had been brought into the Assembly room by force, contrary to his wishes, by a number of citizens he did not know. He asked to be dismissed from the House.

Fitzsimons replied that he would be glad to know if any member of the House had been guilty of forcing the gentleman from his determination to absent himself. If so, the House should mark such conduct with its disapprobation, he said.

Brackenridge added: "If the member has been conducted by the citizens of Philadelphia to his seat in the legislature, and they have not treated him with the respect and veneration he deserves, it must lie with him to obtain satisfaction, but not with us. How he came here can form no part of our enquiry. Whether his friends brought him (and I should think they could not be his enemies who would compel him to do his duty and avoid wrong), I say, Sir, whether his friends brought him, or by the influence of good advice persuaded him to come, and he did come; or whether to ease his difficulty in walking to this room they brought him in a sedan chair, or by whatever ways or means he introduced himself among us, all we are to decide whether he shall have leave of absence."

McCalmont: "I desire that the rules may be read, and I will agree to stand by the decision of the House."

The rules were read, and they were found to state that "every member who did not answer on calling the roll should pay two shillings and six pence, or, if there was not a quorum without him, five shillings."

McCalmont rose, took some loose silver from his pocket, held it out, and said, "Well, Sir, here is your five shillings to let me go."

The crowd gathered behind the railing roared with laughter. The Speaker declared that the person appointed to receive fines was not in his place, and that even if he had been, the member should not pay a fine. McCalmont had not broken the rule, the Speaker said. He had appeared and answered to his name and therefore could keep his money.

Mr. Robinson of Philadelphia County, though a Federalist, had some uneasy qualms of conscience. He opined that the House had no authority to detain the member as though he were in prison. Mr. Wynkoop expressed his amazement at this solicitude for a member who had absconded "from his duty at the bar of the House." Mr. McCalmont declared that he had to answer for his conduct at a more important bar than that of the House.

Fitzsimons was stern. He declared that he was a true friend to good order and decorum, but that he believed the gentleman's complaint was not to be redressed by the House of Assembly. The member himself had trespassed, Fitzsimons said; McCalmont had perhaps offered the greatest indignity to the legislature of Pennsylvania that could be offered. He had tendered a pittance, a fine of five shillings, in order to be permitted to destroy the business, if not the good government, of the state. The member was now present, Fitzsimons said, and should stay, not only on constitutional grounds, but from the law of nature that would not suffer any body to destroy its own existence prematurely.

Robinson: "Suppose the House determine that he shall not leave, and yet he should attempt to withdraw. Certainly you will not lock your doors."

Fitzsimons: "Yes, Sir, if no other method could retain him."

A moment later McCalmont rose and made a dash for the door. The crowd yelled, "Stop him!" and those about the door barred his way. McCalmont returned to his seat.

The Speaker put the question: "Shall Mr. McCalmont have leave of absence?" It was voted "almost unanimously in the negative."

Brackenridge then moved that the delegates to the state convention be elected on the first Tuesday in November. McCalmont objected that this was much too early and moved the last Tuesday in December. His motion failed. He moved the third Tuesday in December, then the second Tuesday, with the same result. He moved that the site of the convention be moved from Philadelphia to Carlisle, but he was not upheld. He moved that the change be made to Lancaster and was enthusiastically supported by the member from Lancaster. Fifteen members voted for Lancaster in a defeated motion.

The formal resolution was now put: That the election of delegates be held on November 6, 1787, and that the convention meet in the State House in Philadelphia on the third Tuesday in November. It was passed by a vote of 44 to 2. The Federalists had won their victory. The Assembly adjourned. McCalmont and Miley were released.

In the campaign that followed for election of delegates, Democrats and Federalists attacked one another with arguments and invective and sometimes with clubs, stones, and fists.

October 5, 1787: The first of twenty-four letters of "Centinel" (sentinel of the people's liberties) appeared in the *Gazetteer*. These papers, running through the next fourteen months, still of undetermined authorship, were the Democratic counterpart of the eight-five papers (*The Federalist*) produced by "Publius" in New York. Centinel attacked Publius on many points and brilliantly set forth the Democratic case against the Constitution, the "harpies of power," and "the wealthy and ambitious, who in every community think they have a right to lord it over their fellow creatures." The treatment accorded McCalmont and Miley, Centinel said, showed what would happen to free citizens under the Federalist Constitution.

October 6: At a public meeting in the State House yard, James Wilson cogently answered the Democratic arguments point by point, and in so doing assumed the role of the country's most effective proponent of the Constitution in debate. His speech was widely distributed, reprinted, copied, and quoted. The Democrats attacked it as a "train of pitiful sophistries and evasions," compared Wilson (unfavorably) with Tiberius, Caligula, and Nero, and charged that he was "strongly tainted with the spirit of *high aristocracy.*"

November 6: The Federalists scored an overwhelming victory in the election of delegates, losing only six western counties. Their majority was 2 to 1, or 46 convention votes to 23. Elated at their victory, several dozen Federalists gathered on election night before Major Boyd's, reviled the "damned rascals" housed therein, flung stones through the newly repaired windows, and broke the door with large rocks.

November 21: The convention convened in the State House. The delegates spent the first week arguing about procedure. James Wilson distinguished himself with five powerful, if somewhat florid, speeches. Robert Whitehill, the Democrat from Cumberland County, submitted fifteen proposed amendments to the Constitution as a bill of rights. They were ignored. On a number of occasions the members were close to physical assault on one another.

December 7: Delaware ratified the Constitution, won over by the compromise that gave the small states equal representation in the Senate (the Constitution's only irrevocable article). John Smilie of Fayette County, who with Whitehill and Findley was leading the fight against ratification in the Pennsylvania convention, sneered that Delaware had "reaped the honor of having first surrendered the liberties of the people."

December 12: Pennsylvania became the second state—and the first large state—"to assent to and ratify" the Constitution. The vote was, predictably, 46 to 23. A transcript of the convention proceedings was made for publication, but the Federalists persuaded the court printer to release only the Federalist speeches.

December 13: The delegates marched in procession to the Court House at Market and Second streets, accompanied by members of the new Assembly, state and city officials, and other local dignitaries. The ratification was read from a balcony to a great gathering of citizens. The city bells rang out, and thirteen cannons fired salvos.

December 18: The defeated Democratic delegates issued a pamphlet titled *Reasons for Dissent* and mailed a copy to every printer in the country. No copies were delivered. Democrats charged that they were destroyed by "the sons of power" who controlled the Pennsylvania post-office system.

December 27: Federalists in Carlisle, a Scotch-Irish town of three hundred houses in the Cumberland Valley some 120 miles west of Philadelphia, staged a public celebration in honor of the ratification. They procured James Wilson for an oration, dragged a cannon to the public square, and heaped up a great stack of barrels for a bonfire. Antifederalists charged the crowd, upset the barrels, spiked the cannon, burned a copy of the Constitution, and began to beat Wilson with bludgeons. An old soldier saved his life by throwing himself over the body and taking the blows until help came.

Two days of riots followed. John Montgomery, venerable Federalist, one of the founders of Dickinson College in Carlisle five years earlier, wrote to a friend, "They are violent on both sides. . . . We [Federalists] are in a very disagreeable unhapey situation in this place nothing ever happened so bad amongst us neaghbours pass each other without speaking."

June 21, 1788: The Constitution became law and the United States a new nation with ratification by New Hampshire, the ninth state.

July 4: Philadelphia mounted on all-day celebration to mark the day of Independence and the forming of the new Union. Some five thousand marched or rode in a Federal Procession a mile and a half long. All the trades, crafts, and professions were represented, many of them with elaborate floats, in a spectacle such as no American had ever seen before. High point of the procession was a structure called the "New Roof or Grand Federal Ediface," 36 feet high, drawn by ten white horses. Benjamin Rush called the Ediface "truly sublime" and observed approvingly that of the thousands who took part in the ceremonies that day, very few engaged in quarrels and almost no one was intoxicated.

On an open field at the parade's end, James Wilson, standing on the Grand Ediface, delivered the Fourth of July oration. Some of his passages were drowned out by the ill-timed firing of thirteen cannons on vessels anchored in the Delaware, but his soaring closing words were loud and clear: "PEACE walks *serene* and *unalarmed* over all the unmolested regions—while LIBERTY, VIRTUE, and RELIGION go hand in hand harmoniously *protecting, enlivening,* and *exalting* all! HAPPY COUNTRY, MAY THY HAPPINESS BE PERPETUAL!"

*   *   *

The Pennsylvania Democrats made their peace with the new form of government. Within two years they got the Bill of Rights they had fought for: ten amendments to the Constitution that were remarkably like the amendments Robert Whitehill had vainly offered to the Pennsylvania state convention. James McCalmont became a judge, and Jacob Miley a representative, under the new Pennsylvania constitution. Robert Whitehill served four terms and John Smilie served eight terms in the House of Representatives of the United States. William Findley served eleven terms, and in one of them, in 1795, he moved the creation of the first standing congressional committee—a body of honest representatives called the Ways and Means Committee, formed to keep a sharp eye on the financial operations of a Federalist administration.

The high-flown political skullduggery described in this article was discovered by Robert C. Alberts in doing research for his most recent book, The Golden Voyage: The Life and Times of William Bingham, 1752–1804, *published by Houghton Mifflin in 1969. Mr. Alberts is now Contributing Editor of this magazine.*

Part Three
The Early National Period

Just as the victory in the War for Independence did not guarantee success in the American experiment with home rule, so the ratification of the Constitution did not guarantee success in American government. It remained to that remarkable generation of American leaders to add substance and function to the bare outline which was the Constitution. In achieving this task, George Washington made his greatest contribution to the nation. However, as it developed policies intended to solve the most pressing problems of the day, the Washington Administration aroused serious opposition. The most pressing problem in domestic affairs was the national debt; in foreign affairs, the problems of neutrality and maritime rights.

Since the burden of formulating policy fell to Alexander Hamilton as Secretary of the Treasury, he became the most controversial figure in the Administration. He became the major target of criticism from the growing camp of the opposition. The reasons for the opposition were not hard to find. What may have appealed to Hamilton as reasonable and statesmenlike proposals, seemed to men like Jefferson and Madison as self-serving and dangerous. And one policy in particular, Hamilton's reliance on excise taxes as a source of revenue, gave rise to the first armed protests against the government under the Constitution. In his article, ''A Tax on Whiskey? Never!'', Gerald Carson explains the origins and the course of the Whiskey Rebellion of 1794.

Hamilton justified the massive show of force in the suppression of the Whiskey Rebellion as necessary to save the Constitution. But his actions only increased the feelings of alienation and resentment against the Administration. When foreign policy decisions also aroused opposition, national politics became deeply embittered, hastening the formation of rival political parties in the American system of government. Thomas J. Fleming traces these developments in his article, ''A Scandalous, Malicious and Seditious Libel.''

The nation survived the crucial but divisive decade of Federalist rule, and in the election of 1800 the voters turned out the Federalists for good. In 1801 Jefferson took over the Presidency, and national politics assumed a more placid bearing. In his second term, Jefferson was forced to deal with the recurring problem of maritime rights. His recourse to economic sanctions, however, compelled the United States to become more self-sufficient. The Embargo Act had the effect of stimulating the nation's first industrial revolution. Ironically, Jefferson, an advocate of American agrarianism thus became the promoter of American industrialism. Arnold Welles chronicles the story of early industrialization through the life of Samuel Slater in his article, "Father of Our Factory System."

The apparent failure of Jefferson's Embargo prompted President Madison to pursue other approaches to economic sanctions in order to protect maritime rights, but without success. Finally, frustration and other irritations in United States-British relations led the president to ask for war in 1812. These developments are explained by Irving Brant in his article, "Timid President? Futile War?" The war was far from inconsequential. It greatly stimulated United States economic development and territorial expansion. Industry spread from the northeast to the upper midwest. Agriculture expanded in the west and the south. By 1815, the nation was on the road to economic specialization. But after only one decade, such specialization also brought on disputes over conflicting sectional self-interests. With that, politics again became divisive. The Era of Jefferson gave way to the Age of Jackson.

A Tax on Whiskey? Never!

Gerald Carson

When one recalls that the President of the United States, the Secretary of War, the Secretary of the Treasury, and the governors of four states once mobilized against the farmers of western Pennsylvania an army almost as large as ever took the field in the Revolutionary War, the event appears at first glance one of the more improbable episodes in the annals of this country. Equipped with mountains of ammunition, forage, baggage, and a bountiful stock of tax-paid whiskey, thirteen thousand grenadiers, dragoons, foot soldiers, pioneers, a train of artillery with six-pounders, mortars, and several "grasshoppers," paraded over the mountains to Pittsburgh against a gaggle of homespun rebels who had already dispersed.

Yet the march had a rationale. President George Washington and his Secretary of the Treasury, Alexander Hamilton, moved to counter civil commotion with overwhelming force because they well understood that the survival of the new U.S. Constitution was involved. Soon after he assumed his post at the Treasury, Hamilton had proposed, to the astonishment of the country, that the United States should meet fully and promptly its financial obligations, including the assumption of the debts contracted by the states in the struggle for independence. Part of the money was to be raised by laying an excise tax upon distilled spirits. The tax became law on March 3, 1791.

In the back country settlements that produced the whiskey and drank the lion's share of it, the news of the passage of the measure was greeted with a roar of indignation. The duty was laid uniformly upon all the states, as the Constitution provided; if the West had to pay more, the Secretary of the Treasury explained, it was only because it used more whiskey. The East could, if it so desired, forego beverage spirits and fall back on cider and beer. The South and the frontier West could not, for they had neither orchards nor breweries. To Virginia and Maryland the excise tax appeared to be as unjust and oppressive as the well-remembered Molasses Act and the tea duties of George III. "The time will come," predicted Georgia's fiery James Jackson in the House of Representatives, "when a shirt shall not be washed without an excise."

Kentucky, then thinly settled, but already producing its characteristic handmade, copper-fired, whole-souled liquor, was of the opinion that the law was unconstitutional. Deputy revenue collectors throughout the Bluegrass region were assaulted, their papers stolen, their horses' ears cropped, and their saddles cut to pieces. On one wild night the people of Lexington dragged a stuffed dummy through the streets and hanged in effigy Colonel Thomas Marshall, the chief collector for the district.

Yet, in no other place did popular fury rise so high, spread so rapidly, involve a whole population so completely, or express so many assorted grievances as in the Pennsylvania frontier counties of Fayette, Allegheny, Westmoreland, and Washington. There, in 1791, a light plume of wood smoke rose from no less than five thousand log stillhouses. The rates went into effect on July 1. The whiskey-maker could choose whether he would pay a yearly levy on his still capacity or a gallonage tax on his actual production.

Before the month was out, "committees of correspondence," in the old Revolutionary phrase, were speeding horsemen over the ridges and through the valleys to arouse the people to arm and assemble. The majority, but not all, of the men who made the whiskey decided to "forbear" from paying the tax. Revenue officers were thoroughly worked over. Robert Johnson, for example, collector for Washington and Allegheny counties, was waylaid near Pigeon Creek by a mob disguised in women's clothing. They cut off his hair, gave him a coat of tar and feathers, and stole his horse.

The Pennsylvania troubles were rooted in the economic importance and impregnable social position of mellow old Monongahela rye whiskey. The frontier people had been reared from childhood on the family jug. They found the taste pleasant, the effect agreeable. Whiskey kept the population cool in summer. In winter, it was the old settlers' equivalent of central heating. Whiskey was usually involved when there was kissing or fighting. It beatified the rituals of birth and death. It provided almost the only diversion, while enjoying at the same time a high reputation as the West's greatest therapeutic agent, effective against fevers, ague, snake bite, or general decline. The doctor kept a bottle in his office for his own use, with the protective label, "Arsenic—Deadly Poison."

Whiskey lubricated the machinery of government. The lawyer produced the bottle when the papers were signed. Whiskey was available at the prothonotary's office when the trial list was made up. Jurors got their dram, and the constable drew his ration for his services on election day. The hospitable barrel and the tin cup were the mark of the successful political candidate. The United States Army issued a gill to a man every day. Ministers of the gospel were paid in rye whiskey, for they were shepherds of a devout flock, Presbyterians mostly, who took their Bible straight, especially where it said:

"Give strong drink unto him that is ready to perish, and wine unto those that be of heavy hearts."

"Let him drink, and forget his poverty, and remember his misery no more."

With grain the most abundant commodity west of the mountains, the farmers could eat it or drink it, but they couldn't sell it in distant markets unless it was reduced in bulk and enhanced in value. Thus a Pennsylvania farmer's "best holt" was whiskey. A pack horse could move only four bushels of grain. But it could carry twenty-four bushels if it was condensed into two large wooden kegs of whiskey slung across its back, while the price of the goods would double when they reached the eastern markets. So whiskey became the frontier remittance for salt, sugar, nails, bars iron, pewter plates, powder and shot. Along the western rivers, where men saw few shilling pieces, a gallon of good, sound rye whiskey was a stable measure of value.

The bitter resistance of the western men to the whiskey tax involved both practical considerations and principles. First, the excise payment was due and must be paid in scarce hard money as soon as the waterwhite distillate flowed from the condensing coil. The principle concerned the whole repulsive idea of an internal revenue levy. The settlers of western Pennsylvania were a bold, hardy, emigrant race from Scotland and northern Ireland, who had set up their mashing tubs, fermenters, and pot stills before the last Indian war whoop ceased to echo among the hills. They brought with them also bitter memories of oppression in the old country under the excise laws, involving invasion of their homes, confiscation of their property, and a system of paid informers. Revenue collectors were social outcasts in a society which might have warmly seconded Doctor Samuel Johnson's definition of excise: "a hateful tax levied upon commodities, and adjudged not by the common judges of property, but wretches hired by those to whom excise is paid."

The whiskey boys of Pennsylvania, then, saw it was simply a matter of sound Whig principles to resist the exciseman as he made his rounds with a Dicas hydrometer to measure the proof of the whiskey and his marking iron to brand the casks with his findings. Earlier, the state had taxed spirits, except that whiskey produced for purely private use was exempt. William Findley of Westmoreland County, a member of Congress at the time and a sympathetic interpreter of the western point of view, looked into this angle. To his astonishment, he learned that all the whiskey distilled in the west was for purely personal use. So far as the excise tax was concerned, or any other state tax, the sturdy Celtic peoples of the Monongahela region had cheerfully returned to a state of nature: they just didn't pay. About every sixth man made whiskey. But all were involved in the problem, since the other five took their rye and corn to the stillhouse where the master distiller turned it into liquid form.

But now matters had taken a more serious turn. The new federal government in Philadelphia was dividing the whole country up into "districts" for the purpose of collecting the money, and cutting the districts up into smaller inspection "surveys." The transmontane Pennsylvanians found themselves in the grip of something known as the fourth survey, with General John Neville, hitherto a popular citizen and leader, getting ready to enforce the law. Rewards would be paid to informers and a percentage of the taxes given to the collectors, who appeared to be a rapacious set.

The first meeting of public protest against the United States excise of 1791 was held in July at Redstone Old Fort (now Brownsville, Pennsylvania). The proceedings were moderate on that occasion, and scarcely went beyond the right of petition. Another meeting in August, more characteristic of others which were to follow, was radical in tone, disorderly, threatening. It passed resolves that any person taking office under the revenue law was an enemy of society.

When warrants were issued in the affair of the molested revenue agent, Robert Johnson, the process server was robbed, beaten, tarred and feathered, and left tied to a tree in the forest. As the inspectors' offices were established, they were systematically raided. The familiar Liberty poles of the Revolution reappeared as whiskey poles. The stills of operators who paid the tax were riddled with bullets in attacks sardonically described as "mending" the stills. This led to a popular description of the whiskey boys as "Tom the Tinker's Men," an ironical reference to the familiar, itinerant repairer of pots and kettles. Notices proposing measures for thwarting the law, or aimed at coercing the law-abiding distillers, were posted on trees or published in the Pittsburgh *Gazette* signed, "Tom and Tinker," nom de plume of John Holcroft and other antitax propagandists. Congressman Findley, one of the prominent men of the region who tried to build a bridge of understanding between the backwoodsmen and the central government, described the outbreak as not the result of any concerted plan, but rather as a flame, "an infatuation almost incredible."

An additional complaint against the tax grew out of the circumstance that offenders were required to appear in the federal court at Philadelphia, three hundred miles away. The whiskey-makers saw this distant government as being no less oppressive than one in London, and often drew the parallel. Some democrats, oriented sympathetically toward the Jacobin Clubs of Paris, whispered that the whole whiskey issue was a scheme of the Federalists to transfer the powers of government from the people to an aristocratic junto.

A mounting clamor of protest led Congress to modify the severity of the excise tax law in 1792 and again in 1794. A further conciliatory step was taken. To ease the hardships of the judicial process, Congress gave to the state courts jurisdiction in excise offenses so that accused persons might be tried in their own vicinity. But some fifty or sixty writs already issued and returnable at Philadelphia resulted in men being carried away from their fields during harvest time. This convinced the western leaders that the aristocrats in the east were seeking a pretext to discipline the democratic west.

One day in July, 1794, while the processes were being served, William Miller, a delinquent farmer-distiller and political supporter of General Neville, saw the General riding up his lane accompanied by a stranger who turned out to be a United States marshal from Philadelphia. The marshal unlimbered a paper and began to read a summons. It ordered the said Miller to "set aside all manner of business and excuses" and appear in his "proper person" before a judge in Philadelphia. Miller had been planning to sell his property and remove to Kentucky, but the cost of the trip to Philadelphia and the fine for which he was liable would eat up the value of his land and betterments.

"I felt my blood boil, at seeing General Neville along, to pilot the sheriff to my very door," Miller said afterward. "I felt myself mad with passion."

As Neville and the marshal rode away, a party from the county militia which was mustered at Mingo Creek fired upon them, but there were no casualties. When the General reached Bower Hill, his country home above the Chartiers Valley, another party, under the command of John Holcroft, awaited him and demanded his commission and official papers. The demand was refused, and both sides began to shoot. As the rebels closed in on the main house, a flanking fire came from the Negro cabins on the plantation. The whiskey boys were drinken off with one killed and four wounded.

The next day, Major James McFarlane, a veteran of the Revolutionary War, led an attack in force upon Neville's painted and papered mansion, furnished with such marvels as carpets, mirrors, pictures and prints, and an eight-day clock. The house was now defended by a dozen soldiers from Fort Fayette at Pittsburgh. A fight followed during which a soldier was shot and McFarlane was killed—by treachery, the rebels said, when a white flag was displayed. The soldiers surrendered and were either released or allowed to escape. Neville was not found, but his cabins, barns, outbuildings, and finally the residence were all burned down. Stocks of grain were destroyed, all fences levelled, as the victors broke up the furniture, liberated the mirrors and clock, and distributed the General's supply of liquor to the thirsty.

The funeral of McFarlane caused great excitement. Among those present were Hugh Henry Brackenridge, author, lawyer, and one of the western moderates, and David Bradford, prosecuting attorney for Washington County. The former wished to find ways to reduce the tension; the latter to increase it. Bradford was a rash, impetuous Marylander, ambitious for power and position. Some thought him a second-rate lawyer. Others disagreed. They said he was third-rate. But he had a gift for rough mob eloquence. Bradford had already robbed the United States mails to find out what information was being sent east against the conspirators. He had already called for the people to make a choice of "*submission or opposition* . . . with *head, heart, hand* and *voice.*"

At the McFarlane funeral service Bradford worked powerfully upon the feelings of the mourners as he described "the murder of McFarlane." Brackenridge also spoke, using wit and drollery to relieve the pressure and to make palatable his warning to the rebels that they were flirting with the possibility of being hanged. But the temper of the throng was for Bradford, as clearly revealed in the epitaph set over McFarlane's grave: "He fell . . . by the hands of an unprincipled villain in the support of what he supposed to be the rights of his country."

The high-water mark of the insurrection was the occupation of Pittsburgh. After the fight and the funeral, Bradford called out the militia regiments of the four disaffected counties. They were commanded to rendezvous at Braddock's Field, near Pittsburgh, with arms, full equipment, and four days' rations. At the field there was a great beating of drums, much marching and counter-marching, almost a holiday spirit. Men in hunting shirts practiced shooting at the mark until a dense pall of smoke hung over the plain, as there had been thirty-nine years before at General Braddock's disaster. There were between five and seven thousand men on the field, many meditating in an ugly mood upon their enemies holed up in Pittsburgh, talking of storming Fort Fayette and burning the town as "a second Sodom."

Bradford's dream was the establishment of an independent state with himself cast as a sort of Washington of the west. Elected major general by acclaim, he dashed about the field on a superb horse, in a fancy uniform, his sword flashing, plumes floating out from his hat as he issued orders, harangued the multitude, and received applications for commissions in the service of—what? No one quite knew.

Marching in good order, strung out over the two-and-a-half miles of road, the rebels advanced on August 1, 1794, toward Pittsburgh in what was hopefully termed a "visit," though the temper of the citizen-soldiers was perhaps nearer to that of one man who twirled his hat on the muzzle of his rifle and shouted, "I have a bad hat now, but I expect to have a better one soon." While the panic-stricken burghers buried the silver and locked up the girls, the mob marched in on what is now Fourth Avenue to the vicinity of the present Baltimore & Ohio Railroad station. A reception committee extended nervous hospitality in the form of hams, poultry, dried venison, bear meat, water, and whiskey, and agreed to banish certain citizens obnoxious to the insurrectionists. One building on a nearby farm was burned; another attempt at arson failed to come off. The day cost Brackenridge four barrels of good old Monongahela. It was better, he reflected, "to be employed in extinguishing the fire of their thirst than of my house."

Later in the month of August armed bands continued to patrol the roads as a "scrub Congress"—in the phrase of one scoffer—met at Parkinson's Ferry, now Monongahela, to debate, pass resolutions, and move somewhat uncertainly toward separation from the United States. Wild and unfounded rumors won belief. It was said that Congress was extending the excise levy to plows at a dollar each, that every wagon entering Philadelphia would be forced to pay a dollar, that a tax was soon to be established at Pittsburgh of fifteen shillings for the birth of every boy baby, and ten for each girl.

It was evident that the crisis had arrived. The President requisitioned 15,000 militia (of whom about 13,000 actually marched) from Pennsylvania, New Jersey, Virginia, and Maryland. Would the citizens of one state invade another to compel obedience to federal law? Here one gets a glimpse of the larger importance of the affair. Both the national government and the state of Pennsylvania sent commissioners to the west with offers of pardon upon satisfactory assurances that the people would obey the laws. Albert Gallatin, William Findley, Brackenridge, and others made a desperate effort to win the people to submission, though their motives were often questioned by both the rebels and the federal authorities. The response to the offer of amnesty was judged not to be sufficiently positive. Pressed by the Secretary of the Treasury, Alexander Hamilton, to have federal authority show its teeth, Washington announced that the troops would march.

The Army was aroused. In particular, the New Jersey militia were ready to exercise lynch law because they had been derided in a western newspaper as a "Watermelon Army" and an uncomplimentary estimate made of their military capabilities. The piece was written as a take-off on the kind of negotiations which preceded an Indian treaty. Possibly the idea was suggested by the fact that the whiskey boys were often called "White Indians." At any rate, in the satire the Indians admonished the great council in Philadelphia: ". . . Brothers, we have that powerful monarch, Capt. Whiskey, to command us. By the power of his influence, and a love to *his person* we are compelled to every great and heroic act . . . We, the Six United Nations of White Indians . . . have all imbibed his principles and passions—that is a love of whiskey . . . Brothers, you must not think to frighten us with . . . infantry, cavalry and artillery, composed of your watermelon armies from the Jersey shores; they would cut a much better figure in warring with the crabs and oysters about the Capes of Delaware."

Captain Whiskey was answered hotly by "A Jersey Blue." He pointed out that "the water-melon army of New Jersey" was going to march westward shortly with "ten-inch howitzers for throwing a species of melon very useful for curing a *gravel occasioned by whiskey!*" The expedition was tagged thereafter as the "Watermelon Army."

The troops moved in two wings under the command of General Henry (Light Horse Harry) Lee, Governor of Virginia. Old Dan Morgan was there and young Meriwether Lewis, five nephews of President Washington, the governors of Pennsylvania and New Jersey, too, and many a veteran blooded in Revolutionary fighting, including Captain John Fries of the Bucks County militia and his dog, which he had named after a drink he occasionally enjoyed—Whiskey.

The left wing marched west during October, 1794, from Virginia and Maryland to Fort Cumberland on the Potomac, then northwest into Pennsylvania, to join forces with the right wing at Bedford. The Pennsylvania and New Jersey corps proceeded via Norristown and Reading to Harrisburg and Carlisle. There, on October 4, President Washington arrived, accompanied by Colonel Alexander Hamilton. The western representatives told the President at Carlisle that the army was not needed, but Hamilton convinced him that it was. Washington rode down to Fort Cumberland on October 16 to review the troops of the left wing, which had assembled there. He then went on to Bedford, the rendezvous, to survey final plans before returning to Philadelphia for the meeting of Congress. Meanwhile Hamilton ordered a roundup of many of the rebels and personally interrogated the most important ones. Brackenridge, incidentally, came off well in his encounter with Hamilton, who declared that he was satisfied with Brackenridge's conduct.

By the time the expedition had crossed the mountains, the rebellion was already coming apart at the seams. David Bradford, who was excluded from the subsequent amnesty, fled to Spanish Louisiana, where he finished out his life as a planter. About 2,000 of the best riflemen in the west left the country, including many a distiller who loaded his pot stills on a pack horse or a Kentucky boat and sought asylum in Kentucky, where, hopefully, a man could distill "the creature" without giving the public debt a lift.

The punitive expedition moved forward in glorious autumn weather, raiding chicken coops, consuming prodigious quantities of the commodity which lay at the heart of the controversy. Richard Howell, governor of New Jersey and commander of the right wing, revived the spirits of the Jersey troops by composing a marching song, "Dash to the Mountains, Jersey Blue":

> To arms once more, our hero cries,
> Sedition lives and order dies;
> To peace and ease them bid adieu
> And dash to the mountains, Jersey Blue.

Faded diaries, old letters, and orderly books preserve something of the gala atmosphere of the expedition. At Trenton, New Jersey, a Miss Forman and a Miss Milnor were most amiable. Newtown, Pennsylvania, was noted as a poor place for hay. At Potts Grove a captain of a cavalry troop got kicked in the shin by his horse. Among the Virginians, Meriwether Lewis enjoyed the martial excitement and wrote to his mother in high spirits of the "mountains of beef and oceans of Whiskey," sent regards "to all the girls," and announced that he would bring "an Insergiant Girl to se them next fall bearing the title of Mrs. Lewis." If there was such a girl, he soon forgot her.

Yet where there is an army in being, there are unpleasant occurrences. Men were lashed. Quartermasters stole government poverty. A soldier was ordered to put an insurgent under guard. In execution of the order, he ran the rebel through with his bayonet, of which wound the prisoner died. At Carlisle, a dragoon's pistol went off and hit a countryman in the groin; he too died. On November 13, long remembered in many a cabin and clearing as "the dismal night," the Jersey Horse rounded up suspects whom they described grimly as "the whiskey pole gentry," dragging them out of bed, tying them back to back.

In late November, finding no one to fight, the army turned east again, leaving a volunteer force under General Morgan to conciliate and consolidate the position during the winter. Twenty "Yahoos" were carried back to Philadelphia and were paraded by the Philadelphia Horse through the streets of the city with "Insurrection" labels on their hats. It was an odd Federalist version of a Roman triumph. The troop was composed, as an admirer said, of "young gentlemen of the first property of the city," with beautiful mounts and uniforms of the finest blue broadcloth. They held their swords elevated in the right hand, while the light flashed from the silver stirrups, martingales, and jingling bridles. Stretched over half a mile they came, first two cavalrymen abreast, then a pair of prisoners, walking; then two more mounted men, and so on.

The army, meditating upon their fatigues and hardships, called for a substantial number of hangings. Samuel Hodgson, the commissary-general, wrote to a Pittsburgh confidant: "We all lament that so few of the insurgents fell—such disorders can only be cured by copious bleedings. . . ," while Philip Freneau, friend and literary colleague of Brackenridge, suggested in retrospect—ironically, of course—the benefits which would have accured to the country "If Washington had drawn and quartered thirty or forty of the whiskey boys . . ." Most of the captives escaped any punishment other than that of being held in jail without a trial for ten or twelve months. One died. Two were finally tried and sentenced to death. Eventually both were let off.

If the rising was a failure, so was the liquor tax. The military adventure alone, without ordinary costs of collection, ran up a bill of $1,500,000, or about one-third of all the money that was realized during the life of the act. Meanwhile the movement of the army to the Pennsylvania hinterland had brought with it a flood of cash which furnished the distillers with currency for paying their taxes. Gradually the bitterness receded. During Jefferson's administration, the tax was quietly repealed. Yet the watermelon armies and the whiskey boys made a not inconsiderable contribution to our constitutional history. Through them, the year 1794 completed what 1787 had begun; for it established the reality of a federal union whose law was not a suggestion but a command.

Gerald Carson's latest book, The Social History of Bourbon, *will be published this fall by Dodd, Mead. Another of his excursions into the habits and history of American drinking, "The Saloon," appeared in the April, 1963, issue of* AMERICAN HERITAGE.

For further reading: Whiskey Rebels, *by Leland D. Baldwin (University of Pittsburgh Press, 1939).*

"A Scandalous, Malicious and Seditious Libel"

Thomas J. Fleming

"At a Court of general Sessions of the Peace, holden at Claverack, in and for the county of Columbia, it is presented that Harry Croswell, late of the city of Hudson, in the county of Columbia aforesaid, Printer, being a malicious and seditious man, and of a depraved mind and wicked and diaboli-cal disposition, and also deceitfully, wickedly and maliciously devising, contriving and intending, Thomas Jefferson, Esquire, President of the United States of America, to detract from, scandalize, traduce, and vilify, and to represent him, the said Thomas Jef-ferson, as unworthy of the confidence, respect and attachment of the People of the said United States, . . . and wickedly and seditiously to disturb the Peace and tranquility as well of the People of the State of New York as of the United States; . . . the said Harry Croswell did on the ninth day of September, in the year of our Lord 1802, with force and arms, at the said city of Hudson, in the said county of Columbia, wickedly, mali-ciously and seditiously print and publish and cause and procure to be printed and pub-lished, a certain scandalous, malicious and seditious libel, in a certain paper or publication entitled 'The Wasp.' . . ."

All history is a mingling of the great and small, of kings losing kingdoms for want of a horse-shoe nail, of presidents assassinated because a guard needed a smoke. But seldom has there been a stranger concatenation of the petty and the magnificent, the comic and the tragic, the trivial and the profound, than in the case of the *People v. Croswell,* in 1803. By an odd blend of good and bad luck, an obscure twenty-four-year-old printer wrote himself into the *Dictionary of American Biography,* established the libel law on which contemporary press freedom still rests, jarred the political security of

President Thomas Jefferson, and indirectly helped to involve Alexander Hamilton in his fatal duel and Aaron Burr.

In 1803 the infant American Republic was running a high political fever. The ferocity of the verbal warfare raging between the Federalists, the party created by Alexander Hamilton, and the Democratic-Republicans, led by President Jefferson, has rarely been matched in American politics, even by the diatribes of today's New Left and Ultra Right.

The first fusilladers had been fired during Washington's Presidency. The Jeffersonians, with not a little help from the Sage of Monticello himself, had set up journalists such as Philip Freneau and Benjamin Franklin Bache with one mission, to deflate and discredit an administration that was, in Jefferson's view, "galloping fast into monarchy." They soon had the Father of His Country in a state of near apoplexy. "That rascal Freneau," as Washington called him, insisted on sending his scurrilous *National Gazette,* published in Philadelphia, to the President's house even after he had cancelled his subscription. Freneau spent most of his abuse on Hamilton. Bache preferred Washington as a target, calling him "treacherous," "mischievous," "inefficient," and sneering at his "farce of disinterestedness" and his "stately journeyings through the American continent in search of personal incense."

These verbal guerrillas soon had imitators. Among the more savage was William Duane, Bache's successor as editor of the Philadelphia *Aurora.* Washington, he wrote, had "discharged the loathings of a sick mind." Even this was topped by an English newcomer, James T. Callender. In the Richmond *Examiner* he declared that "Mr. Washington has been twice a traitor."

The Federalists, the upholders of upper-class dignity, labored under a difficult handicap in such a war. They soon became afraid, in Washington's words, that "there seems to be no bounds to . . . attempts to destroy all confidence, that the People might, and . . . ought to have, in their government; thereby dissolving it, and producing a disunion of the States." The Alien and Sedition Acts of 1798 were an expression of his fear. Passed by a Federalist Congress with Washington's public approval, the Alien Act gave President John Adams the power to deport any foreigners he deemed dangerous to public peace. The Sedition Act empowered the federal judiciary to punish anyone convicted of false or malicious writing against the nation, the President, or Congress with a fine of not more than $2,000 and imprisonment for not more than two years.

Federalist judges immediately went to work and soon had indictments against Bache, Duane, Callender, and a dozen other Democratic-Republican editors. The Jeffersonians responded at the state level with the Kentucky and Virginia resolutions of 1798, which declared the Alien and Sedition Acts altogether void and introduced the doctrine of nullification into American constitutional thinking—a seed that would bear ominous fruit in a later era. Up and down the land, Jeffersonian editors bellowed mightily that the Federalists were attempting to erase the First Amendment and destroy the free press.

The Jeffersonian counterattack was beautifully executed: the Federalist judges retreated in disarray and all but abandoned the unpopular prosecutions after a mere ten convictions. The nation roared into the election of 1800 with both sides strenuously exercising their right of free speech. But except for a few slugging editors who sneered at "Massa Jefferson" the slave owner, most of the Federalist propaganda came from pulpits, where clergymen pictured the election of the pro-French and "atheistic" Jefferson as the beginning of a Jacobinical reign of terror against religion. In the print shops the Jeffersonians had the bigger, more vituperative guns. James Callender's pamphlet, *The Prospect Before Us*, slandered Washington and Adams with such recklessness that it achieved an unenviable literary fame. Although Federalist papers theoretically outnumbered the Jeffersonians 103 to 64, most of them maintained a tepid semineutrality that permitted the Democratic-Republicans to run away with public opinion and the election. Defeated John Adams wrote mournfully, "If we had been blessed with common sense, we should not have been overthrown by Philip Freneau, Duane, Callender. . . . A group of foreign liars have discomfited the education, the talents, the virtues, and the property of the country."

But the Federalists were down, not out. Older leaders like John Jay might retire to their estates in dismay, but there were numerous young, vigorous Federalists in the prime of middle life, such as Hamilton and Fisher Ames of Massachusetts, who did not feel it was time for them to abandon politics. They decided Federalism was not dead, it had just been misrepresented, distorted, and smeared without rebuttal. It was time to junk the older Federalist ideas about the vulgarity of appealing to the people through the press. Ames suggested a Latin motto as a guide: *Fas est et ab hoste doceri ("It is perfectly proper to be taught by one's enemy"). Up and down the Republic, Federalists began founding papers in which, Ames declared, "wit and satire should flash like the electrical fire." At the same time, the paper he helped found, the New England Palladium*, would, he predicted, be "fastidiously polite and well-bred. It should whip Jacobins as a gentleman would a chimney sweeper, at arms length, and keeping aloof from his soot."

In New York, Alexander Hamilton soon gathered a group of well-heeled Federalists who put up $10,000 for a daily to be called the *Evening Post* (Still in business today, as the *New York Post*). Its editor, William Coleman, met Alexander Hamilton by night and took down his editorials from the very lips of the great man himself. Throughout the other states, similar papers suddenly blossomed: in Baltimore, for example, the *Republican, or, Anti-Democrat;* in South Carolina, the Charleston *Courier*. In Hudson, New York, another group of Federalists led by Elisha Williams, one of the state's most noted attorneys, backed Ezra Sampson as the editor of the *Balance and Columbian Repositor*. As a junior editor Sampson hired twenty-two-year-old Harry Croswell.

Connecticut born, this well-built, dignified young man had studied for a time in the household of Noah Webster, later of dictionary fame and a high Federalist of the old school. (Webster's solution for rampant Jeffersonianism was to raise the voting age to forty-five.) Temperamentally, Harry Croswell was a born Federalist. He was religious, had a natural deference for older, wiser, richer man, and tended to see political developments of the day as a clash between the forces of darkness and light.

Hudson at this time was not the somnolent little river town it is today. In the decade after the Revolution it carried more ships on its registers than the city of New York. Much of western Massachusetts and northern Connecticut used Hudson for a shipping center. One March day in 1802, a reporter counted 2,800 sleighs loaded with goods on Hudson's streets, creating a traffic jam of prodigious dimensions. At the same time, with Albany, the state capital, a mere twenty-eight miles upriver, it was hardly surprising that Hudson and surrounding Columbia County were politically sensitive areas. Later in the century one local historian unabashedly claimed that the county had produced more distinguished politicians than any other comparable area in the entire country.

The Jeffersonians were strongly entrenched there. In 1802, the attorney general of the state of New York was sharp-eyed, hatchet-faced Ambrose Spencer, a native son of Columbia County. Morgan Lewis, chief justice of the state supreme court, was married to Gertrude Livingston, whose family's vast upstate holdings included a large chunk of the southern portion of the county. The Livingstons were the most potent voice in the Jeffersonian party at that time.

It was hardly surprising, therefore, that the Jeffersonians decided to set up a rival to the Federalist *Balance*. For their printer they close Charles Holt, former editor of the New London *Bee* and a Sedition Act martyr who had been convicted in 1800 for libel and spent several months in jail. Holt prepared to launch a *Bee* in Hudson and made it clear it would buzz impertinently in the face of the dignified *Balance*.

Young Harry Croswell forthwith saw an opportunity to prove his extreme devotion to Federalism. He persuaded his senior editor, Sampson, to let him publish in the garret of the *Balance* office a paper entitled the *Wasp*. As an editorial pseudonym, Croswell chose "Robert Rusticoat"; for a motto, "To lash the Rascals naked through the world." Down in New York, an observer in the *Evening Post* told the story in doggerel obviously modelled on "Yankee Doodle."

> *There's Charlie Holt is come to town*
> *A proper lad with types, sir.*
> *The Democrats have fetched him here*
> *To give the federals stripes, sir.*
>
> *The Balance-folks seem cruel 'fraid*
> *That he'll pull down their scales, sir.*
> *And so they got a pokerish wasp,*
> *To sting him with his tail, sir.*

Croswell's opening number was nothing less than a declaration of war:

Wherever the Bee ranges, the Wasp will follow over the same fields and on the same flowers—Without attempting to please his friends, the Wasp will only strive to displease, vex and torment his enemies. . . . The Wasp has a dirty and disagreeable job to perform. He has undertaken the chastisement of a set of fellows who are entrenched in filth—who like lazy swine are wallowing in a puddle. He must therefore wade knee deep in smut before he can meet his enemies on their own ground.

At his opposite number, Holt, Croswell levelled the following blast:

It is well known that you was bro't here by virtue of $500 raised for that purpose by the leading Democrats in this city. That the public may know, therefore, with how much purity and independence you will conduct in your editorial labors, would you be kind enough to answer the following questions:

Did the contributors to the $500 purchase you, as they purchase Negroes in Virginia, or hire you as they hire servants in New England?

Are you not a mere automaton in the hands of your masters; pledged to publish whatever slanders of falsehoods they shall dictate? And by your contract with them if you refuse to pollute your sheets have they not a right to ship you back again to your 350 subscribers in New London?

Croswell soon made it clear that this was more than a local war. Down in Virginia, James Callender was demonstrating his lack of principle by turning on his former idol, Thomas Jefferson. After Jefferson became President, Callender, working on the assumption that his slanderous attack on Washington and Adams had done much to swing the election, coolly asked to be made postmaster of Richmond. Jefferson declined, whereupon Callender revealed in print that while he was working on *The Prospect Before Us,* Jefferson had sent him a hundred dollars and had even read part of the manuscript, returning it with the declaration, "Such papers cannot fail to produce the best affect. They inform the thinking part of the nation. . .''

This was sensational stuff, the kind of thing that could hurt Jefferson politically. Washington was now in his grave two years and already the process of canonization was in full swing. Federalist printers rushed to their presses to discuss Jefferson's rather lame explanation that he had sent Callender the hundred dollars out of charity, and because he was a Sedition Act victim. But few equalled the savagery with which the *Wasp* pilloried this explanation.

It amounts to this then. He [Jefferson] read the book and from that book inferred that Callender was an object of charity. Why! One who presented a face bloated with vices, a heart black as hell—one who could be guilty of such foul falsehoods, such vile aspersions of the best and greatest man the world has yet known—he an object of charity! No! He is the very man, that an aspiring mean and hollow hypocrite would press into the service of crime. He is precisely qualified to become a tool—to spit the venom and scatter the malicious, poisonous slanders of his employer. He, in short, is the very man that a dissembling patriot, pretended "man of the people" would employ to plunge for him the dagger, or administer the arsenic.

Again and again Croswell sank his stinger into this Jeffersonian blister.

Will the reader turn to that inaugural speech of 1801 and see how this incarnate [Jefferson] speaks of Washington. There he makes him a demigod—having already paid Callender for making him a devil. . . Will the word hypocrite describe this man? There is not strength enough in the term.

When Holt attempted to answer Croswell by impugning Callender's character, the young Federalist editor hoisted him with another petard.

About the time of Callender's trial, you [Holt] printed a paper in New London—in that paper Callender was extolled to the skies. He was then an "excellent Republican," a "virtuous man," a "good citizen," a "suffering patriot." . . . If there is anything on earth to be pitied, it is a miser-"able editor" constantly tumbling into the mire; and whose every struggle but sinks him deeper.

The disarray of his antagonists emboldened Croswell to aim some shafts at local Democratic-Republicans. In the September 9, 1802, issue of the *Wasp* appeared the following poem:

> *Th' attorney general chanc'd one day to meet*
> *A dirty, ragged fellow in the street*
> > *A noisy swaggering beast*
> > *With run half drunk at least*
> *Th' attorney, too, was drunk—but not with grog—*
> *Power and pride had set his head agog.*

The poem went on to describe how the attorney general, "madly frowning on the clown," asked him how he had the insolence to address him as a "fellow lab'rer for the common good."

> *"Why," said the fellow with a smile,*
> *"You weekly in the paper toil,*
> *"Condemn the old administration*
> *"And do your best to 'save the nation'*
> *"While I with just the same pretenses*
> *"Chalk 'Damn the Feds' on gates and fences."*

Croswell lampooned other leading local characters who were perfectly recognizable even when he named no names. One satire described a prominent judge who spent an evening eating and drinking at a nearby tavern and then refused to pay his bill. In a memoir that he attached to one of the few surviving complete sets of the *Wasp* (now at the New-York Historical Society), Croswell told how he was walking through the streets of Hudson, not long after publication of the latter tale, when up thundered a local justice of the peace, a big man named Hagedorn, who leaped off his wagon, shook his horsewhip under Croswell's nose, and vowed that he considered the tavern story slander and was going to extract instant revenge.

"I had no cane or other means of defense," Croswell wrote. "But I stood erect and dropping my hands to my sides looked him full in the face and in the most cool and collected manner apprised him that . . . neither he nor any other man could ever whip me and it was a mistake for him to talk so loud about it. He . . . broke out again in a tempest of oaths, turned shortly on his heel, mounted his wagon and drove off at a furious pace, his poor horse having received the rash intended for me."

Looking around him, Croswell noticed a staunch Federalist friend in a nearby doorway laughing heartily at the exchange. "Harry Croswell," said he, "how could you be so sure that he would not whip you?"

"Mainly," Croswell replied, "because I planned to run away if he had attempted it."

It never seemed to occur to Croswell that he was a David taking on a number of political Goliaths. One reason may have been the illusion created by the preponderance of Federalists in Hudson. Among his prominent contributors was a young attorney, Thomas Grosvenor, who was the brother-in-law of Elisha Williams. Williams did more than merely threaten Charlie Holt when the *Bee* turned some of its venom in his direction. He caught the small, thin Holt, described as a "cripple" by a Columbia County antiquarian, and with several supporters nearby, thrashed him thoroughly.

Meanwhile, Croswell broadened his attacks on Jefferson with other choice tidbits from Callender's pen. He quoted the erstwhile Jeffersonian as declaring that "Mr. Jefferson has for years past while his wife was living and does now since she is dead, keep a woolly headed concubine by the name of Sally—that by her he had had several children, and that one by the name of Tom has since his father's election taken upon himself many airs of importance, and boasted his extraction from a President." To this, Croswell added another noxious tale: how Jefferson, before his marriage, attempted to seduce Mrs. John Walker, the wife of a close friend.

Other extremist Federalist papers were printing the same stories. Publicly, Jefferson always maintained a philosopher's stance toward the abuse he was getting. In 1803 he wrote to a European friend, "[It] is so difficult to draw a line of separation between the abuse and the wholesome use of the press, that as yet we have found it better to trust the public judgment, rather than the magistrate, with the discrimination between truth and falsehood." But his actions in 1803, belied that view. One reason may have been that two out of the three stories the Federalists were spreading were uncomfortably close to the truth. The slave concubine would seem to be sheer slander, but three years later Jefferson admitted privately that the Walker story was essentially accurate; and even his most benevolent biographers find it hard to explain away his relations with Callender.

By private letter and person messenger, in his wonted style, Jefferson passed the word to his state leaders. "[The] press ought to be restored to its credibility if possible," he told Thomas McKean, the governor of Pennsylvania. ". . . I have therefore long thought that a few prosecutions of the most prominent offenders would have a wholesome effect. . . . Not a general prosecution, for that would look like persecution:

but a selected one." For the already infuriated Jeffersonians in states where Federalists were most impudent, this was what they had been waiting for. Joseph Dennie, the arch-Federalist editor of the Philadelphia *Port Folio,* was promptly charged with seditious libel against the state and the United States. In New York, the selected victim was Harry Croswell.

Several historians have wondered why this obscure editor was singled out rather than the presitigious William Coleman of the *Evening Post,* who had also reprinted Callender's anti-Jefferson blasts. But even a rudimentary sketch of New York politics in 1802 makes it easy to see why Croswell was Attorney General Ambrose Spencer's number-one choice. There is nothing like smiting the enemy when he has had the effrontery to invade one of your most powerful bastions. To underscore this fact, Spencer himself appeared to prosecute the case, with the local district attorney, Ebenezer Foote, serving merely as an assistant.

Spencer was an ex-Federalist who had "gone over" to the other party, and seeing this turncoat undoubtedly made Harry Croswell seethe when he was brought on a bench warrant before three local judges at the Court of General Sessions sitting at Claverack, then the Columbia County seat. The fiery young editor was indicted for libel on two counts, which were duly read to him. One was based on the fourth issue of the *Wasp,* August 12, 1802, in which he had listed "a few 'squally' facts"—five executive acts by President Jefferson which, Croswell maintained, grossly violated the federal Constitution. The second and more serious charge was based on a paragraph that had appeared in the *Wasp* on September 9, 1802:

> Holt says, the burden of the Federal song is, that Mr. Jefferson paid Callender for writing against the late administration. This is wholly false. The charge is explicitly this:—Jefferson paid Callender for calling Washington a traitor, a robber, and a perjurer—. For calling Adams, a hoary headed incendiary; and for most grossly slandering the private characters of men, who, he well knew were virtuous. These charges, not a democratic editor has yet dared, or ever will dare to meet in an open manly discussion.

Croswell was not deserted by his Federalist friends. Standing beside him at the bar were Elisha Williams, Jacob Rutsen Van Rensselaer, and William W. Van Ness. Williams was already established as a legal giant. Oliver Wendell Holmes, in *The Poet at the Breakfast-Table,* wrote that he once asked a distinguished New Yorker, "Who on the whole seems the most considerable person you ever met?" Quite to Holmes's bemusement, the man replied without hesitation, "Elisha Williams." Van Rensselaer was a vigorous descendant of the great patron family that had once owned 62,000 acres of land on the east side of the Hudson River, including the entire town of Claverack. Van Ness at twenty-seven was considered the most brilliant young attorney in Columbia County. His folksy courtroom manner was typical of the younger Federalists' new style. He often interrupted his speeches to ask the foreman of the jury for a chew of tobacco.

The tone of the trial was set from the very first defense motion. Croswell's counsel demanded copies of the indictments before entering a plea. The Attorney General objected and was sustained by the all-Republican bench, and Croswell pleaded not guilty. (In his *Wasp* memoir Croswell says that the Jefferson-Callender passage, which was to become the heart of the case, had actually been written by Thomas Grosvenor, but he declined to implicate this young man and took his chances before the court. This required courage. A sojourn in a crude county jail was no laughing matter in 1803.) The defense then requested a postponement until the next session of the circuit courts. They argued that on an issue as legally complex as the law of libel, a state supreme court justice should sit. The Attorney General objected; he was promptly upheld.

The defense now made a most significant motion—a request for postponement in order to bring from Virginia James Callender himself, who would testify to the truth of the libel. Attorney General Spencer sprang to his feet, quivering like a wire. Under no circumstances would he tolerate such a procedure. They were trying this case according to the law of New York states. The truth or falsehood of the libel was irrelevant! All he had to prove to the twelve good men and true in the jury box was the question of fact. Did Harry Croswell publish these libelous statements against the President of the United States?

Thus in the small country courtroom before three farmer justices of the peace, the political-legal giants of the Empire State drew historic—and ironic—battle lines. Here was the Jeffersonian attorney general, backed by Jeffersonian justices, vociferously upholding the Royalist doctrine that had been brought to bear against John Peter Zenger at his famous trial in 1735.

But the Zenger case is by no means the landmark in the history of press freedom that has sometimes been supposed. The German printer's acquittal on charges of seditious libel against Governor William Cosby changed very little. The jury had simply disregarded the judge's admonition to disregard the question of the truth of the alleged libel, and the law remained as it was. Subsequent cases in New York and other colonies made it clear that American legislators and most voters were ready to support freedom of the press only when the press printed what they approved.

Essentially, in fact, what colonial and post-Revolutionary liberals meant by freedom of the press was a press free from licensing and prior censorship. When the framers wrote in the First Amendment, "Congress shall make no law . . . abridging the freedom of speech, or of the press," the key word to them was "Congress." The reason Jefferson had considered the Sedition Act null was not because it had muzzled his party's press, but because he was convinced that Congress, under the Constitution, had no power to enact such legislation. Writing to Abigail Adams in 1804, Jefferson would declare, "While we deny that Congress have a right to control the freedom of the press, we have ever asserted the right of the States, and their exclusive right, to do so."

Thus the Jeffersonians were not as inconsistent as they seemed to be in their stand on Harry Croswell. They rooted their opinion in the common-law tradition of England, best summed up by the great commentator Sir William Blackstone:

The liberty of the press is indeed essential to the nature of a free state; but this consists in laying no previous restraints upon publications and not in freedom from censure for criminal matter when published. Every free man has an undoubted right to lay what sentiments he pleases before the public; to forbid this is to destroy the freedom of the press; but if he publishes what is improper, mischievous or illegal, he must take the consequences of his own temerity.

But legal principles, even legal traditions, while they may be revered by lawyers and utilized in emergencies like the one in which Ambrose Spencer found himself, are not so sacred to the man in the street, and Croswell's trial soon made it clear that the Jeffersonians were riding a tiger of their own creation. The moment Spencer declared that "the truth cannot be given in evidence." Elisha Williams unlimbered his heaviest rhetorical artillery. Hitherto, he pointed out, it had been the first article in Spencer's political creed that the people possessed the sovereignty and that governors and Presidents were their servants; and that whenever the people should write on their ballots, "Turn them out. Turn them out," those whom they had rejected must fall. But how could this power, this sovereignty, be correctly exercised, how could the people "pluck down the vicious demagogue and raise and support the virtuous patriot unless their variant conduct could be faithfully represented? And what printer would dare to represent such conduct if the truth of the fact so represented could not shield him from destruction?"

Almost immediately Spencer began to backwater. He first agreed to postpone trial of the indictment based on the *Wasp's* claim that Jefferson had violated the Constitution. But he insisted on taking up the second indictment, the charge in regard to Callender, the next day.

Croswell's attorneys appeared in court the next evening and entering a formal affidavit stating that the Federalists intended and expected to prove the truth of the facts as stated in the *Wasp* in regard to Callender and President Jefferson. Like a shrewd fencer, the Attorney General returned an unexpected riposte. He wanted Croswell bound with $5,000 bail on each indictment "to keep the peace and be of good behavior." Croswell's attorneys exploded in a chorus of objections. Not only was such a demand illegal and a violation of Croswell's liberty as a free citizen of the United States—it was indirectly an attack upon the freedom of the press.

Elisha Williams and his confreres spent most of the next day debating this motion with Spencer. Again the political deficiencies of the Jeffersonian case were evident. Spencer, representative of the party that claimed to be the repository of the true spirit of the American Revolution, spent most of his time quoting cases out of English common law. The principal citation was a statute from the reign of Edward III which granted justices power to bind over "such as be not of good fame" to be of good behavior. Williams came back with a rain of English citations, including the still politically potent name of John Wilkes. When this erratic friend of the American Revolution had been arrested for libel in 1763 and the King's attorney attempted to have him bound, the

Chief Justice of England dismissed the motion, "whereupon there was a loud huzzah in Westminster Hall."

The Attorney General rose with a rebuttal that the reporter for the *Balance* grudgingly admitted was, "with the exception of a few indecent expressions . . . one of Mr. Spencer's most ingenious speeches." But in spite of his ingenuity, Spencer's motion to bind Croswell was denied. The Republican judges could not bring themselves to gag Croswell quite so flagrantly.

Six months of legal jousting followed. The Croswell attorneys fought to get the entire case transferred to the circuit court, under a New York supreme court justice, and Spencer struggled to retain it in the lower court, where he would have a local Jeffersonian bench and jury. In the interim, however, the Federalists scored a resounding electoral victory in Hudson and duplicated it in five other Columbia County towns.

The legal battle reached a climax on June 14, 1803, when Spencer and the Croswell legal trio once more clashed at Claverack. After a long and acrimonious debate, Spencer gave way and agreed that both indictments could be tried before a supreme court justice on the next circuit through the county. It soon became evident that Spencer had a good reason for accommodating his opponents. Chief Justice Morgan Lewis appeared as the circuit judge. A thorough Jeffersonian, Lewis interrupted Croswell's lawyers as they once more attempted to request a delay in order to obtain evidence from James Callender in Virginia. Such evidence, Lewis declared, concerned the truth of the charge for which the defendant was indicted and in his opinion the law was "settled, that the truth could not be given in evidence to the jury as a justification."

Croswell's lawyers argued manfully against this prejudgment. They maintained that Croswell's case involved a public libel, which made the truth of vital consideration. On that ground, they requested a delay until a commission appointed by the court could examine Callender. (At this point in his career, Callender was on his way to becoming a hopeless drunkard, and Croswell's lawyers probably felt that he would be a sorry witness at best; hence the shift to a commission to examine him at a distance.)

Judge Lewis was unmoved by the Federalist eloquence. When the Attorney General rose to reply, the Chief Justice told him it was necessary. He said he was "astonished" at the application, and repeated his view that "the law is settled, that the truth of the matter published cannot be given in evidence." Then, suggesting the nervous state of the Jeffersonian position, his Honor hastened to add, "I very much regreat that the law is not otherwise; but as I am to declare what the law is, I cannot on this ground put off the trial."

The outcome of the trial was easily predictable. The only thing that really mattered was the Chief Justice's charge to the jury, in which he instructed them that they had but one thing to decide: whether Harry Croswell did in fact publish the scurrilous statements in the *Wasp*. It was left to the court to weigh matters of truth or falsehood, and also of malice, in determining the sentence. The jury retired at "sunsetting" with nothing to debate. Nevertheless, they remained out the whole night, and not until eight o'clock the next morning did they come to the bar with a verdict of guilty.

Croswell's attorneys immediately moved for a new trial, arguing that Lewis had misdirected the jury, and reiterating that the truth should be given in evidence. The motion was granted and the case was carried over first to the November term of the New York supreme court, and finally to the January, 1804, term.

In the meantime, both sides regrouped for the climax of the battle. The Federalist sought out their chief intellect, Alexander Hamilton. As early as June 23, 1803, they had persuaded General Philip Schuyler, Hamilton's father-in-law, to write the brilliant former Secretary of the Treasury for help. (In a style that typified the primeval Federalist, the patrician Schuyler described the case as "a libel against that Jefferson, who disgraces not only the place he fills but produces immorality by his pernicious example.") There is some evidence that Hamilton advised Croswell's counsel before the circuit court trial. Now, with the proceedings at stage center, he agreed to appear in person, gratis.

Down in Virginia during the same months, fate put a dent in Croswell's cause. In the midst of a drunken spree his potential star witness, Callender, fell out of a boat to find a final resting place, as one writer put it, "in congenial mud" at the bottom of the James River. But he left behind him his published works, including letters Jefferson had written expressing his approval of *The Prospect Before Us,* so his dirty work was very much alive when the supreme court convened February 13, 1804, to hear the final round of *People v. Croswell.*

For Hamilton the case represented an opportunity for revenge against his great rival, who was riding high on the crest of political triumph. Some of it Jefferson owed to Hamilton, whose unwise attempt to dump John Adams as the Federalist candidate in 1800 had done much to hand Jefferson the election. Aaron Burr had in the same year destroyed Hamilton's political power base in New York, manipulating the votes of the Tammany Society to elect a Jeffersonian governor, George Clinton. Discredited with his own party, Hamilton had retreated to his law practice, where he had already established himself by his sheer brilliance as a thinker and speaker.

More than revenge may have stirred Hamilton in the Croswell case. This strange, often contradictory giant, who was considered by Talleyrand to be one of the three greatest men of the age along with Napoleon and Pitt, had a deep, instinctive love of liberty which was never extinguished by his vision of a compact organic society, organized and run by a natural aristocracy at the top. Now free from the inhibitions and necessities of party intrigue, which had prompted him to approve the Sedition Act, he flung himself whole-heartedly into Croswell's defense.

He brought with him from New York an old friend and staunch Federalist, Richard Harrison, who had shared Hamilton's mind and heart since their days together as Washington's aides-de-camp. With these two lawyers of the first rank was young William Van Ness, to provide continuity from the earlier court battles.

The opposition, meanwhile, had made a notable change. On February 3, 1804, Attorney General Ambrose Spencer had been nominated to the supreme court, but he properly abstained from sitting on the case, and summoned one of his political followers, George Caines, as his associate before the bar. Spencer's abstention left a four-man court: Chief Justice Lewis, who had already proved himself a devout Jeffersonian; Brockholst Livingston, who, true to his family reputation, was of a similar political faith; a third Jeffersonian, Smith Thompson; and a lone Federalist, James Kent.

But in force of personality and weight of learning, Kent more than equalled the three Jeffersonian justices. "The American Blackstone," as he was later called for his *Commentaries on American Law,* the most influential legal volumes of the nineteenth century, had been converted to Federalism by listening to Alexander Hamilton's magnificient speeches in favor of the Constitution during the New York state ratifying convention in 1789, and by the still more cogent reasoning of the *Federalist Papers.* It was from a friendship with Hamilton begun in those days that he had acquired his conviction that the common-law tradition was essential to the nation's future. Not all lawyers agreed with this in 1804. In most states, the best legal minds were debating whether they should not scrap the common law and create a whole new code, as the French had done under Napoleon.

The problems—and the advantages—of the common law were all too evident in Croswell's case. All of the first day of the trial and most of the second were consumed by excursions far back into the mazes of English common law, with both sides endeavoring to show that the legal tradition of an earlier and supposedly purer age upheld their view of the central question: whether the truth could be admitted as evidence in a case of seditious libel. It was something of a stand-off; but it did clear away legal debris and effectively set the stage for Alexander Hamilton.

By now the hearing was absorbing the attention of both the judicial and legislative wings of New York's state government. According to Charles Holt's *Bee,* almost the entire state senate and assembly poured into the supreme court chambers to hear the climax of the debate. They were there for more than the excitement of seeing Hamilton in action. Already a legislator had submitted a bill that would permit the truth to be heard in libel cases. The British Parliament had passed a similar bill in 1792.

No exact record of Hamilton's speeches in the Croswell case exists, but New York papers reported them quite fully and Justice James Kent kept ample notes. Hamilton began by emphasizing the importance of the subject and went on to examine what he called "the two Great Points"—the truth as evidence, and the jury's right to examine Croswell's intent. He insisted he was not arguing for "the pestilential Doctrine of an unchecked Press." The best man on earth (Washington) had had his great character besmirched by such a press. No, he was contending for the right to publish "the truth, with good motives, though the censure light on government or individuals." Above all he wanted to see "the check" on the press deposited not in a permanent body of magistrates, but in an "occasionally and fluctuating Body, the jury." He pointed out that in the American system judges were not as independent from the executive and legislative branches as they were in England. All the more reason, therefore, to anchor freedom of the press in the right of trial by jury.

Hamilton ranged up and down English legal history and even dipped into Roman law and scriptural texts, to prove that the common law had always maintained these rights, until it was corrupted by the Star Chamber courts, which only proved his point—"a permanent body of men without the wholesome check of a jury grows absolute." Then he turned and indirectly defended the Sedition Act, which despite its repressive intent had been directed against slander which could be proved to be "false." He declared that he "gloried in" the fact that the United States had "by act" established this doctrine.

From here Hamilton soared into a long paean to the juror's duties and rights. What if this were a "capital case" and the jury decided that it did not agree with the court's interpretation of the law? Everyone knew that jurors were bound by their oaths, in such a case, to vote according to their convictions. Were he himself a juror, Hamilton declared, he would "die on the rack" before he would "immolate his convictions on the altar of power."

Throughout the afternoon, Hamilton all but hypnotized his audience with his dazzling oratory. Kent noted that he was *"sublimely eloquent."* The court adjourned at 5 P.M., and the next morning Hamilton took up the argument again. Once more he worked his way through an impressive number of citations of bolster his argument, but he soon got to the political meat in his morning's work, a digression that Judge Kent in his notes called *"impassioned & most eloquent,"* on the danger to American liberty, not from provisional armies but from "dependent Judges, from *selected* Juries, from *stifling* the Press & the voices of leaders & Patriots."

"We ought to resist, resist, resist, till we hurl the Demagogues & Tyrants from their imaginary Thrones," he cried. Never was there a libel case where the question of truth was more important. "It ought to be distinctly known," he thundered, "whether Mr. Jefferson be guilty or not of so foul an act as the one charged." This catapulted him into a eulogy of the dead Washington that in Kent's opinion was "never surpassed—never equalled."

Finally, he paid sarcastic tribute to the "other party" and especially to their "strange & unexpected compliments on the *Freedom* of the English nation." But, he reiterated, a country is free only where the people have a representation in the government, and where they have a trial by jury. If America abandoned the principles of the common law, a faction in power could construe the Constitution to make "any political Tenet or any Indiscretion a Crime." Sacrificing and crushing individuals "by the perverted Forms & mask of law" was the "most dangerous & destructive Tyranny."

As the stocky figure of the man whom Talleyrand said had "made the fortune of his country" bowed before the black-robbed justices and retired to his seat, James Kent jotted a final note—"I never heard him so great." Thus inspired, Kent wrote a masterful opinion decreeing a new trial for Croswell. The power of his personality and his reasoning persuaded his fellow associate justices, Livingston and Thompson, to abandon their Jeffersonian principles and agree with him—at first. But Chief Justice Lewis, by now running hard for Governor, wrote a contrary opinion of his own. He also paid Justice Livingston a little visit, whereupon Livingston suddenly changed his mind. The court thus divided two and two, and the motion for a new trial was denied.

The prosecution could have moved immediately for a judgment against Croswell, but no such motion was made. The Jeffersonians were already badly clawed by their ride on this legal tiger, and they had no penchant for further gouges. Moreover, the New York senators and assemblymen, having heard Hamilton's eloquence, had set to work on a truth-in-libel bill that was certain to pass; the Chief Justice was upholding a legal principle that was about to be officially invalidated. So the case was simply dropped. Its impact, however, was important: other states would soon follow New York's lead, transforming Harry Croswell's case from a *cause célèbre* into one of the bulwarks of our free press.

Croswell's personal troubles were not yet over. Ambrose Spencer returned to Hudson and brought a new suit against Croswell and his mentor, Sampson, for libel. Sampson settled out of court, but the stubborn Croswell refused to back away from the scathing comments he had made about both Spencer and his henchman, District Attorney Ebenezer Foote, in the farewell issue of the *Wasp*, which had appeared on January 26, 1803. Foote submitted a suit of his own. Spencer recovered $126 in damages, poor Foote, attempting to prove he was not a swindler and a blockhead, was ambushed by a host of witnesses who solemnly vowed they had seen him cheat at cards, among other things. The jury awarded him damages of six cents. This final act of low comedy was gleefully reported in the *Balance*.

Croswell now became senior editor of the *Balance* and continued to do battle in the Federalist cause in Hudson until 1809, when he transferred his paper to Albany. This was a mistake. The Federalists there were in disarray, and his support was meager. Debts piled up; in 1811 a leading Federalist who had loaned him money obtained a judgment against him, and the harassed editor served a short sentence in a debtor's prison. It was one indication of the fatal deficiencies of the Federalists as a party. The "best people" were too interested in lining their own purses to make the sacrifices that a successful political machine demanded.

Totally disgusted, Croswell quit newspapering, took Episopal orders, and after serving briefly as rector of Christ Church in Hudson, moved to Trinity Church in New Haven. He remained in this post, respected and eventually revered, for the next forty-three years. But he never attended another political meeting, or even exercised his rights as a voter. "His revulsion from Federalism was so entire," said one of his acquaintances after his death, "that in later life his tacit sympathy was evidently with the Democratic party."

Thus exit Harry Croswell. As for Alexander Hamilton, the sequel of the Croswell case was tragedy. During the hearings he had stayed at a friend's house near Albany, and in an evening's conversation, he delivered some scathing denunciations of Vice President Aaron Burr, who was soon to run against Chief Justice Lewis for the governorship of New York. In the course of the election campaign, the friend unwisely quoted Hamilton in a letter that got into the newspapers. Lewis won, finishing Burr politically in New York, and the embittered Vice President challenged Hamilton to a duel. The acclaim he won at Croswell's trial may well have played a part in persuading Hamilton to accept—in spite of his personal detestation of duelling, which had been redoubled by the death of his son Philip in a politically inspired duel two years before. Having regained not a little of the stature he had lost within his party, Hamilton may have been more inclined to risk the morning visit to Weehawken in the hope that it would be another step toward undoing his great rival in the White House, Jefferson. He guessed wrong, and paid for it with his life.

Primary materials such as court records and files of early newspapers were Mr. Fleming's principal sources for this article. Recommended for further reading: Legacy of Suppression: Freedom of Speech and Press in Early American History, *by Leonard W. Levy (Harvard University Press, 1960);* The Presidents and the Press, *by James E. Pollard (Macmillan, 1947).*

Timid President? Futile War?

Irving Brant

Of all the major events in American history, the War of 1812 is least known to the most people. Its naval glories are exploited in popular narrative. Its military failures, formerly glossed over, are emphasized by more objective historians with something akin to pleasure. Lease known of all is the part taken by President Madison, who by virtue of the Constitution was commander in chief of the Armed Forces, charged with the duty of "making" the war that Congress "declared."

Through the years, however, a picture of James Madison has been built up by the brushes or palette knives of historians and popular word-artists. He appears as a pacifistic little man overshadowed by the ample figure of his wife, Dolley; a great political philosopher overwhelmed by the responsibilities of a war into which he was projected, at the age of sixty-one, against his will and with no capacity for executive leadership.

The purpose of this article is to appraise, not to acquit or indict. But in the case of Madison, the adverse preconceptions are embedded so deeply that they stand in the way of a fair appraisal. Historians have rejected the Federalist charge that he carried the United States into war to help Napoleon master the Old World. But with few exceptions they have treated him as the dupe of the French Emperor, tricked into war with England by the apparent repeal by the French of the Berlin and Milan Decrees at a time when both countries were despoiling American commerce. (*See* "If Only Mr. Madison Had Waited," American Heritage, April, 1956.) As for his conduct of the war, Madison has received little credit for victories and plenty of blame for misfortunes. Finally, the Treaty of Ghent satisfied none of the grievances cited in the declaration of war, and the one decisive military victory—that of General Andrew Jackson at New Orleans—was won two weeks after the signing of the peace treaty. It all adds up to the picture of a useless and costly conflict, saved by mere luck from being a disaster, and coming to an inconclusive end.

"Everybody knew" in 1812, just as everybody "knows" today, that Madison was timid, hesitant, ruled by stronger men. Everybody knew it, that is, except the foreign diplomats who were sent to overawe him. "Curt, spiteful, passionate." France's Louis

Turreau called him. "Madison is now as obstinate as a mule," wrote England's "Copenhagen" Jackson (the Francis James Jackson who in 1807 had burned Denmark's capital) just before the President kicked him out of the country. Turreau's friendlier successor, Louis Sérurier, heard that the Chief of State was ruled by his Cabinet. He waited several months before he wrote to Paris: "Mr. Madison governs by himself."

Expelling an obnoxious minister was a civilian job. But how could Madison be anything of a war leader when "everybody knew" that he had been kicked into the war by Clay, Calhoun, Grundy, and other congressional War Hawks? There were certain things that "everybody" did not know. They did not know that in March, 1809, two weeks after he became President, Madison authorized British Minister David M. Erskine to inform his government that if she would relax her Orders in Council, he would ask Congress "to enter upon immediate measures of hostility against France."

They did not know of a simultaneous notice to France that if she ceased her commercial aggressions and Great Britian did not, "the President of the United States will advise to an immediate war with the latter." Neither Congress nor the public ever learned that when President Madison proclaimed nonintercourse with England on November 2, 1810, he informed General Turreau that continued interference with American trade by England "will necessarily lead to war"—as it did. The 1809 offer to join England against France brought gasps of astonishment in Congress when Madison revealed it in asking for the declaration of war against England. It brought no gasps of any sort from writers of history. It didn't fit their conception of Madison, so they disposed of it by silence.

England first, then France, was Madison's schedule of redress. In August, 1812, the moment he was notified that England had repealed her Orders in Council, he offered to settle the one remaining issue—impressment of seamen—by informal agreement. At the same time he wrote to his minister in Paris that if England made peace and France failed to repair American wrongs, war would be declared against France as soon as Congress convened, and that if England did not make peace he might even recommend a double war. Joel Barlow was directed to show that letter to the French government. As a result, Barlow was called to Poland to confer with Napoleon in the field and complete a treaty, but Napoleon's defeat at Berezina intervened, and Barlow died of pneumonia near Cracow on his way back to Paris. Madison's letter has been in print for nearly a hundred years, ignored even by historians who knew that it was described in the French foreign office as an ultimatum of war.

The same Federalist editors who jeered at "poor Madison" in 1812 denounced him as a dictator in 1814. They were free to do so. Open sedition and silent resistance forced the United States to fight the war with one arm—New England—tied behind her back. That was more crippling than incompetent generals, raw militia, and an empty treasury. Yet the President rejected every counsel that would have narrowed the constitutional liberties of those who gave vocal aid to the enemy. They would hang themselves, he said, and they did. Among all the words of praise addressed to him when he left office, he may have felt keenest pride in those of the Citizens' Committee of Washington:

> Power and national glory, sir, have often before been acquired by the sword; but rarely without the sacrifice of civil or political liberty. When we reflect that this sword was drawn under your guidance, we cannot resist offering you our own as well as a nation's thanks for the vigilance . . . the energy . . . and the safety with which you have wielded an armed force of 50,000 men . . . without infringing a political, civil or religious right.

It takes time, of course, for people to accept a portrait after a hundred years of caricature. At the risk of being abrupt, let us turn to Madison's actions as war leader. Expecting hostilities with England, why did he not call for adequate preparations? He did, but in Congress a vote for taxes was looked on as political suicide. Madison's first action in national defense was to lay up most of President Jefferson's little gunboats as wasteful of men and money in proportion to gunpower and to order laid-up frigates refitted. Congress cut the requested appropriation and stopped the work. In September, 1811, Sérurier told his government that the President was stimulating a nationwide debate on the question of whether it suited the Republic to have a navy, and if so, should it not be "such as can make the American flag respected"? The proposition had to be presented "in this questioning and deferential form," said the Minister, to avoid exciting state jealousy of federal power.

At the ensuing session of Congress the administration asked for twelve seventy-four-gun ships and ten new frigates, and the repair or reconstruction of six of the ten existing frigates. The new construction was voted down and the reconditioning limited to three ships.

To prepare for the land war, which would have to be fought either on American or Canadian soil, the President wanted a quick build-up of military forces. Then, if the expected bad news came from England, the troops would be ready to march on weakly defended Montreal and Quebec before reinforcements could cross the ocean.

With an authorized personnel of ten thousand, the Army had only about four thousand. The President asked that the old regiments be filled up, that ten thousand additional regulars be recruited, and that provision be made for fifty thousand volunteers. Senator William Branch Giles of Virginia, leader of the anti-Madison Democrats, shook the roof as he decried these puny measures. He demanded thirty-five thousand regulars and five-year enlistments, making it necessary to build a large and costly officer corps before men could be recruited, "The efforts of General [Senator Samuel] Smith and of Mr. Giles of Virginia," British Minister Augustus J. Foster reported, "have been added to those of the Federalists as a means to overthrow Mr. Madison and his administration." Congress talked most of the winter and Giles won. The bill for fifty thousand volunteers occasioned a lengthy constitutional harangue and a decision for state-appointed officers. The result, many believed, would be a militia that could refuse to go onto foreign soil. Skeptically, Madison signed the bills for the regulars and the volunteers.

His skepticism had warrant. On June 8 the number of recruits was estimated at five thousand, and there were few unbalky volunteers except in the West.

With England unyielding, the President on March 31 notified the House Committee on Foreign Relations that he was ready to ask for a shipping embargo—a prelude to war. But "the Executive will not take upon itself the responsibility of declaring that we are prepared for war." Congress must make the final decision with its eyes open. Four days later it did so, the embargo taking effect on April 4.

By that time, military and naval decisions were crowding in upon the Executive. In those fields, two stories are told which carry the suggestion that Madison was stupid, or at least indecisive. The fact that they are still in circulation proves that some writers have been a trifle credulous. One story says that the President decided to make an untrained civilian, Henry Clay, supreme military commander but was dissuaded by his Cabinet. The other is that Madison made up his mind to keep the American Navy tied up for harbor defense, but reversed himself on the pleas of Navy Captains Charles Stewart and William Bainbridge.

The story of the abortive appointment of Henry Clay reached full and rounded form in Calvin Colton's 1857 biography of Clay. It can be traced backward in print and manuscript, diminishing as it recedes—back to Colonel Isaac Cole's recollection, in 1838, of what he once heard from General John Mason, back to Mason's memory of what he was told by his brother-in-law, General Ben Howard. And that was: a group of Clay's friends suggested Clay's appointment to President Madison, who "assented to their opinion of [Clay's] fitness, etc., but said he could not be spared out of Congress." That was the molehill out of which the mountain grew.

The naval history was no third-hand, dry-land scuttlebutt. It came from Captain Stewart himself. As Stewart published the story in 1845, he and Captain Bainbridge went to the Navy Department on June 21, 1812, three days after the declaration of war, to solicit commands at sea. They were told by Secretary Paul Hamilton that the President and Cabinet had decided to keep the ships tied up. They protested, and the argument was continued before the President, who agreed with the captains but gave way to the Cabinet at a special meeting called that evening. Bainbridge and Stewart thereupon drafted a joint letter to the President, who overruled the Cabinet and ordered the Navy into action. Capping Stewart's story was his account of a great naval ball in the following December to which a courier brought news of Captain Stephen Decatur's victory over the frigate *Macedonian*. Whereupon President Madison told the assembled guests that if it had not been for Bainbridge and Stewart, the warships never would have gone to sea.

All rather convincing, unless you happen to know that Madison did not attend that December ball, that on June 23 Bainbridge wrote from Boston (he was not in Washington at all at the time) asking for a fighting command, and that all major warships ready for action were ordered to sea on the day war was declared. Stewart did not invent his 1845 story. It arose out of his muddled recollection and grandiose enlargement of a discussion held at the White House in February, 1812, some months before the declaration of war, in which the President sided with the captains against the Secretary of the Navy. Congress had just rejected the administration's request for twenty-two new warships. The captains, arguing with Hamilton, conceded that even if an American vessel were victorious it might, without reinforcements, he overwhelmed and captured by the enemy. To which Madison replied: "It is victories we want; if you give us them and lose your ships afterwards, they can be replaced by others."

The February discussion between the captains and the President was prophetic. For when Madison made his next request for greater sea power, in the closing weeks of 1812, it was dramatized by the *Constitution's* victory over the *Guerriére* in August, the capture of the *Macedonian* by the *United States* in October, and especially by the gallant exploit of the sloop *Wasp,* which ran into exactly the kind of trouble Stewart and Bainbridge had predicted. Victorious over the *Frolic,* the *Wasp* was unable to hoist a sail when a lumbering British seventy-four came along and took both victor and prize to Bermuda. Captain Stewart, in this campaign for funds, furnished Secretary Hamilton with the technical arguments that helped persuade Congress to authorize four ships of the line, four heavy frigates, and as many sloops of war.

In one critical area the issue of naval power could not wait until the war began. In March, 1812, Stewart was called to Washington and offered a yet-uncreated command on the Great Lakes, controlled then by a few British armed vessels. The President intended to ask Congress for money to build a fleet; in the meantime enough would be scraped up for an eighteen-gun brig. Stewart refused; he was a deep-sea man.

The matter was given a new turn just then by Governor William Hull of Michigan Territory, a veteran of the Revolution. Offered a commission as brigadier general, he urged the building of lake squadrons. But with Stewart rejecting the command and Congress hostile to naval construction, Hull assured the President that he could lead an army across the Detroit River and down the north shore of Lake Erie to the Niagara River. That would restrain the northwestern Indians, deliver much of upper Canada into American hands, and win control of the lakes in less time and at less cost than the building of a fleet would require.

A Detroit campaign was being forced on the government anyway. Early operations against Montreal were made impossible by the dearth of regulars and the refusal of New England governors to furnish militia for federal service. On the other hand, western volunteers were so eager to break up the British-Indian alliance, Clay and others reported, that inaction might chill their spirit. Madison accepted Hull's promise of lake control by land action and thereby made the biggest strategic error of the war.

The appointment of Hull was a major blunder, but hardly a foreseeable one. Thirty years of peace with the Army almost nonexistent forced the President to choose his generals either from aging Revolutionary veterans with fighting experience and reputation, or from young regimental officers who had never seen action. Among the veterans called back, Hull had an unsurpassed Revolutionary record. Even Federalist editors applauded Madison's selection.

Hull commanded twenty-five hundred confident Kentuckians, Ohioans, regulars, and Michigan territorials. He crossed into Canada on July 12, 1812, skirmished with the vastly outnumbered enemy, and retreated to Fort Detroit. There, on August 16, without firing a shot, without consulting his officers, he surrendered his entire army to General Isaac Brock, who was advancing at the head of 330 British regulars and 400 Canadian militiamen, with several hundred Indians whooping in the woods.

Hull's claim that he was short of supplies was categorically denied by his officers but avidly accepted by the Federalist press, with a resultant impact on historians. His most startling assertion was that he had only one day's supply of powder. When he made the same remark to Sir George Prevost, the British commander handed him "the return of the large supply found in the fort; it did not create a blush." Those were the words of British Adjutant General Edward Baynes. Hull's actions, wrote another member of Prevost's staff, "stamp him either for a coward or a traitor." With such comments coming from the captors, it seems just a trifle severe to blame the surrender on either the President or the War Department.

Suppose, instead, we find out how the President reacted to the disaster. New land forces, he said, could be counted on to redeem the country's honor. The immediate necessity was to speed up the building of warships to gain control of the lakes—a method that would have been adopted at the outset "if the easy conquest of them by land held out to us [by Hull] had not misled our calculations." The strength of his feeling was recorded by Richard Rush, who wrote to John Adams the following June: "I know the President to be so convinced upon this subject that I heard him say last fall if the British build thirty frigates upon [the lakes] we ought to build forty."

Madison's insistence produced the warships with which Commodore Perry defeated and captured the British squadron on Lake Erie in September, 1813, changing the whole complexion of the war. He ordered the building of ship after ship on Lake Ontario. Superiority swung back and forth on that lake like reversing winds, but neither side could force a decision because each had protected bases—the British at York (now Toronto) and Kingston, the Americans at Sackets Harbor—to retire to when the other was ahead.

Far more important and more critical was the state of affairs in 1814 on Lake Champlain, the great sluice that opened a supply route northward to Montreal and southward to the Hudson River valley. By summer, more than twenty thousand seasoned veterans of the Peninsular War, released for transatlantic service by Napoleon's downfall, were crowding onto British transports bound for Canada, Chesapeake Bay, and New Orleans. On Lake Champlain, the American ship *Saratoga* was launched thirty-five days after the laying of her keel. Sailors were in short supply both there and on Lake Ontario. Madison ordered the crews filled up with soldiers and told the protesting Secretary of War that naval efficiency was essential even for land operations.

Then came news that the enemy was building a new vessel on Lake Champlain, the *Confiance,* far more powerful than the twenty-six-gun *Saratoga.* Loss of the lake might still be averted, Captain Thomas Macdonough believed, by the swifter building of a light brig. Navy Secretary William Jones, though far more vigorous and capable than his predecessor, said the limit of available funds had been reached.

Madison ordered the ship built anyhow. Its keel had been laid when Jones again drew back. "God knows where the money is to come from," he wrote. The President reaffirmed the order and obtained a pledge of the utmost speed. On July 15 the timbers of the twenty-gun *Eagle* were still standing in the forest. The vessel was launched on August 11 and furnished the margin of power that changed sure defeat into a victory which resounded from Washington to Ghent.

"The battle of Lake Champlain, more than any other incident of the War of 1812, merits the epithet 'decisive,'" wrote the distinguished naval historian Alfred Thayer Mahan many years later. Within earshot of the battle, many of them within sight, nearly fourteen thousand of Wellington's battle-hardened soldiers waited for the Royal Navy to open the way to Albany and New York. When the British fleet surrendered, the army of invasion marched back to Canada and never returned.

In naval affairs, Madison could rely on officers unsurpassed anywhere in the world for knowledge and ability. In army matters he had to learn by hard experience. His first Secretary of War, William Eustis, was a Massachusetts medical man of bustling energy who bore a tremendous load of work in a War Department consisting of himself and eight clerks. Eustis, even in the opinion of some congressmen who wanted him fired, outperformed what anybody had a right to expect in equipping the Army as war approached. But he had no more than a civilian's knowledge of military operations, did little to systematize the nation's defenses, and seemed unable to recognize incompetence in field officers before it was demonstrated in battle. The President shared this last fault. When Adjutant General Baynes visited Major General Henry Dearborn under a flag of truce, he saw at a glance that the American commander lacked energy. Neither Madison nor Eustis sensed this, and the President couldn't see the deficiencies of Eustis. His resignation, after failures on the Niagara front followed the Hull catastrophe, was a concession to public opinion.

Brigadier General John Armstrong, who succeeded Eustis, was notorious for political intrigue but had enough of a military reputation to warrant his selection. The President chose him reluctantly, after Secretary of State James Monroe and Senator William Harris Crawford had refused the place.

During the next year and a half, until the burning of Washington forced him to resign, Armstrong performed his work with one eye on the war and the other on the 1816 presidential race. His good and bad traits showed up at once but not in equal measure. He drove the competent Andrew Jackson to fury and disobedience with a brusque, unappreciative dismissal of his temporary Tennessee volunteers in a distant wilderness. He removed the incompetent General Dearborn with a note even more callous. Both men wrote to the President, Jackson boiling with indignation, Dearborn heartbroken. Madison forced Armstrong to make amends to Jackson. He himself consoled Dearborn but affirmed the removal.

Armstrong's strategy to gain the presidential nomination paralleled that of his rival, James Monroe. Each hoped to be made a lieutenant general and win the war. Monroe's chance vanished when Armstrong took the War Department. Armstrong's opportunity seemed to open when the President, in June of 1813, was stricken with an almost fatal illness followed by several months' convalescence in Virginia. Freed of effective presidential supervision, Armstrong went north under the pretense of making an inspection trip and did not come back until Christmas. During the interval he assumed personal direction of a two-pronged campaign against Montreal, failed to co-ordinate the mishandled offensive movements, and ducked away to Albany to watch the approaching double fiasco as a detached observer.

Personal ambition and laziness turned Armstrong's strategic ideas, even when sound, into flashy gambits, without the preparation or drive required to follow through. Two weeks before the event that drove him out of office, he received a written rebuke from Madison that would have pierced the hide of a rhinoceros—though it did not penetrate his—for secretly exercising powers delegated by Congress to the President, ordering military operations without consultation, suppressing letters intended for the President, accepting the resignation of General William Henry Harrison without authority, and posing to Harrison's successor as the bestower of the appointment.

Nevertheless, Armstrong possessed capabilities that, combined with Madison's ability to thwart their misuse, gave a new look to the American Army. Both men recognized youthful talent, and Armstrong was ruthless enough to get rid of old incompetents.

Zebulon Pike, promoted to brigadier general, was killed in winning his first victory. Jacob Brown and George Izard, lately raised to the same rank, stood out in the Montreal campaign in contrast to their soon-to-be-ousted commanders, Major Generals James Wilkinson and Wade Hampton. Shining talents were displayed by Colonels E. P. Gaines and Winfield Scott; solid performance by Alexander Macomb, T. A. Smith, E. W. Ripley. Every one of these eight men was recommended by Armstrong for promotion, with the exception of Brown. He advised the President that for major generals, not a moment should be lost in promoting Brigadiers Izard and Thomas Flournoy.

Flournoy, a nobody at New Orleans! His promotion, by making Andrew Jackson his subordinate instead of his superior, would have knocked Jackson straight out of the military service—if not into apoplexy. But it also would have barricaded the upward path of Brown—the man most likely to stand in Armstrong's way if Armstrong succeeded in establishing the grade of lieutenant general—by filling all the major-generalships allowed by law.

The President nominated Izard—*and Brown.* It could almost be said that at that moment the Battle of New Orleans was won, although Jackson's appointment as major general still awaited a future vacancy. Also, the leadership was established that retrieved American prestige in the 1814 battles of the Niagara peninsula and helped persuade England that the time was ripe for peace.

The location of that Niagara campaign, illogical because of its limited objective, resulted from troop movements made by Armstrong without consulting the President. To remedy that feature, the Secretary sent a proposal to Madison at Montpelier that Brown's army bypass the peninsula and swing around Lake Ontario to Burlington and York. Madison imposed the same restriction that was to be recognized a hundred years later by Admiral Mahan: control of the lake must first be won to prevent the landing of an army in the American rear. The civilian commander in chief was learning the art of war. By a succession of decisions affecting strength, strategy, and leadership on Lake Champlain, at New Orleans, and on the Niagara front—overruling his subordinates in every instance—Madison went far to determine the outcome.

In spite of their conflicts over appointments, Armstrong and the President worked effectively together in a fundamental regeneration of the military command. On the day war was declared the United States Army had eight generals, most of them just appointed. Their average age was sixty years. Two years later all of them were out of service or assigned to quiescence. In the first half of 1814 nine generals were appointed or promoted—their average age was thirty-six—and these men turned raw American recruits into disciplined soldiers. When the war ended they had just begun to fight.

These redeeming events of 1814 are obscured in popular narrative and even in histories by the burning of Washington and the miserable failure of its defenders. (*See* "The Day They Burned the Capitol," American Heritage, December, 1954.) For that occurrence President Madison bore an inescapable responsibility: constitutionally, he was commander in chief; physically, he was in Washington when the enemy approached. Why did he not foresee the attack, or, if he did, why didn't he guard against it?

The answer to the first question accentuates the second. On May 24, after reading a British proclamation calling for a general uprising of southern slaves, the President wrote to Armstrong that this presaged a campaign of ruthless devastation in which the national capital could not fail to be "a favorite target." On July 1, without dissent but with skepticism concerning the danger (so wrote Navy Secretary William Jones), the Cabinet approved Madison's proposal that ten thousand militiamen be drawn out to help guard the Washington-Baltimore area. When Brigadier General William H. Winder wished to summon them, Secretary Armstrong (the chief skeptic) made the fatal reply that the best mode of using militia "was upon the spur of the occasion." Nevertheless, the power and responsibility belonged to the President, and his own recorded foresight called for vigorous defensive measures. He intervened again and again, to overcome Armstrong's sloth and skepticism, but never forced action on a large enough scale.

Almost in another world is the popular word-picture of the Madisons at this time. It is a composite of Dolley saving the portrait of George Washington as the enemy approached, and of the President—as depicted by the scurrilous (and anonymous) versifier of "The Bladensburg Races"—galloping in terrified flight forty miles into Maryland.

The rhapsodic glee with which the versifier danced in the ashes of the Capitol and White House may not impeach his veracity, but his figurative observation post hardly matched the physical one of Sérurier, who had a panoramic view from the unmenaced Octagon House. The President, Sérurier wrote to Talleyrand two days before the battle, "has just gone to the camp to encourage, by his presence, the army to defend the capital." Madison returned to the White House from the actual battlefield (where Congreve rockets fell near him) after Dolley left the House. He remained there, the French minister said, until after the Georgetown and Washington militia streamed by in confused flight toward Frederick. The manner of his departure as described by Sérurier would be of little moment except that it emphasizes still further how different Madison's character was from the one history has bestowed on him:

> It was then, my lord, that the President, who, in the midst of all this disorder, had displayed to stop it a firmness and constancy worthy of a better success . . . coolly mounted his horse, accompanied by some friends, and slowly gained the bridge that separates Washington from Virginia.

By the time the news of the burning of Washington reached London, the bellicosity and bad temper that had given rise to Admiral Alexander Cochrane's "treat 'em rough" instructions were things of the past. War weariness in England, fresh dangers emerging in chaotic Europe, and the sharp improvement in the American position, strength, and morale in the north, all helped produce a sudden reversal of British policy at Ghent. Peace was signed the day before Christmas, and the fighting ended on January 8, 1815, when two thousand British soldiers—a third of the entire assaulting army—fell dead or wounded at New Orleans.

The Treaty of Ghent left things as they were. Did the war itself leave them unchanged? Impressment and the Orders in Council both vanished before the treaty was signed. European peace removed them as immediate future hazards. If the war had lifted American prestige, no treaty was needed to abolish them forever. By that measurement the New Orleans victory was climax, not epilogue. In 1815, Justice Joseph Story weighed the results of the war and found them massive:

> Never did a country occupy more lofty ground; we have stood the contest, single-handed, against the conqueror of Europe; and we are at peace, with all our blushing victories thick crowding on us. If I do not much mistake, we shall attain to a very high character abroad as well as crush domestic faction.

Domestic faction was crushed in the next election. Those who would fix the time at which the country attained international stature might ask themselves; Could there have been a Monroe Doctrine in 1823 without the War of 1812? It was under the quiet guiding hand of President James Madison that the struggling young republic won an equal position among the free nations of the world, and began its long climb to leadership.

Irving Brant, journalist and historian, has been an editorial writer for newspapers in St. Louis and Chicago. He is the author of, among many other books, a multivolume biography of President Madison.

Father of Our Factory System

Arnold Welles

Feats of memory, particularly of the kind of memory derided as "photographic"—for all the cornucopias of wealth they sometimes pour over television contestants—are looked down on in modern times, but they have their role in history. Consider, for example, the story of Samuel Slater. It would be impolite to call him a spy, for he would not have considered himself one. Furthermore, he was a man of peace. Yet in his own time this cotton spinner's apprentice achieved with his prodigious memory an effect as great as or greater than any successful military espionage has brought about in our own. For he successfully transplanted the infant Industrial Revolution, which was in many ways an English monopoly, across an ocean to a new country.

To understand Slater's feat, one must look back to the economic situation of England and America in the days directly after the Colonies had achieved their independence. If Britain no longer ruled her former colonies, she clung tenaciously to her trade with them. Thanks to her flourishing new textile industry, she was able to sell large quantities of cotton goods in the United States at prices so low there was little incentive left for making cloth over here by the old-fashioned hand methods. To maintain this favorable dependency as long as possible, England went to fantastic lengths to guard the secrets that had mechanized her cotton industry, and so effective were these measures that America might well have continued solely as an agricultural nation for years, had it not been for Samuel Slater.

Slater was born in 1768 on his family's property, Holly House, in Derbyshire, England. His father, William Slater, was an educated, independent farmer and timber merchant, the close friend and neighbor of Jedediah Strutt, successively farmer, textile manufacturer, and partner of England's famous inventor, Sir Richard Arkwright, whose spinning frame had revolutionized the manufacture of cotton yarn. Three years after Samuel Slater's birth, Strutt had financed Arkwright's factory at Cromford—the world's earliest authentic cotton mill—where water power replaced humans and animals in moving the machinery, and where the whole operation of spinning yarn could be accomplished for the first time automatically under one roof. Within five years Arkwright's mills were employing over 5,000 workers, and England's factory system was launched.

It was in this atmosphere of industrial revolution that young Slater grew up. He showed signs of his future mechanical bent at a tender age by making himself a polished steel spindle with which to help wind worsted for his mother, and whenever he had the chance, he would walk over to nearby Cromford or Belper on the Derewent River to see the cotton mills which Strutt and Arkwright owned. In 1782 Strutt began to erect a large hosiery factory at Milford, a mile from the Slater property, and he asked William Slater's permission to engage his eldest son as clerk. Slater, who had noticed the ability and inclinations of his younger son, Samuel, recommended him instead, observing that he not only "wrote well and was good at figures" but was also of a decided mechanical bent.

Thus, at the age of fourteen, Samuel Slater went to live and work with Strutt. When William Slater died shortly afterward, in 1783, young Samuel Slater signed his own indenture to learn cotton spinning as an apprentice in Strutt's factory until the age of 21.

During the early days of his term the boy became so engrossed in the business that he would go for six months without seeing his family, despite the fact that they lived only a mile away, and he would frequently spend his only free day, Sunday, experimenting alone on machinery. In those days millowners had to build all their own machinery, and Slater acquired valuable experience in its design, as well as its operation, and in the processes of spinning yarn. Even before completing his term of indenture he was made superintendent of Strutt's new hosiery mill.

But Slater had become concerned about the chances for an independent career in England. Arkwright's patents having expired, factories had sprung up everywhere, and Slater could see that to launch out on his own he would need more and more capital to stay ahead of the technical improvements constantly taking place. His attention had been drawn to the United States by an article in a Philadelphia paper saying that a bounty of £100 had been granted by the Pennsylvania legislature to a man who had designed a textile machine. Young Slater made up his mind that he would go to the United States and introduce the Arkwright methods there. As his first step, even before his term with Strutt expired, Slater obtained his employer's permission to supervise the erection of the new cotton works Arkwright was then starting, and from his experience he gained valuable knowledge for the future.

There were, it was true, grave risks to consider. Britain still strictly forbade the export of textile machinery or the designs for it. With France entering a period of revolution which might unsettle the economy of the Old World, it was even more important that the large American market be safeguarded for British commerce. As a result, the Arkwright machines and techniques were nowhere in use in America at the time, and various attempts—in Pennsylvania, Massachusetts, Connecticut, Maryland, and

South Carolina—to produce satisfactory cotton textiles borne little fruit. Without Arkwright's inventions it was impossible to make cotton yarn strong enough for the warps needed in hand-loom weaving.

Enterprising Yankees undertook all kinds of ingenious attempts to smuggle out modern machines or drawings. Even the American minister to France was involved in some of them: machinery would be quietly purchased in England, dismantled, and sent in pieces to our Paris legation for transshipment to the United States in boxes labeled "glassware" or "farm implements." British agents and the Royal Navy managed to intercept almost all such shipments, however, and skilled workers who attempted to slip away with drawings or models were apprehended on the high seas and brought back. Passengers leaving England for American ports were thoroughly searched by customs agents before boarding ship.

Slater knew of these handicaps and determined to take along nothing in writing save his indenture papers. Even these he was careful to conceal. As the time of his departure drew near he did not reveal his plans even to his family, telling his mother only that he was taking a trip to London. On September 1, 1789, in the warm sunlight of late summer, he cast one last look at the pleasant meadows and orchards of Holly House and set off through the lovely Derbyshire countryside.

In London he decided to spend a few days sightseeing, inasmuch as this was to be his first and last visit to the capital. Then, after posting a letter home revealing his intended journey, he boarded ship for New York, assuming the guise of a farmer to escape detection. The role was not difficult for the son of a Derbyshire yeoman, and except for the hidden indenture there was nothing to link the young man with the cotton textile industry. But he was carrying with him in a very remarkable memory the complete details of a modern cotton mill.

After a passage of 66 days, Slater's ship reached New York. He had originally intended to go to Philadelphia, but when he learned of the existence of the New York Manufacturing Company on Vesey Street in downtown Manhattan, he showed his indenture and got a job there instead. The company had recently been organized to make yarns and cloth, but the yarn was linen and the machinery, hand-operated, was copied from antiquated English models. This was a far cry from the factories Slater had supervised in Derbyshire, and he was unimpressed.

Fortunately, about this time, the newcomer happened to meet the captain of a packet sailing between New York and Providence, Rhode Island, and from him learned of the interest in textile manufacturing shown by a wealthy, retired merchant of Providence, Moses Brown, later to become one of the founders of Brown University. A converted Quaker and a man of large imagination and business acumen, Brown had invested considerable cash in two rough, hand-operated spinning frames and a crude carding machine as well as in a couple of obsolete "jennies." But all his attempts to produce cotton yarns had ended in failure, and he could find little use for his expensive machinery. Such was the situation when he received a letter from Slater:

New York, December 2d, 1789

Sir,—

A few days ago I was informed that you wanted a manager of *cotton spinning,* etc., in which business I flatter myself that I can give the greatest satisfaction, in making machinery, making good yarn, either for *stockings* or *twist,* as any that is made in England; as I have had opportunity, and an oversight of Sir Richard Arkwright's works, and in Mr. Strutt's mill upwards of eight years. If you are not provided for, should be glad to serve you; though I am in the New York manufactory, and have been for three weeks since I arrived from England. But we have but *one card, two machines,* two spinning jennies, which I think are not worth using. My *intention* is to erect a *perpetual card and spinning.* (Meaning the Arkwright patents). If you please to drop a line respecting the amount of encouragement you wish to give, by favor of Captain Brown, you will much oblige, sir, your most obedient humble servant.

SAMUEL SLATER

N.B.—Please to direct to me at No. 37, Golden Hill, New York.

Slater's letter fired the shrewd Quaker's imagination, and he hastened to reply, declaring that he and his associates were "destitute of a person acquainted with water-frame spinning" and offering Slater all the profits from successful operation of their machinery over and above interest on the capital invested and depreciation charges. His invitation concluded: "If the present situation does not come up to what thou wishes, and, from thy knowledge of the business, can be ascertained of the advantages of the mills, so as to induce thee to come and work ours, and have the *credit* as well as the advantage of perfecting the first water-mill in America, we should be glad to engage thy care so long as they can be made profitable to both, and we can agree."

Tempted and flattered, and assuming that the Providence operation needed only an experienced overseer to make it a success, Slater decided to accept. He took a boat in January, 1790, reached Providence on the eighteenth of the month, and immediately called on Moses Brown.

The two men were in striking contrast. Slater, only 21, was nearly six feet tall and powerfully built, with ruddy complexion and fair hair. Moses Brown, in his soft, broad-brimmed Quaker hat, was well past middle age, of small stature, with a pair of bright, bespectacled eyes set in a benevolent face framed by flowing gray locks. Satisfied from a glance at the Strutt indenture that his young caller was bona fide, Brown took Slater in a sleigh to the little hamlet of Pawtucket, a community consisting of a dozen or so cottages on both sides of the Blackstone River, just outside Providence. They stopped at a small clothier's shop on the river's bank, close by a bridge which linked Rhode Island and Massachusetts. Here was assembled Brown's ill-assorted machinery.

Slater took one look and shook his head, his disappointment obvious. Compared to Strutt's splendid mill this was almost a caricature. He spoke bluntly: "These will not do; they are good for nothing in their present condition, nor can they be made to answer." Brown urged him to reconsider, to give the machines a try, but the young

122

Englishman was not to be persuaded. At last, in desperation, the old merchant threw Slater a challenge:

"Thee said thee could make machinery. Why not do it?"

Reluctantly, Slater finally agreed to build a new mill, using such parts of the old as would answer, but only on one condition: that Brown provide a trusted mechanic to make the machinery which Slater would design and that the man be put under bond neither to disclose the nature of the work nor to copy it.

"If I don't make as good yard as they do in England," Slater declared, "I will have nothing for my services, but will throw the whole of what I have attempted over the bridge!" Brown agreed, arranging in addition to pay Slater's living expenses.

Then the old merchant took his visitor to the cottage of Oziel Wilkinson, an ingenious ironmaster, with whom Slater could board. Wilkinson, also a Quaker, operated a small anchor forge using water power from the river, and there he turned out ships' chandlery, shovels, scythes, and other tools. As the young English-man entered the Wilkinson home, his host's younger daughter shyly scampered out of sight, but Hannah, the elder, lingered in the doorway to look at the stranger. Slater fell in love with her. (Within two years they would be married, and Hannah Slater would later acquire fame in her own right as the discoverer of cotton sewing thread, which she first produced from the fine yarns her husband manufactured.) In the Wilkinson household young Slater found new parents who helped him overcome his homesickness and encouraged him in the first difficult months.

Part of that winter he spent experimenting with Moses Brown's crude carding machine, and he was able to improve the quality of cotton fleece it turned out. This, when spun by hand on the jennies, produced a better yarn, but one which was still too weak and uneven to be used as warp in the hand-weaving of cloth. Slater was downhearted; he realized that he must build everything from scratch.

The rest of the winter he spent assembling the necessary materials for constructing the Arkwright machines and processes. He lacked even the tools with which to make the complicated equipment, and he was forced to make many of them himself before any building could commence. Furthermore, without models to copy, he had to work out his own computations for all measurements. One of the most ingenious elements of the Arkwright inventions was the variation in speeds of various parts of the machines. Mathematical tables for these were not available anywhere save in England; Slater had to rely on his own extraordinary memory. Nevertheless, by April, 1790, he was ready to sign a firm partnership agreement to build two carding machines, a drawing and roving frame, and two spinning frames, all to be run automatically be water power. He was to receive one dollar a day as wages, half-ownership in the machinery he built, and, in addition, one-half of the mill's net profits after it was in operation. Moses Brown had turned over the supervision of his textile investments to William Almy, his son-in-law, and Smith Brown, his cousin, and these two men became Slater's new partners.

Now, behind shuttered windows in the little clothier's building on the riverbank, young Slater began to design the first successful cotton mill in America. As he drew the plans with chalk on wood, Sylvanus Brown, an experienced local wheelwright, cut out the parts from sturdy oak and fastened them together with wooden dowels. Young David Wilkinson, Slater's future brother-in-law and like his father a skilled ironworker, forged shafts for the spindles, rollers for the frames, and teeth in the cards which Pliny Earle, of Leicester, Massachusetts, prepared for the carding machines. Before iron gearwheels and card rims could be made, Slater and Wilkinson had to go to Mansfield, Massachusetts, to find suitable castings. By autumn, working sixteen hours a day, Slater had more than fulfilled his agreement: he had built not two but three carding machines, as well as the drawing and roving frame and two spinning frames. At last he was ready for a trial.

Taking up a handful of raw cotton, Slater fed it into the carding machine, cranked by hand for the occasion by an elderly Negro. This engine was one of the most important elements of the Arkwright system, for in it the raw cotton was pulled across leather cards studded with small iron teeth which drew out and straightened the fibers, laid them side by side, and formed them into a long, narrow fleece called an "end," or "sliver." This was then placed on the drawing and roving frame to be further stretched, smoothed, and then twisted before being spun into yarn on the spinning frame. Before the cotton was run through the cards, the fibers lay in every direction, and it was essential that the carding be successful if the "end" was to be suitable for the subsequent steps. But when Slater fed the test cotton into his machine it only piled up on the cards.

Slater was greatly perplexed and dismayed. The machinery had already taken a long time to make, and his partners were becoming impatient. Slater sensed their growing doubts and knew he would forfeit their confidence if this first trial failed. Yet he had nobody who could check on the correctness of his designs. The Wilkinson family later described his anxiety. Standing before their fireplace, he sighed deeply, and they saw tears in his eyes. Mrs. Wilkinson, noting his distress, asked, "Art thou sick, Samuel?" Slater answered sadly, "If I am frustrated in my carding machine, they will think me an impostor."

After a number of sleepless nights, Slater determined that the trouble arose from a faulty translation of his design into reality, for Pliny Earle had never before made cards of that description. Slater decided that the teeth stood too far apart, and that under pressure of the raw cotton they fell back from their proper places instead of standing firm and combing the cotton as it moved past. He pointed out the defect to Earle, and together, using a discarded piece of grindstone, they beat the teeth into the correct shape. Another test was made and the machine worked satisfactorily.

The final stage was now at hand. Almost a year had passed in preparation for this moment. Would the machinery operate automatically by water power? That was the miracle of the Arkwright techniques, which gave them their name, "perpetual spinning." A connection was made to the small water wheel which had been used by the clothier in whose little shop Slater's new machinery now stood. It was deep winter, and the Blackstone River was frozen over, so that Slater was obliged to crawl down and break up the ice around the wheel. When the wheel turned over, his machinery began to hum.

On December 20, 1790, Samuel Slater's mill produced the first cotton yarn ever made automatically in America. It was strong and of good quality, suitable for sheetings and other types of heavy cotton goods; soon Slater was turning out yarn fine enough to be woven into shirtings, checks, ginghams, and stockings, all of which had until then been imported from Europe. Good cotton cloth woven at home from English yard had cost from forty to fifty cents per yard, but soon Slater brought the cost down as low as nine cents. For the remainder of that first winter, unable to get anyone else to do the job, Slater spent two or three hours each morning before breakfast breaking the river ice to start the water wheel. Daily it left him soaking wet and numb from exposure; his health was affected for the rest of his life.

The little mill started with four employees, but by the end of one month Slater had nine hands at work, most of them children. In this he was following the practice in England, where entire families were employed in the mills. Early English millowners had found children more agile and dexterous than adults, their quick fingers and small hands tending the moving parts more easily. Slater, like other pioneer millowners dealing with small working forces, was able to maintain a paternalistic attitude toward the young persons in his charge; until the coming of the factory system and absentee ownership, child labor was not the evil it later became. Slater introduced a number of social customs he had learned in the Arkwright and Strutt mills. For his workers he built the first Sunday school in New England and there provided instruction in reading, writing, and arithmetic, as well as in religion. Later he promoted common day schools for his mills hands, often paying the teachers' wages out of his own pocket.

Proudly Slater sent a sample of his yarn back to Strutt in Derbyshire, who pronounced it excellent. Yet Americans hesitated to use it, preferring traditional hand-spun linen yarn or machine-made cotton yarn imported from England. Within four months Moses Brown was writing to the owners of a little factory in Beverly, Massachusetts, run by a relative, proposing a joint petition to Congress: Why not raise the duties on imported cotton goods? Some of the proceeds could be given to southern cotton farmers as a bounty for upgrading their raw cotton, and some could be presented to the infant textile industry as a subsidy.

Next, Brown arranged to transmit to Alexander Hamilton, secretary of the treasury and already known as a supporter of industry, a sample of Slater's yarn and of the first cotton check made from it, along with various suggestions for encouraging the new textile manufactures. He reported to Hamilton that within a year machinery and mills could be erected to supply enough yarn for the entire nation. Two months later, when Hamilton presented to Congress his famous *Report on Manufacturers,* he mentioned "the manufactory at Providence [which] has the merit of being the first in introducing into the United States the celebrated cotton mill."

By the end of their first ten months of operations, Almy, Brown & Slater had sold almost 8,000 yards of cloth produced by home weavers from their yarns. After twenty months the factory was turning out more yarn than the weavers in its immediate vicinity could use; a surplus of 2,000 pounds had piled up. Desperately, Moses Brown appealed to Slater, "Thee must shut down thy gates or thee will spin all my farms into cotton yarn."

It was at this point that the full force of Slater's revolutionary processes began to become apparent. To dispose of their surplus the partners began to employ agents in Salem, New York, Baltimore, and Philadelphia, and so encouraging were the sales that it became obvious to them that their potential market was enormous. In 1791, therefore, they closed the little mill and built nearby a more efficient factory designed to accommodate all the processes of yarn manufacturing under one roof. It was opened in 1793. (Now the Old Slater Mill Museum, the building still stands today.)

As of December, 1792, the partners' ledgers had shown a credit in Slater's name of £882, representing his share of the proceeds from the sale of yarn spun by his mill. From then on both he and the infant industry he had helped to create prospered rapidly. The factory was no longer a neighborhood affair but sought its markets in a wider world. When the War of 1812 had ended, there were 165 mills in Rhode Island, Massachusetts, and Connecticut alone, many of them started by former employees of Slater who had gone into business for themselves. By this time Slater, too, had branched out; he owned at least seven mills, either outright or in partnership. An important mill town in Rhode Island already bore the name of Slatersville. Around three new cotton, woolen, and thread mills which he build in Massachusetts, a new textile center sprang up which became the town of Webster. Later, his far-reaching enterprise carried him to Amoskeag Falls on the Merrimac River; in 1822 he bought an interest in a small mill already established there, and in 1826 erected a new mill which became the famous Amoskeag Manufacturing Company, hub of an even greater textile center—Manchester, New Hampshire.

President James Monroe had come to Pawtucket in 1817 to visit the "Old Mill," which was then the largest cotton mill in the nation, containing 5,170 spindles. It had started with 72. Slater himself conducted his distinguished visitor through the factory and proudly showed him his original spinning frame, still running after 27 years. Some years later another President, Andrew Jackson, visited Pawtucket, and when he was told that Slater was confined to his house by rheumatism brought on from that first winter of breaking the ice on the Blackstone, Old Hickery went to pay his respects to the invalid. Courteously addressing Slater as "the Father of American Manufactures," General Jackson said:

"I understand you taught us how to spin, so as to rival Great Britain in her manufactures; you set all these thousands of spindles to work, which I have been delighted in viewing, and which have made so many happy, by a lucrative employment."

Slater thanked his visitor politely and with the dry wit for which he was well known replied:

"Yes, Sir, I suppose that I gave out the psalm, and they have been singing to the tune ever since."

By the time he died in 1835, Slater had become generally recognized as the country's leading textile industrialist. In addition to his cotton and woolen manufactures, he had founded a bank and a textile-machinery factory and had helped promote several turnpikes, including a road from Providence to Pawtucket and another from Worcester, Massachusetts, to Norwich, Connecticut. At his death Moses Brown, who survived him, estimated Slater's estate at $1,200,000—a remarkable achievement in those early days of the nineteenth century.

The industry Slater had founded 45 years earlier had shown phenomenal growth by the year he died. In 1790 the estimated value of all American manufactured goods barely exceeded $20,000,000, and the domestic cotton crop was about 2,000,000 pounds. By 1835 cotton manufactured goods alone were valued in excess of $47,000,000, and that single industry was consuming almost 80,000,000 pounds of cotton annually. Few men in our history have lived to see such tremendous economic changes wrought in one lifetime by their own efforts.

The social changes which Samuel Slater witnessed and helped to further were even more far-reaching. When he arrived in 1789 America was a nation of small farmers and artisans. By the time he died, and to a considerable extent because of his accomplishments, many artisans had become mill hands.

Three years after Slater's mill began operations, a young Yale graduate named Eli Whitney, visiting a Georgia plantation, devised the cotton gin, and this, in combination with English cotton mills and American ones like Slater's in New England, enormously stimulated the cotton economy (and the slave-labor system) of the South. Simultaneously, and paradoxically, Slater and Whitney helped fasten on the North an industrial economy which would defeat the South when the long-standing economic conflict between the two sections flared out at last in civil war.

Arnold Welles is a great-great-grandson of Samuel Slater. Graduated from Yale with honors in American history, he is now in the investment business and divides his time between Savannah, Georgia, and Northeast Harbor, Maine.

Part Four
The Jacksonian Period

In the United States, the period of the 1830s and 1840s was a time of growth and vitality. Industrialization spread west to the states bordering the Great Lakes, while in both the northwest and the southwest the agricultural frontier extended to the Mississippi River and beyond. Expansion of the economy in turn produced an increasing surplus in production, which lead to a mounting foreign trade. Technological advancements had created first an intricate system of canals which tied the nation together, and before the end of the 1840s railroads had supplanted canals as the national mode of transportation. But closer ties and increasing economic interdependence did not promote national unity. Economic specialization led to recurring conflicts over rival sectional interests. And slavery became a more divisive issue as the period progressed. The South, now committed to its "peculiar institution" faced a mounting challenge from the threat of reform from the North and insurrection at home. In his article, "Children of Darkness," Stephen B. Oates tells the story of the Nat Turner insurrection in Virginia and explains how that abortive revolt affected slavery in the South as well as southern relations with the North.

Another troubling development in American life occurred in the 1830s when nativism reared its ugly head. The renewed influx of immigrants during that decade brought to this country increasingly large numbers of Irish and German Catholics. "Native American" Protestants responded to what they perceived to be a threat with a wave of anti-Catholic bigotry. In his informative article, "The Know-Nothing Uproar," Ray Allen Billington traces the course of this nativist crusade.

As diplomacy resolved conflicting territorial claims with Great Britain in both the northeast and northwest, the lure of Oregon with its promise of fertile lands and mild climate was irresistible to thousands of Americans. But the road west was full of danger and littered with broken dreams. Thomas Froncek relates the tragic experience of one group of pioneers, the Donner Party, in his article "Winterkill, 1846." During that same time, however, Americans marched in triumph to the southwest. War with Mexico attained the old vision of a continental nation. Victory on the battlefield and at the conference table secured for the United States the Rio Grande boundary, the Great Southwest, and California. Richard M. Ketchum relates the complex events behind the diplomatic settlement of the war in his article. "The Thankless Task of Nicholas Trist." Unfortunately, the conquests of 1848 served to reignite the bitter debate over slavery in the territories and ushered in the tragic decade of the 1850s.

Children of Darkness

Stephen B. Oates

Until August, 1831, most Americans had never heard of Virginia's Southampton County, an isolated, impoverished neighborhood located along the border in the southeastern part of the state. It was mostly a small farming area, with cotton fields and apple orchards dotting the flat, wooded landscape. The farmers were singularly fond of their apple crops: from them they made a potent apple brandy, one of the major sources of pleasure in this hardscrabble region. The county seat, or "county town," was Jerusalem, a lethargic little community where pigs rooted in the streets and old-timers spat tobacco juice in the shade of the courthouse. Jerusalem lay on the bank of the Nottoway River some seventy miles south of Richmond. There had never been any large plantations in Southampton County, for the soil had always been too poor for extensive tobacco or cotton cultivation. Although one gentleman did own eighty slaves in 1830, the average was around three or four per family. A number of whites had moved on to new cotton lands in Georgia and Alabama, so that Southampton now had a population that was nearly 60 per cent black. While most of the blacks were still enslaved, an unusual number—some seventeen hundred, in fact—were "free persons of color."

By southern white standards, enlightened benevolence did exist in Southampton County—and it existed in the rest of the state, too. Virginia whites allowed a few slave schools to operate—then a crime by state law—and almost without complaint permitted slaves to hold illegal religious meetings. Indeed, Virginians liked to boast that slavery was not so harsh in their "enlightened" state as it was in the brutal cotton plantations in the Deep South. Still, this was a dark time for southern whites—a time of sporadic insurrection panics, especially in South Carolina, and of rising abolitionist militancy in the North—and Virginians were taking no chances. Even though their slaves, they contended, were too happy and too submissive to strike back, Virginia was nevertheless almost a military garrison, with a militia force of some hundred thousand men to guard against insurrection.

Southampton whites, of course, were caught in the same paradox: most of the white males over twenty-one voluntarily belonged to the militia and turned out for the annual drills, yet none of them thought a slave revolt would happen here. *Their* blacks, they told themselves, had never been more content, more docile. True, they did get a bit carried away in their religious meetings these days, with much too much singing and clapping. And true, there were white preachers who punctuated their sermons with what a local observer called "ranting cant about equality" and who might inspire black exhorters to retail that doctrine to their congregations. But generally things were quiet and unchanged in this remote tidewater county, where time seemed to stand as still as a windless summer day.

It happened with shattering suddenness, an explosion of black rage that rocked Southampton County to its foundations. On August 22, 1831, a band of insurgent slaves, led by a black mystic called Nat Turner, rose up with axes and plunged southeastern Virginia—and much of the rest of the South—into convulsions of fear and racial violence. It turned out to be the bloodiest slave insurrection in southern history, one that was to have a profound and irrevocable impact on the destinies of southern whites and blacks alike.

Afterward, white authorities described him as a small man with "distinct African features." Though his shoulders were broad from work in the fields, he was short, slender, and a little knock-kneed, with thin hair, a complexion like black pearl, and large, deep-set eyes. He wore a mustache and cultivated a tuft of whiskers under his lower lip. Before that fateful August day whites who knew Nat Turner thought him harmless, even though he was intelligent and did gabble on about strange religious powers. Among the slaves, though, he enjoyed a powerful influence as an exhorter and self-proclaimed prophet.

He was born in 1800, the property of Benjamin Turner of Southampton County and the son of two strong-minded parents. Tradition has it that his African-born mother threatened to kill him rather than see him grow up in bondage. His father eventually escaped to the North, but not before he had helped inculcate an enormous sense of self-importance in his son. Both parents praised Nat for his brilliance and extraordinary imagination; his mother even claimed that he could recall episodes that happened before his birth—a power that others insisted only the Almighty could have given him. His mother and father both told him that he was intended for some great purpose, that he would surely become a prophet. Nat was also influenced by his grandmother, who along with his white masters taught him to pray and to take pride in his superior intelligence. He learned to read and write with great ease, prompting those who knew him to remark that he had too much sense to be raised in bondage—he "would never be of any service to any one as a slave," one of them said.

In 1810 Benjamin Turner died, and Nat became the property of Turner's oldest son Samuel. Under Samuel Turner's permissive supervision Nat exploited every opportunity to improve his knowledge: he studied white children's school books and experimented in making paper and gunpowder. But it was religion that interested him the most. He attended Negro religious meetings, where the slaves cried out in ecstasy and sang hymns that expressed their longing for a better life. He listened transfixed as black exhorters preached from the Bible with stabbing gestures, singing out in a rhythmic language that was charged with emotion and vivid imagery. He studied the Bible, too, practically memorizing the books of the Old Testament, and grew to manhood with the words of the prophets roaring in his ears.

Evidently Nat came of age a bit confused if not resentful. Both whites and blacks had said he was too intelligent to be raised a slave; yet here he was, fully grown and still in bondage. Obviously he felt betrayed by false hopes. Obviously he thought he should be liberated like the large number of free blacks who lived in Southampton County and who were not nearly so gifted as he. Still enslaved as a man, he zealously cultivated his image as a prophet, aloof, austere, and mystical. As he said later in an oral autobiographical sketch, "Having soon discovered to be great, I must appear so, and therefore studiously avoided mixing in society, and wrapped myself in mystery, devoting myself to fasting and prayer."

Remote, introspective, Turner had religious fantasies in which the Holy Spirit seemed to speak to him as it had to the prophets of old. "Seek ye the kingdom of Heaven," the Spirit told him, "and all things shall be added unto you." Convinced that he "was ordained for some great purpose in the hands of the Almighty," Turner told his fellow slaves about his communion with the Spirit. "And they believed," Turner recalled, "and said my wisdom came from God." Pleased with their response, he began to prepare them for some unnamed mission. He also started preaching at black religious gatherings and soon rose to prominence as a leading exhorter in the slave church. Although never ordained and never officially a member of any church, he was accepted as a Baptist preacher in the slave community, and once he even baptized a white man in a swampy pond. There can be little doubt that the slave church nourished Turner's self-esteem and his desire for independence, for it was not only a center for underground slave plottings against the master class, but a focal point for an entire alternative culture—a subterranean culture that the slaves sought to construct beyond the white man's control. Moreover, Turner's status as a slave preacher gave him considerable freedom of movement, so that he came to know most of Southampton County intimately.

Sometime around 1821 Turner disappeared. His master had put him under an overseer, who may have whipped him, and he fled for his freedom as his father had done. But thirty days later he voluntarily returned. The other slaves were astonished. No fugitive ever came back on his own. "And the negroes found fault, and murmured against me," Turner recounted later, "saying that if they had my sense they would not serve any master in the world." But in his mind Turner did not serve any earthly master. His master was Jehovah—the angry and vengeful God of ancient Israel—and it was Jehovah, he insisted, who had chastened him and brought him back to bondage.

At about this time Nat married. Evidently his wife was a young slave named Cherry who lived on Samuel Turner's place. But in 1822 Samuel Turner died, and they were sold to different masters—Cherry to Giles Reese and Nat to Thomas Moore. Although they were not far apart and still saw each other from time to time, their separation was nevertheless a painful example of the wretched privations that slavery placed on black people, even here in mellowed Southampton County.

As a perceptive man with a prodigious knowledge of the Bible, Turner was more than aware of the hypocrisies and contradictions loose in this Christian area, where whites gloried in the teachings of Jesus and yet discriminated against the "free coloreds" and kept the other blacks in chains. Here slave owners bragged about their benevolence (in Virginia they took care of their "niggers") and yet broke up families, sold Negroes off to whip-happy slave traders when money was scarce, and denied intelligent and skilled blacks something even the most debauched and useless poor whites enjoyed: freedom. Increasingly embittered about his condition and that of his people, his imagination fired to incandescence by prolonged fasting and Old Testament prayers, Turner began to have apocalyptic visions and bloody fantasies in the fields and woods southwest of Jerusalem. "I saw white spirits and black spirits engaged in battle," he declared later, "and the sun was darkened—the thunder rolled in the heavens, and blood flowed in streams—and I heard a voice saying, 'Such is your luck, such you are called to see, and let it come rough or smooth, you must surely bare it.' " He was awestruck, he recalled, but what did the voice mean? What must he bare? He withdrew from his fellow slaves and prayed for a revelation; and one day when he was plowing in the field, he thought the Spirit called out, "Behold me as I stand in the Heavens," and Turner looked up and saw forms of men there in a variety of attitudes, "and there were lights in the sky to which the children of darkness gave other names than what they really were—for they were the lights of the Saviour's hands, stretched forth from east to west, even as they extended on the cross on Calvary for the redemption of sinners."

Certain that Judgment Day was fast approaching, Turner strove to attain "true holiness" and "the true knowledge of faith." And once he had them, once he was "made perfect," then the Spirit showed him other miracles. While working in the field, he said, he discovered drops of blood on the corn. In the woods he found leaves with hieroglyphic characters and numbers etched on them; other leaves contained forms of men—some drawn in blood—like the figures in the sky. He told his fellow slaves about these signs—they were simply astounded—and claimed that the Spirit had endowed him with a special knowledge of the seasons, the rotation of the planets, and the operation of the tides. He acquired an even greater reputation among the county's slaves, many of whom thought he could control the weather and heal disease. He told his followers that clearly something large was about to happen, that he was soon to fulfill "the great promise that had been made to me."

But he still did not know what his mission was. Then on May 12, 1828, "I heard a loud noise in the heavens," Turner remembered, "and the Spirit instantly appeared to me and said the Serpent was loosened, and Christ had laid down the yoke he had borne for the sins of men, and that I should take it on and fight against the Serpent." Now at last it was clear. By signs in the heavens Jehovah would show him when to commence the great work, whereupon "I should arise and prepare myself, and slay my enemies with their own weapons." Until then he should keep his lips sealed.

But his work was too momentous for him to remain entirely silent. He announced to Thomas Moore that the slaves ought to be free and would be "one day or other." Moore, of course, regarded this as dangerous talk from a slave and gave Turner a thrashing.

In 1829 a convention met in Virginia to draft a new state constitution, and there was talk among the slaves—who communicated along a slave grapevine—that they might be liberated. Their hopes were crushed, though, when the convention emphatically rejected emancipation and restricted suffrage to whites only. There was also a strong backlash against antislavery publications thought to be infiltrating from the North, one of which—David Walker's *Appeal*—actually called on the slaves to revolt. In reaction the Virginia legislature enacted a law against teaching slaves to read and write. True, it was not yet rigorously enforced, but from the blacks' viewpoint slavery seemed more entrenched in "enlightened" Virginia than ever.

There is no evidence that Turner ever read antislavery publications, but he was certainly sensitive to the despair of his people. Still, Jehovah gave him no further signs, and he was carried along in the ebb and flow of ordinary life. Moore had died in 1828, and Turner had become the legal property of Moore's nine-year-old son—something that must have humiliated him. In 1829 a local wheelwright, Joseph Travis, married Moore's widow and soon moved into her house near the Cross Keys, a village located southwest of Jerusalem. Still known as Nat Turner even though he had changed owners several times, Nat considered Travis "a kind master" and later said that Travis "placed the greatest confidence in me."

In February, 1831, there was an eclipse of the sun. The sign Turner had been waiting for—could there be any doubt? Removing the seal from his lips, he gathered around him four slaves in whom he had complete trust—Hark, Henry, Nelson, and Sam—and confided what he was called to do. They would commence "the work of death" on July 4, whose connotation Turner clearly understood. But they formed and rejected so many plans that his mind was affected. He was seized with dread. He fell sick, and Independence Day came and passed.

On August 13 there was another sign. Because of some atmospheric disturbance the sun grew so dim that it could be looked at directly. Then it seemed to change colors—now pale green, now blue, now white—and there was much excitement and consternation in many parts of the eastern United States. By afternoon the sun was like an immense ball of polished silver, and the air was moist and hazy. Then a black spot could be seen, apparently on the sun's surface—a phenomenon that greatly aroused the slaves in southeastern Virginia. For Turner the black spot was unmistakable proof that God wanted him to move. With awakened resolution he told his men that "as the black spot passed over the sun, so shall the blacks pass over the earth."

It was Sunday, August 21, deep in the woods near the Travis house at a place called Cabin Pond. Around a crackling fire Turner's confederates feasted on roast pig and apple brandy. With them were two new recruits—Jack, one of Hark's cronies, and

Will, a powerful man who intended to gain his freedom or die in the attempt. Around midafternoon Turner himself made a dramatic appearance, and in the glare of pine-knot torches they finally made their plans. They would rise that night and "kill all the white people." It was a propitious time to begin, because many whites of the militia were away at a camp meeting. The revolt would be so swift and so terrible that the whites would be too panic-stricken to fight back. Until they had sufficient recruits and equipment, the insurgents would annihilate everybody in their path—women and children included. When one of the slaves complained about their small number (there were only seven of them, after all), Turner was quick to reassure him. He had deliberately avoided an extensive plot involving a lot of slaves. He knew that blacks had "frequently attempted similar things," but their plans had "leaked out." Turner intended for his revolt to happen completely without warning. The "march of destruction," he explained, "should be the first news of the insurrection," whereupon slaves and free blacks alike would rise up and join him. He did not say what their ultimate objective was, but possibly he wanted to fight his way into the Great Dismal Swamp some twenty miles to the east. This immense, snake-filled quagmire had long been a haven for fugitives, and Turner may have planned to establish a slave stronghold there from which to launch punitive raids against Virginia and North Carolina. On the other hand, he may well have had nothing in mind beyond the extermination of every white on the ten-mile route to Jerusalem. There are indications that he thought God would guide him after the revolt began, just as He had directed Gideon against the Midianites. Certainly Turner's command of unremitting carnage was that of the Almighty, who had said through his prophet Ezekiel: "Slay utterly old and young, both maids and little children, and women. . . ."

The slaves talked and schemed through the evening. Night came on. Around two in the morning of August 22 they left the woods, by-passed Giles Reese's farm, where Cherry lived, and headed for the Travis homestead, the first target in their crusade.

All was still at the Travis house. In the darkness the insurgents gathered about the cider press, and all drank except Turner, who never touched liquor. Then they moved across the yard with their axes. Hark placed a ladder against the house, and Turner, armed with a hatchet, climbed up and disappeared through a second-story window. In a moment he unbarred the door, and the slaves spread through the house without a sound. The others wanted Turner the prophet, Turner the black messiah, to strike the first blow and kill Joseph Travis. With Will close behind, Turner entered Travis' bedroom and made his way to the white man's bed. Turner swung his hatchet—a wild blow that glanced off Travis's head and brought him out of bed yelling for his wife. But with a sure killer's instinct Will moved in and hacked Travis to death with his axe. In minutes Will and the others had slaughtered the four whites they found in the house, including Mrs. Travis and young Putnam Moore, Turner's legal owner. With Putnam's death Turner felt that at last, after thirty years in bondage, he was free.

The rebels gathered up a handful of old muskets and followed "General Nat" out to the barn. There turner paraded his men about, leading them through every military maneuver he knew. Not all of them, however, were proud of their work. Jack sank to his knees with his head in his hands and said he was sick. But Hark made him get up and forced him along as they set out across the field to the next farm. Along the way somebody remembered the Travis baby. Will and Henry returned and killed it in its cradle.

And so it went throughout that malignant night, as the rebels took farm after farm by surprise. They used no firearms, in order not to arouse the countryside, instead stabbing and decapitating their victims. Although they confiscated horses, weapons, and brandy, they took only what was necessary to continue the struggle, and they committed no rapes. They even spared a few homesteads, one because Turner believed the poor white inhabitants "thought no better of themselves than they did of negroes." By dawn on Monday there were fifteen insurgents—nine on horses—and they were armed with a motley assortment of guns, clubs, swords, and axes. Turner himself now carried a light dress sword, but for some mysterious reason (a fatal irresolution? the dread again?) he had killed nobody yet.

At Elizabeth Turner's place, which the slaves stormed at sunrise, the prophet tried once again to kill. They broke into the house, and there, in the middle of the room, too frightened to move or cry out, stood Mrs. Turner and a neighbor named Mrs. Newsome. Nat knew Elizabeth Turner very well, for she was the widow of his second master, Samuel Turner. While Will attacked her with his axe the prophet took Mrs. Newsome's hand and hit her over the head with his sword. But evidently he could not bring himself to kill her. Finally Will moved him aside and chopped her to death as methodically as though he were cutting wood.

With the sun low in the east, Turner sent a group on foot to another farm while he and Will led the horsemen at a gallop to Caty Whitehead's place. They surrounded the house in a rush, but not before several people fled into the garden. Turner chased after somebody, but it turned out to be a slave girl, as terrified as the whites, and he let her go. All around him, all over the Whitehead farm, there were scenes of unspeakable violence. He saw Will drag Mrs. Whitehead kicking and screaming out of the house and almost sever her head from her body. Running around the house, Turner came upon young Margaret Whitehead hiding under a cellar cap between two chimneys. She ran crying for her life, and Turner set out after her—a wild chase against the hot August sun. He overtook the girl in a field and hit her again and again with his sword, but she would not die. In desperation he picked up a fence rail and beat her to death. Finally he had killed someone. He was to kill no one else.

After the Whitehead massacre the insurgents united briefly and then divided again, those on foot moving in one direction and Turner and the mounted slaves in another. The riders moved across the fields, kicking their horses and mules faster and faster, until at last they raced down the lane to Richard Porter's house, scattering dogs and chickens as they went. But the Porters had fled—forewarned by their own slaves that a revolt was under way. Turner knew that the alarm was spreading now, knew that the militia would soon be mobilizing, so he set out alone to retrieve the other column.

While he was gone Will took the cavalry and raided Nathaniel Francis' homestead. Young Francis was Will's owner, but he could not have been a harsh master: several free blacks voluntarily lived on his farm. Francis was not home, and his pregnant young wife survived Will's onslaught only because a slave concealed her in the attic. After killing the overseer and Francis' two nephews Will and his men raced on to another farm, and another, and then overran John Barrow's place on the Barrow Road. Old man Barrow fought back manfully while his wife escaped in the woods, but the insurgents overwhelmed him and slit his throat. As a tribute to his courage they wrapped his body in a quilt and left a plug of tobacco on his chest.

Meanwhile Turner rode chaotically around the countryside, chasing after one column and then the other, almost always reaching the farms after his scattered troops had done the killing and gone. Eventually he found both columns waiting for him at another pillaged homestead, took charge again, and sent them down the Barrow Road, which intersected the main highway to Jerusalem. They were forty strong now and all mounted. Many of the new recruits had joined up eager "to kill all the white people." But others had been forced to come along as though they were hostages. A Negro later testified that several slaves—among them three teen-age boys—"were constantly guarded by negroes with guns who were ordered to shoot them if they attempted to escape."

On the Barrow Road, Turner's strategy was to put his twenty most dependable men in front and send them galloping down on the homesteads before anybody could escape. But the cry of insurrection had preceded them, and many families had already escaped to nearby Jerusalem, throwing the village into pandemonium. By midmorning church bells were tolling the terrible news—*insurrection, insurrection*—and shouting men were riding through the countryside in a desperate effort to get the militia together before the slaves overran Jerusalem itself.

As Turner's column moved relentlessly toward Jerusalem one Levi Waller, having heard that the blacks had risen, summoned his children from a nearby schoolhouse (some of the other children came running too) and tried to load his guns. But before he could do so, Turner's advance horsemen swept into his yard, a whirlwind of axes and swords, and chased Waller into some tall weeds. Waller managed to escape, but not before he saw the blacks cut down his wife and children. One small girl also escaped by crawling up a dirt chimney, scarcely daring to breathe as the insurgents decapitated the other children—ten in all—and threw their bodies in a pile.

Turner had stationed himself at the rear of his little army and did not participate in these or any other killings along the Barrow Road. He never explained why. He had been fasting for several days and may well have been too weak to try any more killing himself. Or maybe as God's prophet he preferred to let Will and the eight or nine other lieutenants do the slaughtering. All he said about it afterward was that he "sometimes got in sight in time to see the work of death completed" and that he paused to view the bodies "in silent satisfaction" before riding on.

Around noon on Monday the insurgents reached the Jerusalem highway, and Turner soon joined them. Behind them lay a zigzag path of unredeemable destruction: some fifteen homesteads sacked and approximately sixty whites slain. By now the rebels amounted to fifty or sixty—including three or four free blacks. But even at its zenith Turner's army showed signs of disintegration. A few reluctant slaves had already escaped or deserted. And many others were roaring drunk, so drunk they could scarcely ride their horses, let alone do any fighting. To make matters worse, many of the confiscated muskets were broken or too rusty to fire.

Turner resolved to march on Jerusalem at once and seize all the guns and powder he could find there. But a half mile up the road he stopped at the Parker farm, because some of his men had relatives and friends there. When the insurgents did not return, Turner went after them—and found his men not in the slave quarters but down in Parker's brandy cellar. He ordered them back to the highway at once.

On the way back they met a party of armed men—whites. There were about eighteen of them, as far as Turner could make out. They had already routed his small guard at the gate and were now advancing toward the Parker house. With renewed zeal Turner rallied his remaining troops and ordered an attack. Yelling at the top of their lungs, wielding axes, clubs, and gun butts, the Negroes drove the whites back into Parker's cornfield. But their advantage was short-lived. White reinforcements arrived, and more were on the way from nearby Jerusalem. Regrouping in the cornfield, the whites counterattacked, throwing the rebels back in confusion. In the fighting some of Turner's best men fell wounded though none of them died. Several insurgents, too drunk to fight any more, fled pell-mell into the woods.

If Turner had often seemed irresolute earlier in the revolt, he was now undaunted. Even though his force was considerably reduced, he still wanted to storm Jerusalem. He led his men away from the main highway, which was blocked with militia, and took them along a back road, planning to cross the Cypress Bridge and strike the village from the rear. But the bridge was crawling with armed whites. In desperation the blacks set out to find reinforcements: they fell back to the south and then veered north again, picking up new recruits as they moved. They raided a few more farms, too, only to find them deserted, and finally encamped for the night near the slave quarters on Ridley's plantation.

All Monday night news of the revolt spread beyond Southampton County as express riders carried the alarm up to Petersburg and from there to the capitol in Richmond. Governor John Floyd, fearing a statewide uprising, alerted the militia and set cavalry, infantry, and artillery units to the stricken county. Federal troops from Fortress Monroe were on the way, too, and other volunteers and militia outfits were marching from contiguous counties in Virginia and North Carolina. Soon over three thousand armed whites were in Southampton County, and hundreds more were mobilizing.

With whites swarming the countryside, Turner and his lieutenants did not know what to do. During the night an alarm had stampeded their new recruits, so that by Tuesday morning they had only twenty men left. Frantically they set out for Dr. Simon

Blunt's farm to get volunteers—and rode straight into an ambush. Whites barricaded in the house opened fire on them at pointblank range, killing one or more insurgents and capturing several others—among them Hark Travis. Blunt's own slaves, armed with farm tools, helped in the defense and captured a few rebels themselves.

Repulsed at Blunt's farm, Turner led a handful of the faithful back toward the Cross Keys, still hoping to gather reinforcements. But the signs were truly ominous, for armed whites were everywhere. At last the militia overtook Turner's little band and in a final, desperate skirmish killed Will and scattered the rest. Turner himself, alone and in deep anguish, escaped to the vicinity of the Travis farm and hid in a hole under some fence rails.

By Tuesday evening a full-scale manhunt was under way in southeastern Virginia and North Carolina as armed whites prowled the woods and swamps in search of fugitive rebels and alleged collaborators. They chased the blacks down with howling dogs, killing those who resisted—and many of them resisted zealously—and dragging others back to Jerusalem to stand trial in the county court. One free black insurgent committed suicide rather than be taken by white men. Within a week nearly all the bona fide rebels except Turner had either been executed or imprisoned, but not before white vigilantes—and some militiamen—had perpetrated barbarities on more than a score of innocent blacks. Outraged by the atrocities committed on whites, vigilantes rounded up Negroes in the Cross Keys and decapitated them. Another vigilante gang in North Carolina not only beheaded several blacks but placed their skulls on poles, where they remained for days. In all directions whites took Negroes from their shacks and tortured, shot, and burned them to death and then mutilated their corpses in ways that witnesses refused to describe. No one knows how many innocent Negroes died in this reign of terror—at least a hundred twenty, probably more. Finally the militia commander of Southampton County issued a proclamation that any further outrages would be dealt with according to the articles of war. Many whites publicly regretted these atrocities but argued that they were the inevitable results of slave insurrection. Another revolt, they said, would end with the extermination of every black in the region.

Although Turner's uprising ended on Tuesday, August 24, reports of additional insurrections swept over the South long afterward, and dozens of communities from Virginia to Alabama were seized with hysteria. In North Carolina rumors flew that slave armies had been seen on the highways, that one—maybe led by Turner himself—had burned Wilmington, butchered all the inhabitants, and was now marching on the state capital. The hysteria was even worse in Virginia, where reports of concerted slave rebellions and demands for men and guns swamped the governor's office. For a time it seemed that thousands of slaves had risen, that Virginia and perhaps the entire South would soon be ablaze. But Governor Floyd kept his head, examined the reports carefully, and concluded that no such widespread insurrection had taken place. Actually no additional uprisings had happened anywhere. Out of blind panic whites in many parts of the South had mobilized the militia, chased after imaginary insurgents, and jailed or executed still more innocent blacks. Working in cooperation with other political and military authorities in Virginia and North Carolina, Floyd did all he could to quell the excitement, to reassure the public that the slaves were quiet now. Still, the governor did not think the Turner revolt was the work of a solitary fanatic. Behind it, he believed, was a conspiracy of Yankee agitators and black preachers—especially black preachers. ''The whole of that massacre in Southampton is the work of these Preachers,'' he declared, and demanded that they be suppressed.

Meanwhile the "great bandit chieftain," as the newspapers called him, was still at large. For more than two months Turner managed to elude white patrols, hiding out most of the time near Cabin Pond where the revolt had begun. Hunted by a host of aroused whites (there were various rewards totalling eleven hundred dollars on his head), Turner considered giving himself up and once got within two miles of Jerusalem before turning back. Finally on Sunday, October 30, a white named Benjamin Phipps accidentally discovered him in another hideout near Cabin Pond. Since the man had a loaded shotgun, Turner had no choice but to throw down his sword.

The next day, with lynch mobs crying for his head, a white guard hurried Turner up to Jerusalem to stand trial. By now he was resigned to his fate as the will of Almighty God and was entirely fearless and unrepentant. When a couple of court justices examined him that day, he stated emphatically that *he* had conceived and directed the slaughter of all those white people (even though he had killed only Margaret Whitehead) and announced that God had endowed him with extraordinary powers. The justices ordered this ''fanatic'' locked up in the same small wooden jail where the other captured rebels had been incarcerated.

On November 1 one Thomas Gray, an elderly Jerusalem lawyer and slaveholder, came to interrogate Turner as he lay in his cell ''clothed with rags and covered with chains.'' In Gray's opinion the public was anxious to learn the facts about the insurrection—for whites in Southampton could not fathom why their slaves would revolt. What Gray wanted was to take down and publish a confession from Turner that would tell the public the truth about why the rebellion had happened. It appears that Gray had already gathered a wealth of information about the outbreak from other prisoners, some of whom he had defended as a court-appointed counsel. Evidently he had also written unsigned newspaper accounts of the affair, reporting in one that whites had located Turner's wife and lashed her until she surrendered his papers (remarkable papers, papers with hieroglyphics on them and sketches of the Crucifixion and the sun). According to Gray and to other sources as well, Turner over a period of three days gave him a voluntary and authentic confession about the genesis and execution of the revolt, recounting his religious visions in graphic detail and contending again that he was a prophet of Almighty God. ''Do you not find yourself mistaken now?'' Gray asked. Turner replied testily, ''Was not Christ crucified?'' Turner insisted that the uprising was local in origin but warned that other slaves might see signs and act as he had done. By the end of the confession Turner was in high spirits, perfectly ''willing to suffer the fate that awaits me.'' Although Gray considered him ''a gloomy fanatic,'' he thought Turner was one of the most articulate men he had ever met. And Turner could be frightening. When, in a burst of enthusiasm, he spoke of the killings and raised his manacled hands toward heaven, "I looked on him," Gray said, "and my blood curdled in my veins."

On November 5, with William C. Parker acting as his counsel, Turner came to trial in Jerusalem. The court, of course, found him guilty of committing insurrection and sentenced him to hang. Turner, though, insisted that he was not guilty because he did not feel so. On November 11 he went to his death in resolute silence. In addition to Turner, the county court tried some forty-eight other Negroes on various charges of conspiracy, insurrection, and treason. In all, eighteen blacks—including one woman—were convicted and hanged. Ten others were convicted and "transported"—presumably out of the United States.

But the consequences of the Turner revolt did not end with public hangings in Jerusalem. For southern whites the uprising seemed a monstrous climax to a whole decade of ominous events, a decade of abominable tariffs and economic panics, of obstreperous antislavery activities, and of growing slave unrest and insurrection plots, beginning with the Denmark Vesey conspiracy in Charleston in 1822 and culminating now in the worst insurrection Southerners had ever known. Desperately needing to blame somebody besides themselves for Nat Turner, Southerners linked the revolt to some sinister Yankee-abolitionist plot to destroy their cherished way of life. Southern zealots declared that the antislavery movement, gathering momentum in the North throughout the 1820's, had now burst into a full-blown crusade against the South. In January, 1831, William Lloyd Garrison had started publishing *The Liberator* in Boston, demanding in bold, strident langauge that the slaves be immediately and unconditionally emancipated. If Garrison's rhetoric shocked Southerners, even more disturbing was the fact that about eight months after the appearance of *The Liberator* Nat Turner embarked on his bloody crusade—something southern politicians and newspapers refused to accept as mere coincidence. They charged that Garrison was behind the insurrection, that it was his "bloodthirsty" invective that had incited Turner to violence. Never mind that there was no evidence that Turner had ever heard of *The Liberator;* never mind that Garrison categorically denied any connection with the revolt, saying that he and his abolitionist followers were Christian pacifists who wanted to free the slaves through moral suasion. From 1831 on, northern abolitionism and slave rebellion were inextricably associated in the southern mind.

But if Virginians blamed the insurrection on northern abolitionism, many of them defended emancipation itself as the only way to prevent further violence. In fact, for several months in late 1831 and early 1832 Virginians engaged in a momentous public debate over the feasibility of manumission. Out of the western part of the state, where antislavery and anti-Negro sentiment had long been smoldering, came petitions demanding that Virginia eradicate the "accursed," "evil" slave system and colonize all blacks at state expense. Only by removing the entire black population, the petitions argued, could future revolts be avoided. Newspapers also discussed the idea of emancipation and colonization, prompting one to announce that "Nat Turner and the blood of his innocent victims have conquered the silence of fifty years." The debate moved into the

Virginia legislature, too, and early in 1832 proslavery and antislavery orators harangued one another in an unprecedented legislative struggle over emancipation. In the end most delegates concluded that colonization was too costly and too complicated to carry out. And since they were not about to manumit the blacks and leave them as free men in a white man's country, they rejected emancipation. Indeed, they went on to revise and implement the slave codes in order to restrict blacks so stringently that they could never mount another revolt. The modified codes not only strengthened the patrol and militia systems, but sharply curtailed the rights of free blacks and all but eliminated slave schools, slave religious meetings, and slave preachers. For Turner had taught white Virginians a hard lesson about what might happen if they gave slaves enough education and religion to think for themselves.

In the wake of the Turner revolt, the rise of the abolitionists, and the Virginia debates over slavery, the other southern states also expanded their patrol and militia systems and increased the severity of their slave codes. What followed was the Great Reaction of the 1830's and 1840's, during which the South, threatened it seemed by internal and external enemies, became a closed, martial society determined to preserve its slave-based civilization at whatever cost. If Southerners had once apologized for slavery as a necessary evil, they now trumpeted that institution as a positive good—"the greatest of all the great blessings," as James H. Hammond phrased it, "which a kind providence has bestowed." Southern postmasters set about confiscating abolitionist literature, lest these "incendiary" tracts invite the slaves to violence. Some states actually passed sedition laws and other restrictive measures that prohibited Negroes and whites alike from criticizing slavery. And slave owners all across the South tightened up slave discipline, refusing to let blacks visit other plantations and threatening to hang any slave who even looked rebellious. By the 1840's the Old South had devised such an oppressive slave system that organized insurrection was all but impossible.

Even so, southern whites in the ante-bellum period never escaped the haunting fear that somewhere, maybe even in their own slave quarters, another Nat Turner was plotting to rise up and slit their throats. They never forgot him. His name became for them a symbol of terror and violent retribution.

But for ante-bellum blacks—and for their descendants—the name of Nat Turner took on a profoundly different connotation. He became a legendary black hero who broke his chains and murdered white people because slavery had murdered Negroes. Turner, said an elderly black man in Southampton County only a few years ago, was "God's man. He was a man for war, and for legal rights, and for freedom."

Nat Turner remains an enigmatic and controversial figure in our own time, thanks largely to the furor generated by William Styron's novel The Confessions of Nat Turner *(Random House, 1967). Although principally based on Turner's* Confessions *as given to Thomas Gray, the novel portrayed Turner as a celibate bachelor afflicted with masturbation, fantasies about Margaret Whitehead—a psychosexual supposition unsupported by any known evidence. Styron also violated the historical record in many other details, so that from the point of view of historical scholarship his novel must be regarded as an inaccurate and unacceptable recreation of Turner and his insurrection.*

These shortcomings were emphatically brought to public attention in a volume called William Styron's Nat Turner: Ten Black Writers Respond *(Beacon Press, 1968). Unfortunately, although the book included trenchant essay by Mike Thelwell and Vincent Harding that subjected Styron's novel to valid historical criticism, most of the other selections were mere diatribes, filled with their own inaccuracies and attempting to enshrine the figure of Nat Turner as a flawless black god—a military genius and inflexible white-hater with whom today's blacks ought to identify.*

In reconstructing the Nat Turner story for my own narrative, I made extensive use of Henry Irving Tragle's The Southampton Slave Revolt of 1831 *(Random House, 1973), a valuable collection of documents about virtually all aspects of the rebellion. It includes a detailed, annotated chronology of Turner's life and the revolt itself, numerous contemporary newspaper reports, a verbatim record of the slave trials, Governor Floyd's diary and correspondence, and most of the previously published accounts, including the original* Confessions *to Thomas Gray as published in Baltimore in 1831. I am also indebted to Eric Foner, whose* Nat Turner *(Prentice-Hall, 1971), another compilation of source materials, includes a great deal about the role of the slave church in the genesis of the Turner insurrection.*

Stephen B. Oates, professor of history at the University of Massachusetts, is the author of many books, including a biography of John Brown, To Purge This Land With Blood *(Harper & Row, 1970). Currently he is working on a biography of Abraham Lincoln and is also writing a book-length treatment of Nat Turner.*

The Know-Nothing Uproar

Ray Allen Billington

The congressional and state elections of 1851 and 1855 witnessed one of the most remarkable political upheavals in the nation's; history. Candidates whose names were not even on ballots were thrust into office others who had been given no chance to win triumphed over long-established favorites; and a political party that had operated in such secrecy that few knew its name and still fewer its true purposes was catapulted into control in a half-dozen states, won a strong minority place in several others, and seemed destined to capture the White House in 1856. More remarkable still, the political infant that accomplished these miracles was dedicated to principles that were basically un-American, for its sole claim to popular favor rested on its pledge to check the growth of the Catholic Church and foreign immigration. As befitted such a party, its history was mercifully brief. Yet the racial and religious hatreds that found expression in its short-lived triumphs reached deep into the American past and were rooted in a surprisingly large number of people. The two incidents that started their spread a generation before they found political manifestation during the 1850's were surprisingly trivial, yet they were of the sort that often alters the lives of men or nations. One concerned a hat, the other a slate pencil.

The hat belonged to Samuel F. B. Morse, and was clapped firmly on his head on a bright June day in 1830 as he watched a papal procession wend its way through the streets of Rome. As a New England Puritan Morse had little love for Catholicism, but as an artist he admired its pomp and pageantry—until that day, that is. For, as he watched, his hat was suddenly struck from his head by a soldier, or rather (as he recorded in his diary that night) "by a poltroon in a soldier's costume, and this courteous manoeuvre was accompanied with curses and taunts and the expression of a demon in his countenance." That this ill-mannered gesture should be blamed on the soldier never occurred to Morse. "The blame," he wrote, "lies after all not so much with the pitiful wretch who perpetrates this outrage, as it does with those who gave him such base and indiscriminate orders." From that day the artist-inventor was a sworn enemy of Romanism, and he carried that enmity back to America.

Returning to New York at the end of his grand tour, Morse hurried into print to warn his countrymen of the insidious papal designs on the Unites States. His essays were later published in two volumes: *Foreign Conspiracy Against the Liberties of the United States* and *Imminent Dangers to the Free Institutions of the Untied States through Foreign Immigration.* European despots, he told his thousands of readers, were trembling lest the democratic institutions of America inspire revolts on the part of their own peoples. These institutions could not be overthrown by arms, for the Untied States was too powerful: hence monarchs had allied with the Catholic Church, which Morse considered a giant religious despotism, to dispatch its servile minions across the Atlantic, disguised as immigrants, until they were numerous enough to seize control. "You," he thundered to his fellow Americans, "are marked for their prey, not by foreign bayonets, but by *weapons surer of effecting the conquest of liberty* than all the munitions of physical combat in the military or naval storehouses of Europe." Only by closing the gates to those immigrants, Morse believed, could America be saved.

The slate pencil that reshaped the course of history was accidentally rammed into the head of a young girl named Maria Monk as she played near her childhood home on the outskirts of Montreal. From that day on, her mother later testified, Maria was unable to distinguish right from wrong: she became a wayward Jezebel whose sexual precocity finally led to her confinement in a Catholic asylum for magdalens in Montreal. From there she escaped with the aid of her current lover and, large with his child, made her way to New York, where she fell into the hands of a group of fanatical anti-Catholics who saw in her an opportunity to turn prejudice into profit. The result was the publication in 1836 of Maria's so-called autobiography, *Awful Disclosures of Maria Monk . . . in the Hotel Dieu Nunnery at Montreal,* from that day to this a best-selling tribute to the gullibility of book-buying nativists. The enduring popularity of the *Awful Disclosures* is easy to understand: its frankly pornographic "revelations" of the "criminal intercourse" between priests and nuns were enough to titillate a generation accustomed to the more restricted standards of Victorian morality. And hundreds of thousands who read its lurid pages—and those of her *Further Disclosures,* published the following year—were convinced that Catholicism was a monstrous evil that must no longer be endured.

That books of such unsavory origins and unpalatable contents could command nationwide attention was due less to their own merits than to the spirit of the times. Since the beginning of the 1830's nativistic prejudices had been slowly, almost imperceptibly, but steadily mounting as immigrants from the Catholic nations of Europe flooded into the seaboard states in ever-increasing numbers to create the first sizable non-Protestant group in the nation's history. Resentment against these newcomers whose religious practices seemed so alien to traditionally American ways might have remained vague and undefined had not their coming coincided with the importation of a considerable body of anti-Catholic literature from England. There, anti-Catholics were making attacks on Parliament for adopting the tolerant Catholic Emancipation Act of 1829: and as Americans eagerly purchased English books, pamphlets, and magazines that heaped calumny on the Roman Church, native writers awakened to the realization that here was an unexploited market for their talents. In New York a band of zealots launched a weekly newspaper, *The Protestant,* in 1830 and a year later organized the New York Protestant Association. Books with such flaming titles as *A Master Key to Popery and Female Convents: Secrets of Nunneries Disclosed* began to appear. In 1834 a mob burned down a convent in Charlestown, near Boston. Clearly, by the mid-1830's the time was ripe for a concentrated assault on Romanism, which nativists saw as a growing menace to American liberty and Protestantism.

So they reasoned as they stirred themselves into action—and thus inadvertently set in motion the forces that within two decades would be setting their sights on the White House. Some used the press to preach the No-Popery message: *The Downfall of Babylon,* a weekly published in Philadelphia, and the *American Protestant Vindicator,* a biweekly printed in New York, both appeared as if by magic to carry word of the "Jesuitical abomination" of popery across the land in every edition. Individual nativists, capitalizing on the newly discovered American passion for joining, reorganized the New York Protestant Association along national lines as the Protestant Reformation Society and began flooding the country with propagandist literature and lecturing agents. Still others seized their pens to unleash a torrent of books and pamphlets, all preaching the evils of Romanism, that swept a surprisingly large number of men and women into the nativist fold.

One group of propagandists, expanding on the theme first developed by Morse, capitalized on the nationalist impulses of a generation that was soon to espouse the cause of Manifest Destiny. The pope, they insisted, was anxious to move the Vatican out of decadent Italy, and what was more natural than his selection of the Mississippi Valley, the veritable garden of the world, for its new site? To this end he was cooperating with despotic European monarchs who were anxious to protect their own thrones by stemming the flow of liberal ideas from the democratic United States; together they would flood the land with papal minions disguised as immigrants, then seize control and establish those twins of oppression, despotism and Romanism, as the nation's new order. This was the warning voiced by such sober religious leaders as the Reverend Lyman Beecher in his *Plea for the West* (1835) and re-echoed in every Protestant religious journal as well as in the numerous publications of the influential American Home Missionary Society. To many ethnocentric Americans of that self-assured generation this was an argument that made sense.

Other persons were won by the plea that Catholics were seeking to undermine the American school system. Nativists began developing this theme shortly after 1839, when the American Bible Society, a Protestant group, announced a plan to place a copy of the Scriptures in every classroom of the nation. Catholics, both the hierarchy and the laity, protested when teachers began daily readings of this Protestant version of the Scriptures, and many Protestants interpreted the opposition to mean that Catholics disapproved of both the Bible and education. The issue was most violently joined in New York City, where the schools were under the control of the Protestant-dominated Public

School Society, a private agency that distributed public funds. Led by the vigorous Bishop John Hughes, Catholics carried their fight to the state legislature, where, in 1843, they helped push through a bill abolishing the Public School Society and placing the city's schools under state administration. Protestants retaliated by electing a solidly No-Popery school board that continued Bible reading in the schools. But the harm was done. Protestant America was convinced that this attempt to inflict the minority will on the majority had shown that Catholicism was truly despotic and that Catholics were sworn enemies of the Holy Word.

While the propaganda inspired by the Bible-reading controversy appealed especially to middle-class churchgoers, another brand of calumny was aimed at the semi-literate masses who wanted sensationalism in unadulterated doses. Brazenly paraded before the public in such books as *Open Convents, Priests' Prisons for Women* and *Auricular Confession and Popish Nunneries,* this type of literature capitalized upon the demand for pornography proven by the popularity of Maria Monk's *Awful Disclosures.* Some authors of this school specialized in tales of convent immorality; others fastened upon the confessional to prove that popery stripped the last vestiges of morality from its victims. How, these writers asked, can Catholics be expected to obey the laws of God or man when all sin can be forgiven by a few muttered words from a confessor? How can a maiden remain pure when locked for hours in a confessional booth with a lecherous priest who is more interested in making advances than in saving souls?

In that day, when action spoke louder than words, such lurid sensationalism could not be peddled without inflaming men to violence. Trouble began in Philadelphia during the spring of 1841 when a group of nativists, wrought up by a Bible-reading controversy similar to that in New York, attempted to hold a mass meeting in one of the city's Irish-Catholic sections. In the inevitable clash that followed, a few shots were fired and one of the nativists was fatally wounded. With this, the editor of the leading anti-Catholic newspaper, the *Native American,* completely lost his head. "Another St. Bartholomew's Day is begun on the streets of Philadelphia," he proclaimed. "The bloody hand of the Pope has stretched itself forth to our destruction. We now call on our fellow-citizens, who regard free institutions whether they be native or adopted, to arm." That afternoon rioting began as bands of Protestant workmen marched through Catholic sections, burning and pillaging as they went. Hundreds of homes and two Catholic churches were put to the torch before troops arrived to quell the rioters. A few weeks later the July Fourth celebration touched off another period of carnage in the City of Brotherly Love; it lasted for three days, during which thirteen were killed and fifty wounded.

The Philadelphia riots sent organized nativism into a period of temporary decline. The fruits of anti-Catholicism were church-burning and bloodshed, and the majority of sensible Americans felt a natural revulsion that they took no pains to hide. Amidst their torrents of censure, the Protestant Reformation Society died unmourned, to be replaced at once by the American Protestant Society. This new national organization pledged itself to illuminate the "spiritual darkness" of popery with "Light and Love" rather than violence, and to "awaken Christian feeling and Christian action for the salvation of Romanists," but the time was not ripe for even such a mild form of prejudice. The people, heatedly debating the slavery issue during and after the Mexican War, clearly felt little fear of a mythical papal invasion while the Union stood in real peril. Not until the Compromise of 1850 settled the sectional crisis, apparently for all time to come, could they rekindle their enthusiasm for the No-Popery crusade.

Times were auspicious for a revival of the assault, for by the end of the 1840's a number of tolerant, middle-class people were coming to the belief that the nativists' charges were not without some basis of truth. The Catholic Church, they were well aware, was no temporal-minded despotism bent on the political subjugation of the United States, but they nevertheless felt that the arrogantly uncompromising attitude of some of its clergy, if unchallenged, threatened the traditional values and institutions of their homeland. Immigrants, they knew, were not Jesuit minions in disguise, but they did believe that the newcomers were threatening to corrupt the political parties, disrupt the time-honored tradition of isolation from Europe's storms, lower the living standard of native workers, and cost the nation heavily in pauperism and crime. As they soberly contemplated the results of a generation of Catholic growth and unrestrained immigration, thousands upon thousands of previously unworried Americans began to reconsider the arguments of the nativists.

Certainly there was little to reassure them in the attitude of many overzealous Catholic clergymen who, misled by the rapid increase of their flocks into believing that Catholicism would soon become dominant in the United States, seemed in Protestant eyes to be behaving as though that day were already at hand. When Archbishop Hughes of New York could declare, as he did in his widely circulated address on "The Decline of Protestantism and Its Cause," that Catholics did intend to convert the entire population of the Mississippi Valley, and that the avowed mission of Catholicism was "to convert the world—including the inhabitants of the United States—the people of the cities, and the people of the country . . . the Senate, the Cabinet, the President, and all!" the time had apparently come to pay attention to the warnings of anti-papists. When Catholics could demand, as they did in a dozen states after 1852, that a share of the tax-raised school funds be diverted for the use of their parochial schools, even tolerant citizens felt they must rally to the defense of their most venerated institutions.

Even more fear was engendered among non-nativists by the rising tide of immigration. They might agree that newcomers bolstered the economic and military strength of the United States, but they were brought up short by the results of a generation of uncontrolled migration. Sober facts told the story: In 1850 only 6.5 per cent of the foreign born attended schools, as compared to 20 per cent of the native born. Among aliens, one person in every 32 was a pauper receiving public support, while among natives the ratio was only one in every 260. Nearly half of the 27,000 persons convicted of crimes were aliens, although foreigners constituted only 11 per cent of the population. As sobering as these figures was the less tangible evidence that was there for all to see: quiet city streets transformed into unsightly slums, corrupt political machines truckling to foreign-born voters, American workers displaced by new arrivals accustomed to lower living standards, the decline of national isolation from Europe's stormy politics as Irish and Germans loudly demanded support for the revolutionary movements of their homelands. To men and women who witnessed these changes, there seemed more truth than wit in the tale of the schoolboy called upon to parse "America"; " 'America,' " said he, "is a very common noun, singular number, masculine gender, critical case, and governed by the Irish." Nor did there seem any end to these alterations in the pattern of American life. Boston's foreign-born voting population increased by 195 per cent in the first five years of the 1850's, while the number of its native-born voters mounted by only 15 per cent, indicating a not-too-distant future when the whole United States would be dominated by Catholic aliens.

Doubts such as these haunted Protestant Americans who had scorned organized nativism in the past; to them the time was clearly at hand for an all-out assault on Catholic and immigrant alike. To command their support, a society must be formed that would be free of the taints that had marred earlier nativistic organizations. This emerged when the American Protestant Society joined with two tiny groups dedicated to the herculean task of winning Europe to Protestantism—the Foreign Evangelical Society and the Christian Alliance—to form the American and Foreign Christian Union. Governed by a constitution that did not even mention "popery" or "Romanism," the new society was pledged to "diffuse and promote the principles of Religious Liberty, and a pure and Evangelical Christianity, both at home and abroad, wherever a corrupted Christianity exists." Organized nativism had moved far from the days when Maria Monk and the Protestant Reformation Society spread their crude invective throughout the land.

The new society's relative moderation attracted an unprecedented number of followers from among middle-class, churchgoing Protestants. By 1854 the contributions it received were large enough to support 120 traveling agents, all of them roaming constantly, speaking against Catholicism wherever they could find an audience, and laboring zealously to "save" Catholic souls. More important was the support now attracted from the nation's churches. Almost without exception, the 125 Protestant religious magazines and newspapers published in the United States converted themselves into champions of the crusade, while virtually every Protestant church body opened its doors to agents of the American and Foreign Christian Union, collected funds in the Union's behalf, and encouraged ministers to speak out for the salvation of misguided Romanists. In the same way the powerful interdenominational societies—the American Bible Society, the American Tract Society, and the American Home Missionary Society—all swung into line and became effective organs for disseminating anti-Catholic propaganda. By 1854 American Protestants were caught up in a No-Popery campaign of unprecedented proportions: thousands upon thousands were ready to translate their prejudices into votes whenever the opportunity offered.

Nor did the American and Foreign Christian Union completely ignore the more turbulent working classes in its campaign to save the country from Rome—although its appeal to this group was inadvertent rather than planned. This was inspired by the

American visit of a papal nuncio, Archbishop Gaetano Bedini, who had already alarmed Italian nationalists by his alliance with monarchists in the brutal suppression of northern Italy's abortive struggle for independence from Austria in 1848. The American and Foreign Christian Union, eager to parade the Nuncio's unenviable record before the American people, imported an Italian ex-priest, Alessandro Gavazzi, to denounce Bedini in each city the Nuncio was scheduled to visit.

Gavazzi lived up to his assignment too well when he began his tour in 1853. Garbed in somber monk's robes emblazoned with a fiery cross, he shouted to his audiences: "Popery cannot be reformed. *Destruction to Popery!* No Protestantism; no protestations. Nothing but annihilation!" Here was a message that appealed to sensation-loving Americans in a day when tensions bred of the slavery conflict made violence synonymous with adherence to any cause. Wherever Bedini went Gavazzi had been there before him to whip the people into a frenzy against what he called this "Bloody Butcher of Bologna"; mobs in several cities burned the Nuncio in effigy, shouted insults, or threatened bodily harm.

The Bedini rioting touched off a new era of inflammatory attacks on Catholics and Catholicism. In a dozen cities self-appointed rabble rousers mounted their soapboxes, summoned their street-corner audiences, and unleashed their unrestrained invective; aroused by such tactics, the nativists burned churches and convents, molested immigrants, insulted Catholics, and on one occasion tarred and feathered a priest. These disorders bred a near-hysteria in areas where immigrants were most numerous, notably in the Northeast. There housekeepers refused to employ Irish servant girls lest the family food be poisoned on papal orders; placards everywhere warned the people to be on guard against the Pope's legions; and even the paper used by merchants to wrap parcels admonished buyers against the evils of Rome. In Maine mysterious symbols found on the homes in one community caused a near-panic among those who feared they had been marked for destruction by the Inquisition—until an itinerant hairdresser explained that he had thus chalked the houses he had already canvassed. In the nation's capital a block of marble contributed by the Pope to the Washington Monument was dumped into the Potomac by a raging mob. Clearly a surprisingly large portion of the American people had been swept so far along the No-Popery road that a political party reflecting their views would command support. The stage was set for that remarkable exhibit of political nativism that reached a climax in the election of 1854 and 1855.

Of the dozens of semipolitical nativist groups organized about the beginning of the decade, the one destined to emerge on a national scale was the Order of the Star Spangled Banner. Secretly formed in New York in 1849—probably by Charles B. Allen, a politically ambitious anti-Catholic—it remained so small at first that its influence was scarcely felt beyond the city's borders. But in the spring of 1854 its members, having put their own house in order by healing local schisms, worked out a plan for national expansion on a federal pattern and devised a secret ritual with handshakes, passwords, oaths of membership, and all the other hocus-pocus so dear to Americans to this day. The result was phenomenal. So eager were nativists to express themselves politically that within months the Order, known now as the American party or the Know-Nothing party (from its members' practice of parrying all questions with "I know nothing about it"), had spread over most of the nation and was a political force to be reckoned with.

Its growth was demonstrated in the fall elections of 1854. In the northern and border states the Know-Nothings showed surprising strength, carrying Massachusetts and Delaware solidly and winning a balance of power in Pennsylvania. A year later three more New England states, New Hampshire, Rhode Island, and Connecticut, succumbed; along the middle border Maryland and Kentucky swung into line, with Tennessee almost following; and in the South the party's total vote was only 16,000 less than that of its opponents. Even in the Old Northwest, where the heavy percentage of foreign born doomed any nativist party, the Know-Nothings scored some near-misses, especially in Wisconsin. Little wonder that the party leaders confidently anticipated electing a President in 1856, or that such hostile newspapers as the New York *Herald* were willing to concede them victory.

What was responsible for this amazing political phenomenon? Three factors played an essential role. One was the nativistic propaganda that reached a crescendo just as the party was entering the national scene; hundreds of thousands of Americans voted for the party's candidates because they were sincerely convinced that Catholicism and foreign immigration seriously threatened their institutions. Another was the breakdown of traditional political patterns following the Compromise of 1850; voters during the next years had to decide among Democratic, Whig, Anti-Nebraska, Free Soil, Hard Democratic, Soft Democratic, Conscience Whig, Union Maine Law, and a variety of other candidates. Any well-knit party with a well-defined purpose stood to profit by this disarray. Thirdly, the dramatic reopening of the slavery controversy with the passage of the Kansas-Nebraska Act of 1854 temporarily played into Know-Nothing hands. In the furious debate that followed, thousands deserted the older parties. Many of them joined the Know-Nothings, attracted by the party's neutrality on the slavery issue and its loud promises to preserve the Union.

That these forces were operating in 1854 and 1855 was shown by the Know-Nothings' victory pattern. In the South, where they were only partially successful, their strength was centered in the rich-soil areas, suggesting that they attracted ex-Whig planters who were seeking compromise on the slavery issue rather than expressing dislike of Rome. Yet thousands of poorer southerners also supported the party, probably because their evangelical religions stimulated their hatred of Catholicism just as sectional loyalties sharpened their hostility toward immigrants, who were increasing the population strength of the North. In the border states the party's sweeping victories were traceable more to a desire to compromise the troublesome slavery question than to entrenched nativistic beliefs; men whose homes occupied the probable battlegrounds of a civil war naturally hesitated to support either of the sectional parties that emerged after the Kansas-Nebraska Act. Only in the Northeast did the Know-Nothings match their victories in the border states, and only there was hatred of the Catholic and the immigrant primarily responsible for the party's growth. Yankees and New Yorkers, with no desire to avoid a showdown on slavery, could have rushed into the newly formed Republican party had not their nativistic prejudices taken precedence. Instead they cast their lot with the Know-Nothings because three decades of propaganda had convinced them that Romanism and aliens threatened the institutions of their forefathers.

Whatever their causes, the thumping victories of 1854 and 1855 placed nativists in a position to translate prejudice into action. Yet they failed utterly to do so, and this failure not only revealed the party's weakness but contributed to its decline. Know-Nothings never commanded a majority in Congress, but they did hold a balance of power on several occasions. Despite this favorable position, their crusade against Catholicism could produce nothing more than a few bombastic speeches directed against the alleged temporal designs of the pope, while their anti-alien program degenerated into a single bill that would have extended the period before naturalization to 21 years.

Even this measure failed to reach a vote. Within the states Know-Nothings proved just as impotent. In Massachusetts a bumbling governor and an inept legislature allowed several bills limiting aliens' voting to die in committee, although they did adopt a law requiring Bible reading in the schools and created a "Nunnery Committee" to report on Catholic schools, seminaries, and convents within the state. After frightening a few nuns and lay teachers by poking about parochial schools in search of firearms and other evidence of conspiracy, the committee disbanded amidst the derisive hoots of most of the sensible people of the nation. Nor was the record of the Know-Nothings more impressive in Maryland or other states under their control. Having no tangible program acceptable in a democratic land, the party, as Horace Greeley remarked, was "as devoid of the elements of persistence as an anti-Cholera or anti-Potato-Rot party would be."

These manifestations of Know-Nothing weakness encouraged spokesmen for human decency who had been cowed into silence by the hysteria of the past few years to raise their voices, feebly at first, and then with growing assurance. Some leveled their verbal lances against the party's secrecy; "one might as well study optics in the pyramids of Egypt or the subterranean tombs of Rome," warned Henry Ward Beecher, "as liberty in secret conclaves controlled by hoary knaves versed in political intrigue."

Others poked fun at the Know-Nothings' fantastic fears of a papal invasion or the transfer of the Vatican to the Mississippi Valley. Still more condemned the party for the rioting and bloodshed it inspired, a charge that gained meaning as each new election brought further clashes between nativists and immigrants. This combination of censure and ridicule proved effective; by the end of 1855 Know-Nothingism was on the wane.

The party's end was hurried by the very force that had stimulated its early growth: the reopened slavery controversy. As battle lines formed following the Kansas-Nebraska Act, and as each dispatch from "bleeding Kansas" inflamed the public mind, nativists found themselves catapulted into the conflict, no matter how loudly they protested their neutrality. Northerners, rallying beneath the antislavery banner, began to view the whole Know-Nothing movement as a southern conspiracy to distract attention from the vital issue of the day. Southerners, forming ranks behind their "peculiar institution," began to look upon nativists as enemies of the solidarity needed to protect slavery from Black

Republicans. Thus discredited in North and South, the Know-Nothing party lost its followers in droves, but worse was yet to come. Its 1855 national convention was unable to avoid a debate on slavery and broke up in disorder, with northern and southern Know-Nothings arrayed against each other on this all-prevailing issue.

Thus divided, the party approached the presidential election of 1856 with no chance of victory. Yet its leader clung to a last hope: if the major sectional parties fought to a standstill, they believed, the final decision might be made in the House of Representatives, where they had a strategic position. Thus inspired, they sought unsuccessfully to patch up their internal differences, then nominated former President Millard Fillmore of New York as their candidate.

A more unfortunate choice would have been hard to find. Already hated by northerners for having signed the unpopular Fugitive Slave Act of 1850, Fillmore had not only proven himself inept in the Presidency but had exhibited none of the fiery zeal needed to attract nativists to his standard. Actually he scarcely mentioned Catholicism during his campaign, devoting himself instead to vague plans for saving the Union. When the ballots were counted he had received over 800,000 popular votes—almost a fourth of the total—but received the electoral vote of Maryland alone. The Know-Nothing party was as dead as the dodo.

The defeat of Know-Nothingism was also a setback for intolerance. When put to the test, the bigots who had fomented against Romanists and aliens for a generation had nothing to offer save the timeworn clichés of bigotry and a political ineptitude that revealed their own inferiority. Prophets of hatred were to thrust themselves onto the national scene in the future, as the careers of the American Protective association of the 1890's and the Ku Klux Klan of the 1920's amply demonstrated, yet never was their threat to basic American values so serious as in the 1850's. By discrediting the cause for which they stood, the Know-Nothings, ironically, made a contribution to the principles of human decency that they opposed so violently.

Ray Allen Billington, a member of the Advisory Board of AMERICAN HERITAGE, *is the author of several books, among them* The Protestant Crusade, 1800–1860. *For many years he has been William Smith Mason Professor of History at Northwestern University in Evanston, Illinois.*

GO WEST

Winterkill, 1846

The Tragic Journey
of the Donner Party

Thomas Froncek

To the brothers George and Jacob Donner the way to California seemed clear and simple. Both in their sixties, solid and well-to-do thanks to their own hard work, but beginning now to feel their age and the long Illinois winters in their bones, the two men sat in the glow of the hearth-fire that winter of 1845–46 and turned again the well-thumbed pages of *The Emigrants' Guide to Oregon and California*. With the snow piled outside and the Sangamon River lying frozen in its bed, the brothers read with wonder the books' description of a golden land. In California, winter was warmer than summer, said the author—one Lansford W. Hastings. Hollyhocks and sweet william bloomed at Christmastime. Clover stood five feet high and the cattle never had to be fed or housed. "Here perpetual summer is in the midst of unceasing winter; perennial spring and never failing autumn stand side by side, and towering snow clad mountains forever look down upon eternal verdure."

Oh, yes, Oregon had its virtues, Hastings admitted. It was more like the country most Americans knew: green and wooded. And it was claimed by the United States, not by Mexico. Also, the trail was shorter. But for much of the year Oregon was gray and misty; and the last stretch of the trail—the part that took you through the Cascades— was dreadfully difficult. No, it was better to try for California. Besides, said Hastings, it was possible to shorten the trip.

All you had to do was follow the regular wagon route toward Fort Bridger—the road used by emigrants ever since the first small band of American settlers made its way overland in 1841. You started at the Missouri frontier town of Independence, headed northwest across the grassy plains of what is now Kansas and Nebraska, followed the North Fork of the Platte River to Fort Laramie, and continued westward to South Pass, the broad, gently sloping plain that took you over the crest of the Continental Divide. From there you headed southwest to Fort Bridger.

Then, instead of making the long, northward swing to Fort Hall and down the Humboldt River, you took Hastings' shortcut: "bearing west southwest, to the Salt Lake, and then continuing down to the Bay of St. Francisco."

What could be more sensible? Anyone who glanced at a map could see that the Fort Hall trail made sense for Oregon but not for California. Was it not reasonable to suppose that there was a more direct route across the still unmapped spaces that lay due west of Fort Bridger? Now here was this man Hastings saying it was so. And in print. Between the polished leather covers of a book!

So George and Jacob Donner made their decision: they would venture the new route and get to California just that much sooner. It was a decision that would have them remembering fondly, before another winter was out, the comforts of their Illinois homesteads.

The trouble was that in 1845, when *The Emigrants' Guide* was published, neither its author nor anyone else had yet broken the new route to California. So far, the so-called shortcut existed only in Hastings' imagination. A restless young schemer from Ohio in whose head swirled dreams of empire, Hastings had written his book and created the cutoff as a means of attracting enough American settlers to California to overthrow the Mexican regime and declare an independent republic. Then, of course, the new government would need leaders and there he would be: Lansford Hastings himself, California's own Sam Houston.

Unfortunately the abstract logic of Hastings' new emigrant trail bore no relation to the uncompromising facts of geography. The country that Hastings so blithely swept away with his pen was some of the worst for wagon travel in the United States. Between Fort Bridger and the Great Salt Lake lay the Wasatch Range—boulder-strewn, canyon-cut, and covered in many places with miles of tangled scrub forest. And beyond the Salt Lake lay the alkaline wastes of the Great Salt Lake Desert. It was a country that the Rocky Mountain fur trappers had known and avoided for twenty years but had failed to record except in their own heads. The fact was that in the spring of 1846 the general public had plenty of legend but little hard information about the Far West. It was as though no white man had ever trod the Wasatch or the Salt Desert wilderness. No map showed what that terrible country was like. John Charles Frémont, whose widely read accounts were full of wonderful descriptions and adventure stories, inspired any number of restless young easterners to strike out for the far country—or to dream of doing so. But Frémont did not concern himself with opening new wagon routes, nor did he offer much information that would be useful to emigrants on the trail.

Hence the popularity of Hastings' *Emigrants' Guide*. Grossly inaccurate and not nearly so well written as Frémont's book, it nonetheless seemed to give the emigrants just what they needed—practical information about the Great Trek: how they could prepare for it, what they could expect along the way, and what they would find in the Promised Land. All up and down the Ohio and Mississippi valleys that winter Hastings' book was being read, talked over, and passed from hand to hand.

As to Hastings' proposed new route, vague as it was, there was about it that air of self-evident logic. Moreover, the theory of a more direct route seemed to be confirmed by Frémont's exploration of 1845. Arriving at Sutter's Fort (now Sacramento) at the end of that year, Frémont reported that he had crossed the Salt Desert and had pushed his way over the high Sierra just ahead of the snow. He was gaunt and worn from the ordeal, even though he had made the journey on horseback. Yet he declared grandly that the route he had just explored was "decidedly better" for wagons, being considerably shorter and "less mountainous, with good pasturage and well watered." Frémont, it seems was cut from the same cloth as Hastings. Both were optimistic to the point of being irresponsible.

Encouraged by Frémont's report, Hastings started east from Sutter's Fort in mid-April, 1846, to scout the trail for himself finally and to persuade as many westward-bound emigrants as he could to follow him back to California. The party with which he traveled seems to have included a number of people who did not share his enthusiasm for the golden shore. As the saying went, they "had seen the elephant" and were going home. But Hastings was seldom perturbed by opposition; and at any rate, a man could not always choose his traveling companions. So the party moved east, over the Sierra and along the Humboldt River trail: a trickle of humanity against the westward tide.

In Illinois, meanwhile, George and Jacob Donner, together with their friend James Frazier Reed, a local furniture manufacturer, prepared to join the more than two thousand emigrants who were starting for Oregon and California that spring. Mustering in Springfield on April 15, they made a bustling and prosperous confusion: women in homespun, impatient to get started; white-topped wagons; dogs; children; high-booted teamsters; the unruly herd of cattle and horses.

They were probably among the best-off emigrants on the trail that year. The Donner brothers—with their wives, with twelve children between them, and with four young men hired to help with the animals—were setting off with three wagons apiece: one packed with goods to be used for setting up trade and housekeeping in California; one loaded with supplies for the journey; and one to live in. George Donner's wife Tamsen was taking water colors, oil paints, and "apparatus for preserving botanical specimens." She was bringing books and school supplies for the young ladies' seminary she planned to establish in California; and she was bringing a quilt into which she had sewn ten thousand dollars in bank notes.

Reed, who was forty-six years old, who had served in the Black Hawk War with a would-be politician named Abraham Lincoln, and who had later done well for himself in the furniture business, had loaded his three wagons with all the luxuries of a successful life, including cushions, bunks, a stove, and a store of gourmet wines and brandies. Heading west in hopes of improving his prosperity, he was traveling with his wife, his ailing mother-in-law, four children, and five employees, all in their twenties and all Sangamon County neighbors: Baylis Williams, his sister Eliza, and three young men working their way west.

This was the company that set out from Springfield on April 16, heading west at last along the muddy Illinois springtime roads. At different stages along the trail, the caravan was lengthened by the wagons of other travelers, the numbers fluctuating as emigrant parties grouped and regrouped. There was Patrick Breen, for one. He joined up at Independence, bringing with him his wife, six sons, a daughter, and a friend named

Patrick Dolan. Breen, a transplanted Irishman, had enjoyed enough success at farming on the Iowa side of the Mississippi Valley to be traveling with three wagons and his own substantial herd of horses and cattle.

Then there was an Illinois carriage maker named William Eddy with his wife and two children; and the Fosters; the Pikes, the Graveses; the Kesebergs and Wolfingers (both from Germany); the McCutchens; a cutler named Hardcoop, who was in his sixties; and various unattached young men. Among these last were a few who seem to have come along simply for the adventure.

But there were a number, among both the single men and the married, who neither shared the prosperity of the Donners and the Reeds nor were particularly adventuresome, but who hoped only to escape the hard times that had beaten down so many people in the Mississippi Valley during the depression of the late thirties and early forties. In the West, at least, a man might still be able to buy land cheaply and get a fair price for the fruits of his labor.

So they had headed for Independence. And having traveled first with one party then with another, as chance, convenience, and temperament seemed to dictate, they had fallen in at last with the Donners. One train, after all, was much like another. It was the people that made the difference. The numbers grew, and when the Donner Party was complete it contained a total of eighty-seven men, women, and children.

The trek was hard going right from the start. The emigrants were townspeople and farmers, not frontiersmen. They were used to having regular meals and a roof over their heads. For them, life on the trail took some getting used to. It was not just the strain of traveling for weeks at a time in an unknown country, but also of struggling with the cattle and of repairing broken wagons; of sleeping on the damp ground or on a hard wagon bed; of eating poorly; and of being soaked through by rain and blistered by the sun. Quarrels were frequent even in the first days of the journey. Illness, too, was commonplace: colds, bronchitis, agues, bouts of diarrhea. Reed's mother-in-law, Mrs. Sarah Keyes, aged and feeble, lasted only a few weeks. She was buried under an oak near the Big Blue River in May.

The Donners and their friends were faring neither better nor worse than most bands of emigrants on the trail that spring. Indeed, they were even managing to enjoy themselves a little. Having joined an enormous train of seventy-two wagons (itself a conglomerate of smaller trains), they found in that village on wheels as much congenial company as they wished—more even than they had known at home. There were sewing circles, glee clubs, debating societies, open-air church services on Sundays, the pleasant rituals of the campfire, and any number of playmates for the children. And they enjoyed as much as anyone the ample beauties of the springtime prairie—that luxurious rolling plain of grass and wildflowers, where diarists waxed eloquent at the thought of "prairie schooners" sailing gracefully upon an emerald sea.

But as they climbed the long slope toward the Rockies, a subtle change occurred. The heat of summer was coming on and enthusiasm was giving way to boredom and a gnawing anxiety. The country, too, was different now. Instead of the broad, smooth prairie highway, the wagons had to be pulled through a hard, dry land that was cut up by ravines and dusty alkaline hills. Water and grass had grown scarce, and now there were Indians to worry about. This was Pawnee country, and a man had to be constantly on his guard to prevent his cattle from being driven off or himself from falling behind and becoming a victim of a Pawnee raiding party. Tempers flared and quarrels turned into fist fights. The big parties began splitting up.

Then came new frustrations. Just east of Fort Laramie the now fragmented party to which the Donners were attached met up with a grubby old wanderer named James Clyman, who told them that Hastings' route was a mistake. Clyman, it turned out, was an old friend of James Reed: a mountain man who had first crossed the Missouri in 1823, had later settled in Illinois and Wisconsin, and had been in the same company as Reed (and Lincoln) during the Black Hawk War. Restlessness had turned his needle for California in 1844. But this spring of 1846, satisfied that there was little promise in the Promised Land, he had started for home, traveling east with Lansford Hastings over the very trail the emigrant were planning to take.

That trail, Clyman had found, was appallingly difficult even on horseback. Hastings was waiting at Fort Bridger to tell the emigrants otherwise. But Clyman, nominating himself a one-man safety committee, was riding ahead to warn everyone he met against taking the supposed short-cut. Now, on this night of June 27, 1846, he found himself sitting beside an emigrant campfire, telling his friend Reed and a number of other wagon captains (including, probably, George and Jacob Donner) about the terrible country they would encounter if they took Hastings' route. Clyman's advice (as he later recalled in his journal) was for the emigrants to stick to the regular wagon route. "It is barely possible to get through if you follow it," he told them, "and may be impossible if you don't."

No one welcomed the news. It was too disheartening to think of stretching their tedious journey still further by making the long swing north to Fort Hall. Besides, they were already beginning to feel the pressure of time. By their constant quarreling and reorganizing, by taking time out for fishing and sight-seeing and fist fights, they had fallen behind schedule. After two months of travel they were barely a third of the way to California. At this rate, they would not get to the Sierra until the end of October, when they would be running low on provisions and when the mountain passes were likely to be blocked by snow. Fear of such a prospect had already prompted one of those at the campfire, a Louisville newspaperman named Edwin Bryant, to trade his wagon and oxen for mules and packsaddles. Several of his companions had done likewise.

Bryant put Clyman down for a liar, suspecting ulterior motives, though he had no idea what they might be. Another wagon captain, an old Santa Fe trader and former governor of Missouri named Lilliburn Boggs, took just the opposite view. Impressed by Clyman's report, he decided to take his party to Oregon by way of Fort Hall. But Reed held out. Did Hastings' book count for nothing? And all those months of planning?

Tense and irritable, Reed spoke up: "There is a nigher route," he insisted, "and it is of no use to take so much of a roundabout course."

So in the end it came down to the word of one man against another: the word of Clyman, who had no more to his name than a pack and a horse and a timber claim in Wisconsin (and that probably worthless), against the word of a man who had written a book! No, Reed would go the way he had planned and the Donners would go with him. They were respectable men. They listened to respectable voices.

One chronicler, an Oregon-bound emigrant who took leave of the Donner Party a short time later, noted in his journal that "The Californians were generally much elated and in fine spirits, with the prospect of a better and nearer road to the country of their destination. Mrs. George Donner [Tamsen] was an exception. She was gloomy, sad, and dispirited, in view of the fact that her husband and others could think for a moment of leaving the old road and confide in the statement of a man of whom they knew nothing but who was probably some selfish adventurer."

Yet the soundness of their judgment seemed only to be confirmed when, having trekked across the Wyoming desert and up the long slope to South Pass, Reed and the Donner brothers came down on the westward side of the Great Divide and rolled up to Jim Bridger's ramshackle trading post. There they found that a large party of emigrants had already started westward over the new trail, with Hastings himself at its head. Bryant's party, too, had stuck to its plan despite his misgivings and was taking the new route. Even better, here was Jim Bridger himself, one of the greatest mountain men of all, telling them just what they wanted to hear: that the new trail was open and easy, and that Hastings would be marking the route for those who followed.

Perhaps it was Bridger's name, perhaps it was his manner, or perhaps it was their own anxieties and frustrations that prompted Reed and the Donner brothers to trust "Old Gabe" where they had failed to trust Clyman. In any case, their trust was misplaced. Bridger was lying. Why? Old Gabe had his reasons. Two years before, a new short-cut had been established between South Pass and Fort Hall—one that bypassed Fort Bridger and so threatened to put its proprietor out of business. If, by some fluke, Hastings and his followers did stumble on a new route out of Fort Bridger, why then Old Gabe stood to regain his share of the emigrant trade.

But the members of the Donner Party knew nothing of Bridger's motives. They took him at his word. The matter was settled. After stopping a few days to rest the oxen, the party left Fort Bridger on the last day of July and headed west toward the Wasatch Range.

Meanwhile, the parties that had gone ahead were finding the trail infinitely more difficult than Hastings had led them to believe. Even Bryant and his friends, mounted though they were on mules, were almost beaten by the rugged canyons of the Wasatch, and they were half dead with thirst before they got across the Salt Desert.

For the party of wagons led by Hastings the journey was hellish. Called the Harlan-Young Party, after two of its captains, it consisted of four fragmentary trains totaling about sixty wagons. Having been delayed on the trail, and having found Hastings himself awaiting them at Fort Bridger, the leaders of the party had been persuaded to risk the new route in hopes of saving time. Hastings, confident as ever, had agreed to guide them. At last he had found his following. After that, his only problem was deciding where to lead them.

Hoping to find an easier route over the Wasatch than the one he and Clyman had traveled on their eastward journey, Hastings led them straight into the narrow canyon of the Weber River, where the wagons at times had to be alternately driven and floated in the river bed, and at other times, dragged up and over the sheer cliffs with a windlass. Once on the desert—eighty miles of glaring salt and sand instead of the forty that Hastings had promised—oxen died and wagons were abandoned. The sun wore down even the strongest men.

Eventually the party found its way to the Humboldt River. But instead of gaining time, the emigrants had lost nearly three weeks. Hastings' cutoff had proved to be not only more difficult but also 125 miles *longer* than the Fort Hall route. When the Harlan-Young Party crossed the Sierra in early October the snow was already beginning to fly. They were the last party on the trail that year—except for that of the Donner brothers.

The Donner Party, now numbering its full complement of twenty-three wagons and eighty-seven people, had been running into delays almost from the time it had left Fort Bridger. Thirteen-year-old Eddie Breen broke his leg in a fall from a horse and needed tending. That took time. Then, at the head of Weber canyon, the party found a forked stick with a note stuck on it, instructing any that followed to send a messenger forward to Hastings, who would come back and personally direct them to a better route. So the party went into camp and Reed and two others rode ahead to find Hastings. Five days the party waited, while supplies dwindled and the season grew shorter. When Reed returned he was alone. The other men's horses, he said, had broken down. Hastings had decided he must stay with the Harlan-Young Party, but from the top of arise, he had pointed Reed a new path between the hazy peaks of the Wasatch.

Crossing the forty miles to the valley of the Great Salt Lake took the Donner Party fifteen days of almost unimaginable labor—of pushing aside boulders, hacking through trees and underbrush, bridging swamps and rivers, backtracking out of blind canyons, and dragging the wagons up one ridge after another. The road they cut was a good one—a godsend to the Mormons, who poured over it a year later. But, for their contribution, the men and women of the Donner Party paid dearly in time and energy.

The ordeal was taking its toll. Cumulative fatigue and a growing sense of the danger they faced was beginning to drive them apart. Reed was blamed for the bad trail, another man for not doing his share. Some no doubt blamed the consumptive waif named Halloran for eating but being too weak to work. But Halloran died, his head on Tamsen's lap, and was buried near the trail.

The party went ahead as best it could and reached the oasis east of the Salt Desert at the beginning of September. Another note from Hastings: they should load up with all the grass and water they could carry, for the desert, instead of taking only one day to cross, would take two days and two nights.

The crossing took them six days and most of six nights, and it strained still further the sorry fabric of their morale. A few drove their teams hard, hoping to shorten the journey. Others went slowly, hoping to spare the animals and so insure they got across. Reed and the Donners fell far behind, their progress slowed by their fine wagons, so grandly laden with the comforts of home. Eventually they left the wagons and set off on foot. Reed carrying his three-year-old Tommy on his shoulders.

Everyone made it to the spring at the foot of Pilot Peak. No one died. But they had lost precious days in the crossing, and now they spent more days recuperating, searching for lost and dying cattle; and bringing up their wagons. Few of them had come through without some loss. A number, finding their herds reduced, set about lightening their loads. Reed, who had lost most of his cattle, had to abandon two of his opulent wagons and divide his gourmet delicacies among his companions. Lewis Keseberg left a wagon behind, and so did Jacob Donner, who had exchanged his solid prairie home and his wealth of Illinois land for wagons and teams and cash in hand. But one team was gone now. He had no choice. No matter how painful the decision, a wagon simply had to be left behind.

When they moved on again, September was almost half gone and they were at least a month away from the Sierra. But they had to keep going. They were too far along to turn back (it would have meant the desert again). Ahead, if they were lucky, the mountain passes might still be open. Yet already the fall chill was in the air, and one day, as they pushed on toward the Humboldt, the people of the Donner Party encountered a little desert snowstorm.

Meanwhile, beginning to fear that their food supplies would run out before they even got to the mountains, they sent two men ahead on horseback to appeal to Captain Sutter for provisions. One was young Charles Stanton, a bachelor; the other, a family man. William McCutchen, who left behind a wife and child. The rest pressed on and reached the main Humboldt River trail on September 30. Hoping to make better use of the sparse grass, the company had split into two sections and spread out, traveling a mile or so apart. The Donners led one group, Reed the other.

Everyone was on edge now. The most trifling matters sent men flying into senseless rages. It was an experience common to all parties on this last stretch of the trail, when the novelty of the trip had long since worn off and everyone was travel weary. But the toll was seldom as grievous as it now became for the Donner Party. Shortly after striking the main trail, Reed jumped into a quarrel between two teamsters and ended by killing one of them with a knife. Banished from the company (some had wanted him hanged), Reed rode off toward the mountains, leaving his wife and children in the care of his friends. A short time later, the old cutler Hardcoop fell behind and never caught up, and the men with horses refused to wear out their mounts by going back to look for him. Then another man mysteriously disappeared: the German Wolfinger, who was thought to be carrying a lot of money. Having lost most of his team on a difficult stretch of Nevada desert, he had stayed behind to cache his belongings. Two single men—partners, also from Germany stayed to help, and returned in a few days with a story about how the Indians had killed Wolfinger and burned his outfit. (But later, on his deathbed, one of them confessed to the murder.)

By the time it reached the meadows at the foot of the Sierra, the Donner Party was a party no more, but a straggling collection of individuals bound by family ties alone. There were only a dozen or so wagons left. The great crate of books that was to be the germ of Tamsen Donner's girls' academy had been cached in the Nevada desert. Loosely guarded, the cattle wandered away or were driven off by "Diggers"—impoverished bands of desert Indians, most of them Paiutes. A gun went off by accident and a man was killed. William Eddy, who had lost all his stock, could find no one to take his children into a wagon.

But then at last they had some encouragement: a pack train came loping down the trail out of the west. It was Stanton, returning from Sutter's Fort with seven pack mules loaded with food and with two of Sutter's Indian *vaqueros* to guide them. Here was hope for the first time in weeks: food, and word that Reed had gotten through (though he had nearly starved), and that McCutchen had given out on the crossing and was laid up at Sutter's. Word, too, that the mountain passes were still open. Yes, there had been snow. They could see it on the peaks above them when the clouds gave way. But at this time of year, Stanton had been told, it would be nearly a month before the pass was blocked.

So they still had time, they told themselves. They could even afford to rest a few days in this grassy meadow before starting the push for the summit. (How long it had been since they had seen grass so tall, so green!) And having rested, they started in three small groups up the rugged canyon of the Truckee River, and reached Truckee (now Donner) Lake at the end of October. Just ahead loomed the summit: a wall of granite rising two thousand feet above the lake.

It was the worst obstacle on the whole grueling journey, not least because it came at the end, when men and animals were so worn down. Even the parties that had gone before—in good time and in fair weather—had found the effort exhausting. As many as fifteen yoke of oxen had to be used to pull a single wagon up the steep trail that led to the summit at Emigrant Gap. Every man was needed to handle the ropes and crowbars and to block the wheels. More than one wagon had gone over the side. But the job could be done, and now the first group of the Donner Party began struggling up the slope.

They found the pass already blanketed with five feet of snow—too deep for the wagons. They went back to the lake, waited out a day of rain (snow higher up), and started again, this time with their belongings packed on the backs of oxen. Stanton and one of Sutter's Indians made it to the summit. They could have gone down the western slope, but they turned back to help the others. The others were spent. They could not go on. They camped. They would go over the summit in the morning. But that night a snowstorm blew in and they awoke to find themselves half buried, the cattle gone, the snow too deep for them to move ahead. So again they turned back. Later, when the snow stopped, they could try again. (The season was still early; the snow might still melt.) Meantime, the men set to work building huts of logs and brush and canvas from the wagon tops. The lead group set up near the lake, while the Donner brothers, their families, and their teamsters went into camp five or six miles down the trail, at Alder Creek.

It snowed almost continuously for eight days. Reed and McCutchen, leading a relief train of pack horses up the western slope, pushed through shoulder-deep snow until they could go no further and had to turn back. The Donner Party was on its own.

It numbered eight-two people now, many of them children. And they knew the worst: winter had come early and they were trapped. They could still hope that a relief party would reach them from Sutter's, but in the meantime they would have to survive as best they could by eating their cattle and hunting. But who among them could have imagined that snow could get so deep? They were plains people, not mountaineers. They did not know what to expect of a winter in the Sierra. There, in the high passes, thirty feet of snow has been known to fall in a month. By February it can be packed sixty feet deep.

Day by day the weather grew colder and the snow grew deeper. The people killed most of the cattle, hoping that the snow and cold would preserve the meat. William Eddy, the party's one good shot, managed to bag a coyote with a borrowed rifle: also an owl, two ducks, a squirrel, and then a grizzly bear. But after that there was nothing. The deer and elk had descended below the snow line and the bears were staying in their dens.

Twice in November those who were most able tried to get over the divide in hopes of saving themselves and their children and of bringing relief to the others. The second time, they actually got over and started down the other side. They had been using Sutter's mules to break a trail, however, and when the animals gave out, Stanton refused to go on without them. The mules were Captain Sutter's property; they must be returned. The party went back, and soon afterward another storm broke. All the remaining cattle and horses were lost under the snow, and so were Sutter's mules. The huts, too, were buried, leaving only tunnels to the doorways and holes where the chimneys stood. The light was shut out.

Early in December, young Baylis Williams died—not from starvation, for some food was left, but from malnutrition. A few days later, old Jacob Donner (who had dreamed of warm California) died and was buried in snow. Stanton and Uncle Billy Graves, who knew New England winters, showed the others how to make snowshoes. Thus equipped, a few, perhaps, could get out and get help.

The snowshoers (the party later known as the Forlorn Hope) started for the pass in mid-December—fifteen men and women, including a boy of twelve, Stanton, Eddy, and Sutter's two Indians, who knew the trail. They took with them all the food that could be spared—two mouthfuls a day for six days—for a journey that was to last more than a month.

They were weak from hunger before they even began. The snowshoes slowed them down. They got over the divide, though, and started down the western slope. The first to give out was Stanton. He had been in California once and had come back. He had made the attempt twice in November. But he was finished now. One morning, when the others were preparing to set out, he sat quietly smoking his pipe. "Yes," he said, "I am coming soon." The others went ahead. Stanton never rejoined them.

By the day before Christmas they had been laboring through snow, at eight thousand feet, for more than a week, and had been without food for four days. Pat Breen's friend, Patrick Dolan, was the first to speak what they all were thinking: They should draw lots, Dolan said, to see who should be killed. Some agreed. Others objected. Eddy suggested that two of them, selected by lots, shoot it out with revolvers. Again objections. Then it occurred to them: someone would die soon anyway.

That night a blizzard engulfed them. Most of them were ready to die now. They would have died, except that Eddy remembered a mountain man's trick: he made them huddle together under the blankets, until the snow covered them up and they were warmed by the heat of their bodies. And there they stayed for two days. Delirium overtook many of them. They were raving and shrieking. When it was over, four were dead: Dolan, Uncle Billy, a Mexican herder named Antoine, and the boy Lemuel Murphy. The survivors, crawling out of their mound, managed to strike a fire against a dead pine tree. They cut strips from the legs and arms of Patrick Dolan and roasted them. Eddy and the Indians refused to eat, but after another day, they, too, gave in. The other bodies were butchered and the flesh dried at the fire for the journey ahead.

Back at the huts below the divide Christmas was nearly as grim. The refugees had not yet reached the final extreme. But five were dead, and many of the others were reduced to catching and eating the field mice that came burrowing into the huts. They had begun eating oxhides, which they first boiled into a thick glue, and some of them were easing the pains of hunger by chewing tree bark. At the lake camp, a little frozen meat was still left, and one woman had hoarded a few handfuls of flour, from which she made a kind of gruel for the infant in her care. But probably none felt themselves more fortunate that Christmas than the four children of Mrs. Reed. For nearly eight weeks their mother had kept hidden away the fixings for a holiday stew, which she now brought forth in all its meager glory: a mess of ox tripe, a cupful of white beans, a few dried apples, half a cup of rice, and a tiny square of bacon. "Children, eat slowly," she warned, "there is plenty for all."

Across the divide, the snowshoers stumbled on—ten of them now. The weather cleared and held, and the snow, in places, had finally crusted over enough for them to walk without their snowshoes. Eventually they started to see patches of bare ground. But by then the dried flesh was gone and they were eating the rawhide of their snowshoes. The Indians! Kill the Indians! But Eddy warned them and they slipped away. It was the edge now. Even Eddy was failing. Spotting a deer, he hardly had the strength to lift the rifle to his shoulder. Uncle Billy's daughter, Mary Graves, stood by, weeping. But that night they ate venison and slept soundly.

Another man died. They cut out his heart. His wife saw it roasted on a stick.

Seven of them were left now, five women and two men, one of them mad: William Foster pleaded with Eddy to kill one of the women, pleaded until suddenly Eddy was at him with a knife, threatening to kill him if he said it again.

Days later, food gone, they came upon the two Indians, collapsed and dying. Eddy would not kill them, but left the gun for Foster. They ate again. Eddy ate only grass.

By the end they were crawling as much as they were walking. A small log in the path became a major obstacle. Their feet were bloody pulp. On January 12 they stumbled into a poor Indian camp, were given acorn meal, and were helped on their way. They managed to go five days more before the last bit of strength was used up and they lay down to die. Eddy alone, helped by two Indians, dragged himself the last six miles to Johnson's Ranch, the first settlement on the edge of the Sacramento Valley. His bloody footprints marked the trail for those who would go to rescue his companions.

It was two more weeks before the first relief party got under way. The American settlers in northern California had just fought their last campaign against the Mexicans and it took time to raise enough volunteers. Incredibly, William Eddy, who was determined to rescue his wife and children, was among those who started from Johnson's on February 4; and he got well up into the mountains before being sent back with the horses.

The seven who continued on foot found the climb hard going, even though they were healthy and well fed. Beset by violent rainstorms, fresh snow, and then a blizzard, they would have died if the storms had continued. But they came through it, and crossed over the divide on February 18. When they dropped down to the snowy silence of the lake, they saw nothing but a level plain of snow; no smoke, no sign of life. In the stillness, they wondered if anyone was still alive—until a shout brought a strange, half-human creature clawing its way up out of a hole. Then others appeared. Skinny and white they were, with staring eyes and tiny, lunatic voices. Still others were found under the snow, in their dark, reeking huts: the sick and the dying, who could not move from their beds. The bodies of those who had died since the last storm lay at the top of the ramps, the survivors having had strength to drag them up, but not to bury them.

What had occurred at the camp during the two months since the Forlorn Hope had started for the pass was recorded in the nightmare memories of those who survived and in the diary of Patrick Breen—a spare chronicle of weather and death, of courage, meanness, faith, insanity. The indomitable Mrs. Reed, taking with her her daughter Virginia, Eliza Williams, and a teamster named Milt Elliot, had tried just after New Year's to get over the pass between storms and had to turn back. "I could get along very well while I thought we were going ahead," Virginia later recalled, "but as soon as we had to turn back I could hardly walk." Keseberg's child had died, and Eddy's daughter, and a man named Spitzer, and Eddy's wife, and Milt Elliot. Keseberg had stayed in bed, hoarding valuables that were not his. Eliza Williams' mind had dimmed; she was an infant now.

At Alder Creek, George Donner lay dying, and Tamsen would not leave his side to go with the relief party. She had come with her husband this far, had followed him despite his stubborn insistence on taking Hastings' word when all wisdom went against it. She would not abandon him now, nor would Jacob's wife Elizabeth leave her youngest children or the body of her husband. The rescuers chose the four strongest of the Donner children, and the women dressed them in the good heavy clothes that had been packed the previous spring on the Sangamon. The others would have to wait for the next relief party, which was expected in a few days.

Twenty-three started out with the First Relief, including all of the Reeds. But Tommy and his eight-year-old sister Patty had to be sent back. They were too weak, too slow; they were endangering the whole party. "Well, Mother," Patty said, "if you never see me again, do the best you can."

James Reed, leading the Second Relief up the western slopes, met his wife and two children coming down. On March 1 he arrived in the lake camp, where he found his Tommy and Patty still alive. But Reed had come too late to spare the survivors the final horror. Bones were scattered about, tufts of human hair, half-consumed limbs. Reed recognized the bearded head of his friend Jacob Donner lying in the snow, the skull opened. Inside the Donner hut, he found Jacob's remaining children devouring the half-roasted heart and liver of their father. Elizabeth was dying. She would not eat the food she had prepared for her children. Reed led her and the children and fourteen others back down the mountain.

Eddy and Foster, who had fought viciously in the snow two months before, led the Third Relief over the divide in March. They discovered that their sons had died, and heard the now deranged Keseberg tell them he had eaten the two boys. George Donner, they found, was somehow still alive. Tamsen wrapped her three remaining children in warm clothes and bade them good-bye. Her body had stood her well; she was still in good strength. She would stay to care for her husband and to close his eyes when he died. Foster's mother-in-law, aged and dying, would have to stay; she was too far gone to travel. So, it seemed, was Keseberg.

It was the end of April before the last survivor was brought down from the mountains. The final party of rescuers found only carnage at Donner Lake and Donner Creek (as the campsites were soon being called)—carnage and the demented Keseberg. He was lying down, one of the rescuers remembered, "amidst the human bones, and beside him a large pan full of fresh liver and lights." At the creek, the relief party had found a kettle full of pieces of the body of George Donner. Nearby, on a chair, were ox legs which had been perfectly preserved in the now melting snow but which had not been eaten. Why, they asked Keseberg, had he not use the meat of the bullock instead of human flesh? "Oh! it's too dry eating!" he's answered.

And what of Tamsen, who had been in such good health just three weeks before? The party could find no trace of her body, but they believed that Keseberg had killed her. He denied it for the rest of his life. After George Donner died, Keseberg maintained, she had come to the lake in delirium. Keseberg said he had warmed her and put

her to bed, and the next morning had found her dead. But he also told the rescuers that
"he ate her body and found her flesh the best he had ever tasted. He further stated that
he obtained from her body at least four pounds of fat."

When the Donner Party reached the Sierra, it had included eighty-two people, five
having died on the way there. Thirty-five died in the mountains, along with the two
Indians who had come to rescue them. As Bernard DeVoto points out in his classic
Year of Decision: Eighteen Forty Six, the party had shared the common chance of the
emigrant trail and "the common chance turned against them." But chance alone is not
enough to explain that disastrous combination of events, personalities, and interests that
overwhelmed them. Chance was one factor, but so was the ambition of Lansford Hastings, the business enterprise of Jim Bridger, the cumbersome prosperity of the Donner
wagons, the obstinate temper of Reed, the early winter, the tardiness of the relief parties
. . . perhaps even so little a thing as James Clyman's grubby looks.

Among the forty-seven survivors there were not many who came through without
being haunted for the rest of their lives by the memories of what they had had to endure. The sight of a rising moon forever reminded Mrs. Foster of that moonlit night in
the mountains when her companions in the Forlorn Hope set to work on the body of
Patrick Dolan, while her brother Lemuel Murphy lay dead in her arms. Eliza Donner
never forgot how she had eaten the bark of trees to ease the pain in her stomach.

For the most part the survivors settled into blessedly ordinary lives. Fourteen-year-
old Virginia Reed, for one, received a marriage proposal even before she reached
Sutter's Fort. "Tell the girls that this is the greatest place for marrying they ever saw,"
she wrote home to Illinois. Keseberg, for a time, reveled in his notoriety, finding an
audience for his ghoulish tales in the bars of Gold Rush San Francisco—until the town
grew more respectable and he sometimes found himself taunted and stoned when he
stepped outside his house.

And then there was Lansford Hastings, whom William Eddy set out one day to
kill. But Eddy was dissuaded by a friend from carrying out his plan. The Ohio schemer
lived on, forever optimistic, chasing one elusive dream after another. During the Civil
War he went to Richmond with a plan for seizing Arizona and southern California for
the Confederacy, but nothing came of it. Later, he tried to establish a colony in Brazil
for ex-Confederate soldiers. To forward his scheme he even published an *Emigrants'
Guide to South America.* But in 1870, before his plans were well under way, he died of
a tropical disease. Not for him a cold winter death, starvation in the snow.

Thomas Froncek, a frequent contributor to American Heritage, *has traveled the route
of the Donners. A free-lance writer and editor, he is the author of many magazine articles and* Voices from the Wilderness: The Frontiersman's Own Story *(1974).*

The Thankless Task of Nicholas Trist

Richard M. Ketchum

As winter wore on into the spring of 1847, the hope grew in Washington that the year-old war with Mexico might be settled soon. The nation's first major foreign conflict had been an unpopular affair from the beginning; a large number of Americans seem to have thought it would be a short skirmish, followed by a rich land-grab, and were disappointed when the Mexicans showed no immediate signs of collapsing or negotiating. When President James K. Polk learned of General Winfield Scott's victory on March 27 at Veracruz, he concluded that the moment was auspicious for peace talks and, with the agreement of his Cabinet, looked about for a man he might send to Scott's headquarters to be on the scene should the Mexicans decide to sue for peace.

A Democrat who had already decided not to seek re-election in 1848, the President was eager for the war to end, but he had no intention of appointing someone who would make political hay out of an important peace mission. He realized he had to select someone "who would be satisfactory to the country . . . [yet] such is the jealousy of the different factions of the Democratic party in reference to the next Presidential Election toward each other that it is impossible to appoint any prominent man." And so it was that Nicholas Philip Trist was chosen for one of the strangest, most misunderstood, most productive assignments in American diplomatic history.

At the time Polk plucked him out of near-anonymity for greater things, Trist was the chief clerk in the State Department. This meant that he was second-in-command to the Secretary, James Buchanan—a position he had attained largely through his intimate connections with some of the towering figures in United States politics. Trist had been born in 1800 in Charlottesville, Virginia, where he grandmother was a close friend of Thomas Jefferson, and as a result of that relationship Nicholas and his brothers were invited to come to Monticello for an extended visit in 1817. There Nicholas promptly fell in love with Mr. Jefferson's granddaughter Virginia Jefferson Randolph (a tall girl of "not great personal charms," as Trist's outspoken mother described her) and asked permission to marry her. Virginia's mother and Nicholas' found this prospect chilling, since he was only eighteen and she seventeen; September and young Trist's departure for the Military Academy at West Point came none too soon to suit either of them. At the academy the new cadet showed certain traits that remained with him all his life: he hated restrictions and discipline; he was frequently ill (with his frail constitution— he was 6 feet tall and weighed only 120 pounds—he had difficulty throwing off colds); he worried incessantly; he wrote interminable letters to his family and friends; and he persisted in a belief that Virginians were a very special people, superior to the inhabitants of other parts of the country. At West Point he became a close friend of young Andrew Jackson Donelson, nephew of the hero of New Orleans—an association that was to have an important effect on his later career.

In the summer of 1821 Trist returned to Monticello, determined to quit West Point, marry Virginia Randolph, and take up the law. This time he was granted permission to propose to his inamorata but lost his nerve at the crucial moment and instead wrote her a letter the next day: "The interview of yesterday," he admitted, "was for the purpose of making a declaration of a passion that you must have often read in me." But once again he was rebuffed, this time by the girl herself, who did not want to leave her family just then and suggested that Trist return to Louisiana—where he had grown up— and read law there. He followed her advice, and three years later he was back at Monticello, where they were married at last on September 11, 1824.

Trist continued his study of the law with Thomas Jefferson and became the feeble ex-President's part-time secretary, riding and walking companion, and confidant. In long talks together Jefferson spoke to him about his views on all the events and personalities of the day, and the old man and the young one developed a truly close friendship. When the Trists' first child was born in May, 1826, she was named for Jefferson's wife; the baby was Jefferson's first great-grandchild and the only one he lived to see, for by this time he was confined to bed most of the time. Trist was with him almost constantly, writing his last letters and conversing for hours with the man who had befriended him. The old statesman was determined to live until July 4, the fiftieth anniversary of the Declaration of Independence he had written, and his last weeks were a triumph of will. All through the night of July 3 Trist remained at his side; with an effort Jefferson asked if it were midnight yet, and when Trist replied that it was, the dying man smiled and murmured, "Ah, just as I wished." A few hours later he was dead.

To Trist, as an administrator of Jefferson's estate, fell the chief burden of settling the former President's chaotic financial affairs (less than five thousand dollars remained in his bank account when he died, and the estate was sorely pressed for funds to run Monticello and support the large family that continued to live there). But despite the demands made upon him, Trist completed his law studies and in November, 1826, was admitted to the Virginia bar. Then followed a brief and unsuccessful ownership of a newspaper, until Trist received an offer of a clerkship in the Department of State from the Secretary, Henry Clay. The job paid fourteen hundred dollars a year, and he accepted with pleasure. Luckily, when Andrew Jackson became President in 1829, Trist's friendship with Jefferson, Madison, and Jackson's nephew Donelson was remembered; unlike so many victims of the spoils system, he was allowed to stay on in his job. Soon Trist and his wife became regulars at White House dinners; Jackson was especially interested in hearing from them about Jefferson's political beliefs, his views on emancipation of the slaves, and his ideas concerning religious freedom.

At the Jefferson memorial birthday dinner in 1830 Trist gave what was technically the chief toast—to the memory of the late President—but his remarks were considerably overshadowed by those of Andrew Jackson: this was the famous occasion on which Jackson rose to his feet, fixed would-be secessionist John C. Calhoun with a steely eye, and stated unequivocally, "Our Union: It must be preserved."

At this time Trist's fluent knowledge of Spanish made him one of the principal State Department informants on Latin-American countries; he was also beginning to handle most of the correspondence between the United States and Russia while James Buchanan was minister there. And opportunity knocked, oddly enough, as a result of a grand social brouhaha at the White House. By spring of 1830 the members of Jackson's Cabinet had taken sides over Peggy O'Neale Eaton, a former barmaid who had become the second wife of John Eaton, the Secretary of War, and while the president stubbornly supported her, the Cabinet officers (except Secretary of State Martin Van Buren) and their wives would have nothing to do with her. Mrs. Andrew Jackson Donelson withdrew as the President's hostess rather than call on her, and suddenly, Trist was asked to assume Donelson's place as Jackson's private secretary.

Diplomats, congressmen, and Cabinet officers transacted business through him; it was a demanding, time-consuming position of great responsibility and long hours, from which Trist—fortunately for his relations with his family—was relieved in 1831 by Donelson's reconciliation with his uncle. Then, after two more years in the State Department, Trist received a presidential appointment that promised an opportunity to do something on his own. By now a man of polished manners, impeccable connections, keen insight, and with a broad grounding in foreign affairs, he became consul at the Cuban port of Havana.

He had not been in Havana long before he realized that it had been a mistake to come; it was not a good post for anyone with ambition. The tedious tropical hours found Trist writing incredibly long letters and reports to Washington—reports so full of trivia one wonders if the recipients ever finished reading them (one communication to the Senate Committee on Finance contained fifty-two closely written pages). This was, however, one of the few times in his life that Trist made anything like enough money; he seems to have picked up substantial sums outside his job through notary fees and by investing funds that were deposited with him. But in 1839 some ugly charges were made against Trist—accusations of inefficiency, failure to support American interests, and abetting the slave trade—and his conduct was reviewed by a congressional committee. Although the congressmen gave him a clean bill of health, Trist seems to have been negligent, at the very least, and perhaps even guilty of some of the charges made against him. Certainly many U.S. captains who touched at Havana were highly critical of the consul and his activities. In any case, merit—or the lack of it—sometimes counted for less than the spoils system, and in 1841 Trist received word from the new Whig Secretary of State, Daniel Webster, that he was relieved of his consular duties. Four years later the political tides changed once more, James K. Polk became President, Trist's old friend James Buchanan was appointed Secretary of State, and Trist was named chief clerk of the department. The dying Andrew Jackson, ever a man to support a friend, wrote to Polk endorsing Trist for the job, which paid two thousand dollars a year.

And so it came about, early in 1847, that President Polk decided to send Nicholas P. Trist as his emissary to Mexico, there to await the proper moment to enter into negotiations with a shaky Mexican government. Despite his disappointing performance in Cuba, Trist seemed a natural for the post: in addition to his fluency in Spanish he was thoroughly knowledgeable about the workings of the State Department; as a loyal Democrat he was known to Polk and to members of the Cabinet, yet he had never been active in politics and appeared to have no ambitions in that direction. His assignment, quite simply, was to make his way as inconspicuously as possible to General Winfield Scott's headquarters in Mexico and to forward to the enemy government, via the American commanding general, a proposed treaty of peace drafted by the secretary of State and approved by administration leaders in Washington. If, by the time he arrived there, the Mexicans had already designated a plenipotentiary empowered on conclude a treaty, Trist was to begin negotiations with him on the basis of the American draft. Its terms were quite definite and had been drawn by Polk and Buchanan in the uneasy awareness that the congressional opposition was ready to pounce on the slightest misstep as a means of repudiating the administration on "the Mexican question." This draft treaty had been submitted to the Cabinet on April 13: revised and approved by both President and Cabinet, it was delivered on April 15, 1847, to Nicholas P. Trist, who was designated a "commissioner plenipotentiary" and bidden Godspeed.

Secrecy, of course, was absolutely vital to the mission, and Polk had every confidence in the discretion of his emissary; but Trist had been gone less than a week when reports of his assignment appeared in the New York *Herald,* the *National Intelligence, Niles' Weekly Register,* and other newspapers. Polk was understandably furious and alternated between blaming Trist and the State Department for the unpardonable leak (finally he settled on the latter as the most likely source and took a dislike to Buchanan that hardened as time wore on). From New Orleans the unsuspecting Trist wrote one of his wearisome letters to his chief; in thirty verbose pages the only real news he gave Buchanan was that he had arrived in Louisiana after travelling overland via Charleston, Augusta, and Mobile, whence he had taken a steamer to New Orleans. Traveling incognito as "Doctor Tarreau," a French merchant, he had stayed at a "French auberge, of the economical order," rather than at one of the better hotels where someone might recognize him and become suspicious.

For all his precautions Trist managed to call a good deal of attention to himself by his painstaking selection of a vessel to carry him quickly toward his destination; from New Orleans he sailed across the Gulf of Mexico in eight days, arriving on May 6 at Veracruz, where he learned that a supply train would leave on the eighth for Scott's headquarters. And here Trist made a monumental error.

He bore with him a letter of appointment from Buchanan, giving him "full diplomatic powers" to sign a treaty in the name of the United States. He also had two copies of the treaty *projet,* or draft—one of them sealed, for the Mexicans—and his instructions were to place the sealed copy in the hands of General Scott for forwarding to the Mexican authorities. But unfortunately, instead of delivering this document to Scott personally and informing him of its contents, Trist chose to remain at Veracruz and to write a letter to the General in which he requested that the sealed dispatch be delivered to the Mexican minister of foreign affairs. With this communication he enclosed one from William I. Marcy, the Secretary of War, which ordered Scott to transmit the sealed letter to the Mexicans and informed him that "Mr. Trist, an officer from our department of foreign affairs, next in rank to its chief," was now at Army headquarters.

Scott exploded. Under the best of circumstances he was a proud man, excruciatingly sensitive of his reputation and quick to detect a slight whether or not one was intended. Temperament aside, there was also the fact that he was a prominent Whig—a political foe of the administration in Washington—and had long since fallen out with President Polk. In fact, at the time Polk gave Scott command of the Army in May, 1846, the tactless General had written the President an offensive letter complaining about Democratic place-seekers and then had confided to Secretary of War Marcy that he had no stomach for placing himself "in the most perilous of all positions:—a fire upon my rear, from Washington, and the fire in the front, from the Mexicans." Polk's furious reaction had been to excuse Scott from field command in Mexico, leaving him to stew in the capital while Zachary Taylor won the victories and the glory. Finally, in November, 1846, Scott was sent to command the movement on Veracruz and Mexico City, but Polk neither forgave not forgot. He wrote in his diary:

> General Scott has acted with so little discretion since he assumed the command that the confidential plans of the Government which were confided only to himself have been made so public that every Mexican may know them. . . . His vanity is such that he could not keep the most important secrets of the Government which were given to him. He is . . . making such a parade before the public in all he does that there is danger that the objects of the campaign may be entirely defeated. . . .

Such a background was not one to make Scott warm to Trist, and what was to have been a co-operative mission between the two was immediately thrown into jeopardy. Still in the dark about the contents of the proposed treaty, Scott wrote an outraged answer to Trist's first letter. It began: "I see that the secretary of War proposes to degrade me, requiring that I, as command-in-chief of this army, shall defer to you, the chief clerk in the Dep't of State, the question of continuing or discontinuing hostilities."

After getting that out of his system, he indicated that since there was no real Mexican government, he could not forward the dispatch anyway.

Here Nicholas Trist, had he had his wits about him, would have recognized his initial error and attempted to patch things up with the General. But no, he sent off one of his endless communications—an eighteen-page letter that Scott termed "sarcastic, burning, and impolite." By now Polk's peace mission was completely off the rails. Scott, assuming Trist to be an ally of Polk and Buchanan (both of whom he mistrusted because they had opposed his appointment as commanding general), now believed that the government in Washington was deliberately trying to prevent him from having a voice in a truce with the Mexicans. Trist, no less suspicious, wrote his wife that Scott was "decidedly the greatest imbecile that I have ever had anything to do with" and soon was exchanging further angry letters with him. By May 19—more than three weeks after Trist arrived to negotiate a peace with the Mexican government—he had still not even met the U.S. Commander in chief, who wrote him a curt note referring to one of Trist's thirty-page onslaughts as a "farrago of impudence, conceit, and arrogance."

Fortunately for posterity, both men were now being taken to task by their chiefs: Buchanan wrote Trist telling him that this was no time for a personal vendetta—the government, he said, could not indulge its representatives in a quarrel; Marcy told off Scott in similar fashion. Despite their differences and their abraded nerve ends, both men were good Americans, and they soon realized how detrimental to the nation's interests their conduct was. Nicholas Trist took the initial step to heal the rift: on June 25 he sent Scott a note that was for the first time free of rancor, and Scott replied at once, saying that he would be quite willing to forget the recent unpleasantness. Just then Trist fell ill, causing Scott to feel more compassionate toward him; on July 6 a box of guava marmalade was delivered to the diplomat's sickbed from the Commander in Chief, and with this peace offering the feud ended as suddenly as it had begun. A few days later the two met for the first time and established an immediate *entente cordiale;* soon contrite letters were on their way to Washington from both of them to their respective departments, requesting that the earlier, angry letters of complaint be removed from the files.

But by this time, naturally enough, the President of the United States was thoroughly disgusted with both his representatives. In addition to what he knew from other sources of the Trist-Scott feud, he had been receiving confidential dispatches from Scott's second-in-command, General Gideon J. Pillow, Polk's former law partner in Tennessee, who lost no opportunity to put Scott (and, after the *repproachment,* Trist) in the worst possible light. Pillow was no fool; he wanted the top job himself, and thanks in part to his machinations, Polk gave renewed consideration to removing Scott from command.

Because of the horrendous delays in getting word from the battlefield to Washington—it often took three or four weeks for a message to reach the capital—there was an Alice-in-Wonderland aspect to the whole affair by this time, so that while Polk fumed at the White House over the lack of progress, events in Mexico were actually pushing matters toward a settlement. In August, Trist met for the first time with the Mexican peace commissioners, who balked at parting with Texas south of the Nueces River and a portion of Upper California. Since the Rio Grande boundary was a *sine qua non* of Trist's instructions, he broke off the talks; but he agreed to submit the Mexican proposal to Washington. Meanwhile the course of the war made peace inevitable: on September 14 the Americans captured Mexico City, Santa Anna and the government fled, and Trist observed that "total dissolution" of the country was at hand. In this state of chaos Mexico would neither negotiate nor fight.

But as far as Washington knew, the unpopular war was merely dragging on, and President Polk could take no comfort from the fact that his Democrats were outnumbered in the House 117 to 110. Having heard further from Pillow that Trist was "acting unwisely," he concluded that no good could possibly come of the peace mission and told the Secretary of State to order his "commissioner plenipotentiary" to return home. So on October 6 Buchanan, unaware that Mexico City had fallen, wrote Trist telling him how conditions had changed since the previous April, reminding him of the American lives and treasure that had been squandered since then, and informing him, finally, that he was recalled. If Trist had written a treaty by the time he received these instructions, the Secretary added, he should of course bring it home with him; but if not, he should not delay his departure even though he might be in the midst of negotiations with the Mexicans. The next day, probably out of friendship and to soften the blow of Trist's recall, Buchanan followed up his official letter with a chatty personal note telling his friend how much he looked forward to having him back in the department again.

Two weeks later—on October 21—letters Trist had written on September 28 were received in Washington, making it clear that he had discussed terms with the Mexicans that exceeded his carefully drafted instructions. That was too much for Polk: his commissioner had "embarrassed future negotiations," the President spluttered. His conduct was "much to be regretted," since he had evidently encouraged the Mexicans to hope for better conditions than he had any right to promise them.

In November, when Trist finally received his letter of recall, along with other letters criticizing his actions, he characteristically sat down and wrote a lengthy justification of his conduct during the negotiations. Time and events certainly seemed to support Trist's hopes that a settlement would be reached before long. He was convinced that the Mexican peace party would form a government; Santa Anna, the defeated leader, had resigned the presidency, and the army had not rallied to him when he fled the Mexican capital. He had been succeeded by Manuel de la Peña y Peña, the president of the supreme court, who appointed a peace advocate as his minister of relations. But just at that moment, with the Mexicans on the verge of peace talks, Trist's recall had arrived. To his wife he wrote of his bitter disappointment; he intended to resign from the State Department, he told her, and "bid adieu *forever* to official life." Over and above his personal chagrin he could not understand why his government—if it sincerely desired peace, as he assumed—did not replace him with another peace commissioner. On

December 1, when no word of a replacement had reached him, Trist decided to ignore his recall and stay in Mexico to write a treaty. He had concluded that he could not permit the present opportunity to slip by, and on December 6 he wrote to inform Buchanan of his decision. Even if new commissioners were appointed now, he argued, they could not arrive in time to salvage the situation, and if the opportunity were lost now, it might be gone forever. As for the boundaries, he realized that those limits included in his original instructions were the maximum to which the Mexicans could agree. With great sensitivity Trist wrote, "however helpless a nation may feel, there is necessarily a point beyond which she cannot be expected to go under any circumstances, in surrendering her territory as the price of peace."

One hopes that President Polk was spared the full catalogue of Trist's arguments, since his letter ran to sixty-five pages, but in any event Polk reacted predictable. He ordered Trist out of Army headquarters at once and instructed the Untied States military commander to inform the Mexicans that Nicholas P. Trist was no longer acting for the United States government. Separately, the President had also decided to replace Scott, having heard from Pillow and other subordinate officers that Scott was taking all the credit for victory over the Mexicans. (Robert E. Lee, a young colonel who had participated in that victory, wrote sadly to a friend concerning the dissensions in the army. "No one can regret them more than I do. They have clouded a bright campaign. . . . The affair I suppose will soon be before the court . . . but I suspect that if one party [Scott] has been guilty of harshness . . . the other [Pillow and other dissident officers] has been guilty of insubordination.")

Trist responded to adversity by writing still more letters, assuring Buchanan that it was not personal vanity but devotion to duty that prompted him to remain in Mexico. Since he had not been replaced, he repeated, he would stay and achieve a peaceful settlement out of regard for both nations. At long last, on December 30, 1847, peace negotiations began in the town of Guadalupe Hidalgo, outside Mexico City. Trist was handicapped by having not even a secretary to assist him, so he was obliged to keep minutes while listening to the Mexican proposals. Each night he retired to write voluminous letters to Buchanan and to his wife.

On January 25 he was able to inform the Secretary of State that the terms of a treaty had been agreed upon. He had obtained the boundaries called for in his original instructions with only a slight variation at the western extremity; but he believed that the new line, which included the fine port of San Diego, fulfilled his orders in principle, and it was acceptable to the Mexicans. The defeated government was to be paid an indemnity of $15,00,000 for the territory taken by the United States, and the victors were to assume claims against Mexico up to $3,250,000. On his own hook, Trist had worked out a solution to the status of Mexicans living in the ceded lands. If they elected to move out of what was now U.S. territory, they could take their belongings with them, without penalty; if they decided to remain, they could retain their Mexican citizenship provided that within a year they announced their intention to do so—otherwise they would become U.S. citizens.

On February 2, 1848, after a rash of delays caused by the Mexican commissioners, Trist wrote proudly to Buchanan informing him that the Treaty of Peace, Friendship, Limits, and Settlement had been signed that day at Guadalupe Hidalgo. Since Trist now had to remain in Mexico to testify at a court of inquiry ordered by President Polk to examine the charges brought by several members of Scott's staff concerning the conduct of the war, he asked James I. Freaner, correspondent for the New orleans *Delta*, to carry the treaty back to the Unit States. As Robert Arthur Brent has written, the completed treaty was the most important achievement of Trist's life. If Trist had acted "at times negligently, at others without tact," he had nonetheless never lost sight of his objective, which was the establishing of peace between Mexico and the United States. "His success," Brent adds, "was the glory of the Polk administration; his disgrace was his own to bear."

And the signs all pointed to disgrace now. When Buchanan brought the treaty to Polk at the White House on February 19, the President was still angry over Trist's behavior, although he was forced to admit that the document met all the conditions given to Trist in April, 1847. After thinking the matter over, Polk informed his Cabinet that he would submit the treaty to the Senate. If he did not do so, he reasoned, Congress might react by refusing to appropriate money to keep the Army in Mexico, and Polk would have to withdraw the troops without a peace treaty. The Whigs who had attacked the war so bitterly would surely make political capital out of his failure to end it, especially when the treaty embodied the very terms laid down by Polk himself. And finally, Polk was keenly aware of the immense value of the lands ceded by this treaty to the United States. So on February 23—against the advice of Buchanan, who wanted to demand even more territory from the defeated Mexicans—Polk sent the treaty to the Senate, including with it a remarkable note recommending that it be debated on its own merits and without reference to the unfortunate actions of Nicholas P. Trist. The Senate responded by requesting from the President all correspondence relating to Trist's mission, and members of the Foreign Relations Committee informed Polk that they would recommend rejection—not because of the terms of the treaty but because Trist had written it after his recall.

Polk fought back at once. The senators were usurping the powers of the Chief Executive, he stated firmly; the Senate might consider the treaty itself, but not how it had been made—that was the prerogative of the President. There was formidable opposition to the treaty: Thomas Hart Benton led a group of Democrats who opposed ratification on moral grounds—the Untied States, they said, had no right to any territory other than Texas south to the Nueces River; Daniel Webster, leading the Whig forces, opposed it on the basis that the United States would thereby acquire too much territory; and another group of Democrats was against it because the United States did not get *enough* land. But on March 10, with four senators not voting, the treaty was finally approved by a vote of thirty-eight to fourteen.

And what of the treaty's chief advocate? Poor Trist, after wrangling with Army authorities over his right as an American citizen to remain in Mexico, was placed under arrest as the only means of getting him to leave the country where he had toiled for so long. When he rejoined his family in Washington at last, on May 17, 1848, thirteen months had elapsed since his departure, and he found himself dismissed from government service in disgrace. Buchanan, now completely out of favor with the President, could not help him. (Polk had grown increasingly suspicious of his Secretary of State because of his presidential aspirations: "No candidate for the presidency ought ever to remain in the Cabinet," Polk noted in his diary. "He is an unsafe adviser.") And the President, of course, wanted nothing to do with Trist. Although Trist, more than any other man, was responsible for fulfilling Polk's ambition of rounding out the natural boundaries of the United States, the President could not bring himself to forgive his act of disobedience. Indeed, since Trist had been on a secret mission and therefore was paid out of the President's special funds, he was even denied his full pay by the Chief Executive, who cut off his salary as of November 16, when he received his recall.

In a memorial to Congress, Trist pleaded his cause: he had not sought the appointment as peace commissioner; he had been asked to render a great service to his country; in doing so, he had saved thousands of lives and millions of dollars; he had acquired a vast territory for the United States, extending our western boundary to the Pacific and fixing firm boundaries between Mexico and the Untied States where none had existed. Surely a man who had achieved that deserved recognition? But the Congress was not in a forgiving mood either.

Virtually destitute, Trist and his wife moved to West Chester, Pennsylvania, in July of 1848. Fortunately, a few friends—Winfield Scott among them—offered him help. During his stay there several writers came to him in search of information about the great men he had known: Henry S. Randall, for his biography of Jefferson; James Parton, for his biography of Jackson; Thomas Hart Benton, for assistance on his *Thirty Years' View*. By 1855, with his wife running a school for young ladies, Nicholas Trist was reduced to taking a job as a clerk for the Wilmington and Baltimore Railroad Company, where he eventually worked up to paymaster at a salary of $112.50 a month. It was a bitter lot for a man who had been so close to the nation's great and had done so much for his country.

As the Civil War approached, Trist was drawn again to politics—for the New York *World* he wrote an article quoting Jefferson's and Madison's views on secession. To General Scott, a Virginian who was now commanding general of the Union Army, he wrote that he was also a southerner by birth and a Yankee by adoption, but that his sympathies and those of his wife lay with the North and with preservation of the Union. Now and again Trist's friends tried to help him obtain a government job. In 1861 Scott wrote to the Secretary of the Treasury, Salmon P. Chase, stating that Trist had been wronged by Polk and neglected by Taylor, Fillmore, Pierce, and Buchanan; the nation owed Nicholas Trist a great debt, the old soldier added. But Chase did nothing. Finally, in 1870, Senator Charles Sumner made an eloquent speech in Trist's behalf, reminding the Senate of his signal contributions, and a year later Trist received the sum of $14,559.90—money that was owed him for his salary and expenses in Mexico twenty-three years earlier. It came none too soon, for he had had to give up his railway job a year earlier, and the Trists were poverty-stricken. In the summer of 1870 President Grant appointed him postmaster in Alexandria, Virginia. He was paid $2,900 a year, which was more money than he had earned at any time since 1841, but he had less than four years to enjoy this munificence. On February 11, 1874, after suffering a stoke, Trist died.

Anyone wishing to contemplate the part chance plays in human destiny might give some thought to the career of Nicholas P. Trist. His act of rare courage and principle for a cause he believed to be right cost him the support of the President and brought him dismissal, disgrace, poverty, and the total disregard of posterity. Most historians have neglected him entirely or dismissed him as a man of no ability, overlooking the fact that Trist was a victim of an unpopular war and an administration that neither understood nor sympathized with his difficulties or his aspirations. Immovable on matters of principle, Trist determined to do what he considered right. And for this, as well as for the tangible effects of his deed, he deserves better of his country.

What the nation obtained as a result of the treaty he executed singlehandedly was the boundary of the Rio Grande and the cession of territory between that river and the Pacific Ocean—which includes the present states of California, Nevada, Utah, New Mexico, Arizona, a corner of Wyoming, and the western slope of Colorado. Because of the efforts of Nicholas P. Trist, James K. Polk is remembered as the President who, except for Jefferson, added more territory to the nation than any other. When Polk left office the United states was half again as large as when he took the oath. As a final irony, while Nicholas P. Trist and the Mexicans were reaching final agreement in Guadalupe Hidalgo, gold was discovered at Sutter's Mill in California, with consequences beyond all imagining.

Mr. Ketchum, Senior Editor for Book Publishing of American Heritage Publishing Company, is the author of the "Faces from the Past" series that has appeared frequently in this magazine. These pieces, together with many new ones, will be published soon in book form under the same title by American Heritage Press.

Among the sources for this article were: "Nicholas Philip Trist: Biography of a Disobedient Diplomat," an unpublished doctoral dissertation written in 1950 by Robert Arthur Brent the University of Virginia, and "Nicholas P. Trist, a Diplomat with Ideals," an article in the Mississippi Valley Historical Review *for June, 1924, by Louis M. Sears. A good over-all view of the period is in* The War with Mexico, *by Justin H. Smith (two volumes, Macmillan, 1919).*

Part Five • The Civil War and Reconstruction Period

After a decade of recurring and mounting crises between the North and the South, South Carolina reacted emotionally to the election of Abraham Lincoln in 1860 and seceded from the Union, followed by the states of the Lower South. Before Lincoln took the oath of office in March, 1861, the Confederate States of America had been formed. When conciliation failed to resolve the differences with the South, the mere suggestion of coercion by the National Government precipitated the opening shots of the Civil War. The Upper South joined the Lower South; the sides were drawn and the nation was plunged into the bloodiest conflict in its history. Allan Nevins, in his article, ''The Needless Conflict'' examines one of the major episodes of the 1850s in the widening breach between North and South, the fight over Kansas.

Lincoln was at first determined to confine the conflict to a single cause; save the Union. But by 1862 for reasons both political and diplomatic, Lincoln resolved to move toward emancipation of the slaves. In his thoughtful article, ''The Slaves Freed,'' Stephen B. Oates traces the evolution of Lincoln's policy from emancipation to abolition of slavery. That outcome would be determined by the bloody course of the war. Bruce Catton provides a glimpse of what military life was like for the average soldier in his article, ''Hayfoot, Strawfoot.''

Four years of war demonstrated that the South, although full of courage and determination, was no match for the superior manpower, industrial might, and wealth of the North. The humiliating end came in 1865 with surrender. How Reconstruction would have worked out if Lincoln had lived will never be known. But as David Donald explains in his article, "Why They Impeached Andrew Johnson," Lincoln's successor lacked the political skills and power base that might have carried Lincoln to success. As a result, Johnson not only failed to accomplish Presidential Reconstruction, but he found himself in constant dispute with the Republican Congress. Although impeachment proceedings failed to convict Johnson, he was isolated and ignored for the remainer of his term. Leadership in policy was seized by Congress, and the South was subjected to a prolonged and traumatic period of Reconstruction. As difficult as it was, Reconstruction may have been necessary to change Southern life and bind that section once again to the Union.

The Needless Conflict

Allan Nevins

When James Buchanan, standing in a homespun suit before cheering crowds, took the oath of office on March 4, 1857, he seemed confident that the issues before the nation could be readily settled. He spoke about an army road to California, use of the Treasury surplus to pay all the national debt, and proper guardianship of the public lands. In Kansas, he declared, the path ahead was clear. The simple logical rule that the will of the people should determine the institutions of a territory had brought in sight a happy settlement. The inhabitants would declare for or against slavery as they pleased. Opinions differed as to the proper time for making such a decision; but Buchanan thought that "the appropriate period will be when the number of actual residents in the Territory shall justify the formation of a constitution with a view to its admission as a State." He trusted that the long strife between North and South was nearing its end, and that the sectional party which had almost elected Frémont would die a natural death.

Two days after the inaugural Buchanan took deep satisfaction in a decision by the Supreme Court of which he had improper foreknowledge: the Dred Scott decision handed down by Chief Justice Taney. Its vital element, so far as the nation's destiny was concerned, was the ruling that the Missouri Compromise restriction, by which slavery had been excluded north of the 36°30′ line, was void; that on the contrary, every territory was open to slavery. Not merely was Congress without power to legislate *against* slavery, but by implication it should act to protect it. Much of the northern press denounced the decision fervently. But the country was prosperous; it was clear that time and political action might change the Supreme Court, bringing a new decision; and the explosion of wrath proved brief.

Buchanan had seen his view sustained; slavery might freely enter any territory, the inhabitants of which could not decide whether to keep it or drop it until they wrote their first constitution. In theory, the highway to national peace was as traversible as the Lancaster turnpike. To be sure, Kansas was rent between two bitter parties, proslavery and antislavery; from the moment Stephen A. Douglas' Kansas-Nebraska Act had thrown open the West to popular sovereignty three years earlier, it had been a theater of unrelenting conflict. Popular sovereignty had simply failed to work. In the spring of 1855 about five thousand invading Missourians, swamping the polls, had given Kansas a fanatically proslavery legislature which the free-soil settlers flatly refused to recognize. That fall a free-soil convention in Topeka had adopted a constitution which the slavery men in turn flatly rejected. Some bloody fighting had ensued. But could not all this be thrust into the past?

In theory, the President might now send out an impartial new governor; and if the people wanted statehood, an election might be held for a new constitutional convention. Then the voters could give the nation its sixteenth slave state or it seventeenth free state—everybody behaving quietly and reasonably. Serenity would prevail. Actually, the idea that the people of Kansas, so violently aroused, would show quiet reason, was about as tenable as the idea that Europeans would begin settling boundary quarrels by a quiet game of chess. Behind the two Kansas parties were grim southerners and determined northerners. "Slavery will now yield a greater profit in Kansas," trumpeted a southern propagandist in *De Bow's Review,* "either to hire out or cultivate the soil, than any other place." He wanted proslavery squatters. Meanwhile, Yankees were subsidizing their own settlers. "I know people," said Emerson in a speech, "who are making haste to reduce their expenses and pay their debts . . . to save and earn for the benefit of Kansas emigrants."

Nor was reason in Kansas the only need. Impartiality in Congress, courage in the presidential chair, were also required. The state was dressed for a brief, fateful melodrama, which more than anything else was to fix the position of James Buchanan and Stephen A. Douglas in history, was to shape the circumstances under which Lincoln made his first national reputation, and was to have more potency than any other single event in deciding whether North and South should remain brothers or fly at each other's throats. That melodrama was entitled "Lecompton." Douglas was to go to his grave believing that, had Buchanan played an honest, resolute part in it, rebellion would have been killed in its incipiency. The role that Buchanan did play may be counted one of the signal failures of American statesmanship.

To hold that the Civil War could not have been averted by wise, firm, and timely action is to concede too much to determinism in history. Winston Churchill said that the Second World War should be called "The Unnecessary War"; the same term might as justly be applied to our Civil War. Passionate unreason among large sections of the population was one ingredient in the broth of conflict. Accident, fortuity, fate, or sheer bad luck (these terms are interchangeable) was another; John Brown's raid, so malign in its effects on opinion, North and South, might justly be termed an accident. Nothing in the logic of forces or events required so crazy an act. But beyond these ingredients lies the further element of wretched leadership. Had the United States possessed three farseeing, imaginative, and resolute Presidents instead of Fillmore, Pierce, and Buchanan, the war might have been postponed until time and economic forces killed its roots.

Buchanan was the weakest of the three, and the Lecompton affair lights up his incompetence like a play of lightning across a nocturnal storm front.

The melodrama had two stages, one in faraway, thinly settled Kansas, burning hot in summer, bitter cold in winter, and though reputedly rich, really so poor that settlers were soon on the brink of starvation. Here the most curious fact was the disparity between the mean actors and the great results they effect. A handful of ignorant, reckless, semi-drunken settlers on the southern side, led by a few desperadoes of politics—the delegates of the Lecompton Constitutional Convention—actually had the power to make or mar the nation. The other stage was Washington. The participants here, representing great interests and ideas, had at least a dignity worthy of the scene and the consequences of their action. James Buchanan faced three main groups holding three divergent views of the sectional problem.

The proslavery group (that is, Robert Toombs, Alexander H. Stephens, Jefferson Davis, John Slidell, David Atchison, and many more) demanded that slavery be allowed to expand freely within the territories; soon they were asking also that such expansion be given federal protection against any hostile local action. This stand involved the principle that slavery was morally right, and socially and economically a positive good. Reverdy Johnson of Maryland, in the Dred Scott case, had vehemently argued the beneficence of slavery.

The popular sovereignty group, led by Douglas and particularly strong among northwestern Democrats, maintained that in any territory the issue of slavery or free soil should be determined *at all times* by the settlers therein. Douglas modified the Dred Scott doctrine: local police legislation and action, he said, could exclude slavery even before state-making took place. He sternly rejected the demand for federal protection against such action. His popular sovereignty view implied indifference to or rejection of any moral test of slavery. Whether the institution was socially and economically good or bad depended mainly on climate and soil, and moral ideas were irrelevant. He did not care whether slavery was voted up or voted down; the right to a fair vote was the all-important matter.

The free-soil group, led by Seward and Chase, but soon to find its best voice in Lincoln, held that slavery should be excluded from all territories present or future. They insisted that slavery was morally wrong, had been condemned as such by the Fathers, and was increasingly outlawed by the march of world civilization. It might be argued that the free-soil contention was superfluous, in that climate and aridity forbade a further extension of slavery anyhow. But in Lincoln's eyes this did not touch the heart of the matter. It might or might not be expandable. (Already it existed in Delaware and Missouri, and Cuba and Mexico might be conquered for it.) What was important was for American to accept the fact that, being morally wrong and socially an anachronism, it *ought* not to expand; it *ought* to be put in the way of ultimate eradication. Lincoln was a planner. Once the country accepted nonexpansion, it would thereby accept the idea of ultimate extinction. This crisis met and passed, it could sit down and decide when and how, in God's good time and with suitable compensation to slaveholders, it might be ended.

The Buchanan who faced these three warring groups was victim of the mistaken belief among American politicians (like Pierce, Benjamin Harrison, and Warren G. Harding, for example) that it is better to be a poor President than to stick to honorable but lesser posts. He would have made a respectable diplomat or decent Cabinet officer under a really strong President. Sixty-six in 1857, the obese bachelor felt all his years. He had wound his devious way up through a succession of offices without once showing a flash of inspiration or an ounce of grim courage. James K. Polk had accurately characterized him as an old woman—"It is one of his weaknesses that he takes on and magnifies small matters into great and undeserved importance." His principal characteristic was irresolution." Even among close friends," remarked a southern senator, "he very rarely expressed his opinions at all upon disputed questions, except in language especially marked with a caution circumspection almost amounting to timidity."

He was industrious, capable, and tactful, a well-read Christian gentleman; he had acquired from forty years of public life a rich fund of experience. But he was pedestrian, humorless, calculating, and pliable. He never made a witty remark, never wrote a memorable sentence, and never showed a touch of distinction. Above all (and this was the source of his irresolution) he had no strong convictions. Associating all his life with southern leaders in Washington, this Pennsylvanian leaned toward their views, but he never disclosed a deep adherence to any principle. Like other weak men, he could be stubborn; still oftener, he could show a petulant irascibility when events pushed him into a corner. And like other timid men, he would sometimes flare out in a sudden burst of anger, directed not against enemies who could hurt him but against friends or neutrals who would not. As the sectional crisis deepened, it became his dominant hope to stumble through it, somehow, and anyhow, so as to leave office with the Union yet intact. His successor could bear the storm.

This was the President who had to deal, in Kansas and Washington, with men of fierce conviction, stern courage and, all too often, ruthless methods.

In Kansas the proslavery leaders were determined to strike boldly and unscrupulously for a slave state. They maintained close communications with such southern chieftains in Washington as Senator Slidell, Speaker James L. Orr, and Howell Cobb and Jacob Thompson, Buchanan's secretaries of the Treasury and the Interior. Having gained control of the territorial legislature, they meant to keep and use this mastery. Just before Buchanan became President they passed a bill for a constitutional convention—and a more unfair measure was never put on paper. Nearly all county officers, selected not by popular vote but by the dishonestly chosen legislature, were proslavery men. The bill provided that the sheriffs and their deputies should in March, 1857, register the white residents; that the probate judges should then take from the sheriffs complete lists of qualified voters; and that the county commissioners should finally choose election judges.

Everyone knew that a heavy majority of the Kansas settlers were antislavery. Many, even of the southerners, who had migrated thither opposed the "peculiar institution" as retrogressive and crippling in character. Everybody also knew that Kansas, with hardly thirty thousand people, burdened with debts, and unsupplied with fit roads, schools, or courthouses, was not yet ready for statehood; it still needed the federal government's care. Most Kansans refused to recognize the "bogus" legislature. Yet this legislature was forcing a premature convention, and taking steps to see that the election of delegates was controlled by sheriffs, judges, and county commissioners who were mainly proslavery Democrats. Governor John W. Geary, himself a Democrat appointed by Pierce, indignantly vetoed the bill. But the legislature immediately repassed it over Geary's veto; and when threats against his life increased until citizens laid bets that he would be assassinated within forty days, he resigned in alarm and posted east to apprise the country of imminent perils.

Along the way to Washington, Geary paused to warn the press that a packed convention was about to drag fettered Kansas before Congress with a slavery constitution. This convention would have a free hand, for the bill just passed made no provision for a popular vote on the instrument. Indeed, one legislator admitted that the plan was to avoid popular submission, for he proposed inserting a clause to guard against the possibility that Congress might return the constitution for a referendum. Thus, commented the *Missouri Democrat*, "the felon legislature has provided as effectually for getting the desired result as Louis Napoleon did for getting himself elected Emperor." All this was an ironic commentary on Douglas' maxim: "Let the voice of the people rule."

And Douglas, watching the reckless course of the Kansas legislators with alarms, saw that his principles and his political future were at stake. When his Kansas-Nebraska Act was passed, he had given the North his solemn promise that a free, full, and fair election would decide the future of the two territories. No fraud, no sharp practice, no browbeating would be sanctioned; every male white citizen should have use of the ballot box. He had notified the South that Kansas was almost certain to be free soil. Now he professed confidence that President Buchanan would never permit a breach of fair procedure. He joined Buchanan in persuading one of the nation's ablest men, former Secretary of the Treasury Robert J. Walker, to go out to Kansas in Geary's place as governor. Douglas knew that if he consented to a betrayal of popular sovereignty he would be ruined forever politically in his own state of Illinois.

For a brief space in the spring of 1857 Buchanan seemed to stand firm. In his instructions to Governor Walker he engaged that the new constitution would be laid before the people; and "they must be protected in the exercise of their right of voting for or against that instrument, and the fair expression of the popular will must not be interrupted by fraud or violence."

It is not strange that the rash proslavery gamesters in Kansas prosecuted their designs despite all Buchanan's fair words and Walker's desperate efforts to stay them. They knew that with four fifths of the people already against them, and the odds growing greater every year, only brazen trickery could effect their end. They were aware that the South, which believed that a fair division would give Kansas to slavery and Nebraska to freedom, expected them to stand firm. They were egged on by the two reckless southern Cabinet members, Howell Cobb and Thompson, who sent an agent, H. L. Martin of Mississippi, out to the Kansas convention. This gathering in Lecompton, with 48 of the 60 members hailing from slave states, was the shabbiest conclave of its kind ever held on American soil. One of Buchanan's Kansas correspondents wrote that he had not supposed such a wild set could be found. The *Kansas News* termed them a body of "broken-down political hacks, demagogues, fire-eaters, perjurers, ruffians, ballot-box stuffers, and loafers." But before it broke up with the shout, "Now, boys, let's come and take a drink!" it had written a constitution.

This constitution, the work of a totally unrepresentative body, was a devious repudiation of all the principles Buchanan and Douglas had laid down. Although it contained numerous controversial provisions, such as limitation of banking to one institution and a bar against free Negroes, the main document was not to be submitted to general vote at all. A nominal reference of the great cardinal question was indeed provided. Voters might cast their ballots for the "constitution with slavery" or the "constitution without slavery." But when closely examined this was seen to be actually a piece of chicanery. Whichever form was adopted, the 200 slaves in Kansas would remain, with a constitutional guarantee against interference. Whenever the proslavery party in Kansas could get control of the legislature, they might open the door wide for more slaves. The rigged convention had put its handiwork before the people with a rigged choice: "Heads I win, tails you lose."

Would Buchanan lay this impudent contrivance before Congress, and ask it to vote the admission of Kansas as a state? Or would he contemptuously spurn it? An intrepid man would not have hesitated an instant to take the honest course; he would not have needed the indignant outcry of the northern press, the outraged roar of Douglas, to inspirit him. But Buchanan quailed before the storm of passion into which proslavery extremists had worked themselves.

The hot blood of the South was now up. That section, grossly misinformed upon events in Kansas, believed that *it* was being cheated. The northern free-soilers had vowed that no new slave state (save by a partition of Texas) should ever be admitted. Southerners thought that in pursuance of this resolve, the Yankees had made unscrupulous use of their wealth and numbers to lay hands on Kansas. Did the North think itself entitled to every piece on the board—to take Kansas as well as California, Minnesota, Iowa, Nebraska, Oregon—to give southerners nothing? The Lecompton delegates, from this point of view, were dauntless champions of a wronged section. What if they did use sharp tactics? That was but a necessary response to northern arrogance. Jefferson Davis declared that his section trembled under a sense of insecurity. "You have made it a political war. We are on the defensive. How far are you to push us?" Sharp threats of secession and battle mingled with the southern denunciations. "Sir," Senator Alfred Iverson of Georgia was soon to assert, "I believe that the time will come when the slave States will be compelled, in vindication of their rights, interests, and honor, to separate from the free States, and erect an independent confederacy; and I am not sure, sir, that the time is not at hand.''

Three southern members of the Cabinet, Cobb, Thompson, and John B. Floyd, had taken the measure of Buchanan's pusillanimity. They, with one northern sympathizer, Jeremiah Black, and several White House habitués like John Slidell of Louisiana, constituted a virtual Directory exercising control over the tremulous President. They played on Buchanan's fierce partisan hatred of Republicans, and his jealous dislike of Douglas. They played also on his legalistic cast of mind; after all, the Lecompton constitution was a legal instrument by a legal convention—outwardly. Above all, they played on his fears, his morbid sensitiveness, and his responsiveness to immediate pressures. They could do this the more easily because the threats of disruption and violence were real. Henry S. Foote, a former senator from Mississippi and an enemy of Jefferson Davis, who saw Lecompton in its true light and hurried to Washington to advise the President, writes:

"It was unfortunately of no avail that these efforts to reassure Mr. Buchanan were at that time essayed by myself and others; he had already become thoroughly *panic-stricken;* the howlings of the bulldog of secession had fairly frightened him out of his wits, and he ingloriously resolved to yield without further resistance to the decrial and villification to which he had been so acrimoniously subjected.''

And the well-informed Washington correspondent of the New Orleans *Picayune* a little later told just how aggressively the Chief Executive was bludgeoned into submission:

"The President was informed in November, 1857, that the States of Alabama, Mississippi, and South Carolina, and perhaps others, would hold conventions and secede from the Union if the Lecompton Constitution, which established slavery, should not be accepted by Congress. The reason was that these States, supposing that the South had been cheated out of Kansas, were, whether right or wrong, determined to revolt. The President believed this. Senator Hunter, of Virginia, to my knowledge, believed it. Many other eminent men did, and perhaps not without reason.''

Buchanan, without imagination as without nerve, began to yield to this southern storm in midsummer, and by November, 1857, he was surrendering completely. When Congress met in December his message upheld the Lecompton Constitution with a tissue of false and evasive statements. Seldom in American history has a chief magistrate made a greater error, or missed a larger opportunity. The astute secretary for his predecessor, Franklin Pierce, wrote: "I had considerable hopes of Mr. Buchanan—I really thought he was a statesman—but I have now come to the settled conclusion that he is just the damndest old fool that has ever occupied the presidential chair. He has deliberately walked overboard with his eyes open—let him drown, for he must.''

As Buchanan shrank from the lists, Douglas entered them with that *gaudium certaminis* which was one of his greatest qualities. The finest chapters of his life, his last great contests for the Union, were opening. Obviously he would have had to act under political necessity even if deaf to principle, for had he let popular sovereignty be torn to pieces, Illinois would not have sent him back to the Senate the following year; but he was not the man to turn his back on principle. His struggle against Lecompton was an exhibition of iron determination. The drama of that battle has given it an almost unique place in the record or our party controversies.

"By God, sir!" he exclaimed, "I made James Buchanan, and by God, sir, I will unmake him!" Friends told him that the southern Democrats meant to ruin him. "I have taken a through ticket," rejoined Douglas, "and checked my baggage." He lost no time in facing Buchanan in the White House and denouncing the Lecompton policy. When the President reminded him how Jackson had crushed two party rebels, he was ready with a stringing retort. Douglas was not to be overawed by a man he despised as a weakling. "Mr. President," he snorted, "I wish you to remember that General Jackson is dead."

As for the southern leaders, Douglas' scorn for the extremists who had coerced Buchanan was unbounded. He told the Washington correspondent of the Chicago *Journal* that he had begun his fight as a contest against a single bad measure. But his blow at Lecompton was a blow against slavery extension, and he at once had the whole "slave power" down on him like a pack of wolves. He added: "in making the fight against this power, I was enabled to stand off and view the men with whom I had been acting; I was ashamed I had ever been caught in such company; they are a set of unprincipled demagogues, bent upon perpetuating slavery, and by the exercise of that unequal and unfair power, to control the government or break up the Union; and I intend to prevent their doing either."

After a along, close, and acrid contest, on April 1, 1858, Lecompton was defeated. A coalition of Republicans, Douglasite Democrats, and Know-Nothings struck down the fraudulent constitution in the House, 120 to 112. When the vote was announced, a wild cheer rolled through the galleries. Old Francis P. Blair, Jackson's friend, carried the news to the dying Thomas Hart Benton, who had been intensely aroused by the crisis. Benton could barely speak, but his exultation was unbounded. "In energetic whispers," records Blair, "he told his visitor that the same men who had sought to destroy the republic in 1850 were at the bottom of this accursed Lecompton business. Among the greatest of his consolations in dying was the consciousness that the House of Representatives had baffled these treasonable schemes and put the heels of the people on the neck of the traitors."

The Administration covered its retreat by a hastily concocted measure, the English Bill, under which Kansas was kept waiting on the doorstep—sure in the end to enter a free state. The Kansas plotters, the Cobb-Thompson-Floyd clique in the Cabinet, and Buchanan had all been worsted. But the damage had been done. Southern secessionists had gained fresh strength and greater boldness from their success in coercing the Administration.

The Lecompton struggle left a varied and interesting set of aftereffects. It lifted Stephen A. Douglas to a new plane; he had been a fighting Democratic strategist, but now he became a true national leader, thinking far less of party and more of country. It sharpened the issues which that summer and fall were to form the staple of the memorable Lincoln-Douglas debates in Illinois. At the same time, it deepened the schism which had been growing for some years between southern Democrats and northwestern Democrats, and helped pave the way to that disruption of the party which preceded and facilitated the disruption of the nation. It planted new seeds of dissension in Kansas—seeds which resulted in fresh conflicts between Kansas free-soilers or jayhawkers on one side and Missouri invaders or border ruffians on the other, and in a spirit of border lawlessness which was to give the Civil War some of its darkest pages. The Lecompton battle discredited Buchanan in the eyes of most decent northerners, strengthened southern conviction of his weakness, and left the Administration materially and morally weaker in dealing with the problems of the next two and a half critical years.

For the full measure of Buchanan's failure, however, we must go deeper. Had he shown the courage that to an Adams, a Jackson, a Polk, or a Cleveland would have been second nature, the courage that springs from a deep integrity, he might have done the republic an immeasurable service by grappling with disunion when it was yet weak and unprepared. Ex-Senator Foote wrote later that he knew well that a scheme for destroying the union "had long been on foot in the South." He knew that its leaders "were only waiting for the enfeebling of the Democratic Party in the North, and the general triumph of Free-soilism as a consequence thereof, to alarm the whole South into acquiescence in their policy." Buchanan's support of the unwise and corrupt Lecompton constitution that played into the plotters' hands.

The same view was taken yet more emphatically by Douglas. He had inside information in 1857, he later told the Senate, that four states were threatening Buchanan with secession. Had that threat been met in the right Jacksonian spirit, had the bluff been called—for the four states were unprepared for secession and war— the leaders of the movement would have been utterly discredited. Their conspiracy would have collapsed, and they would have been so routed and humiliated in 1857 that the Democratic party schism in 1860 might never have taken place, and if it had, secession in 1861 would have been impossible.

The roots of the Civil War of course go deep; they go back beyond Douglas' impetuous Kansas-Nebraska Bill, back beyond the Mexican War, back beyond the Missouri compromise. But the last good chance of averting secession and civil strife was perhaps lost in 1857. Even Zachary Taylor in 1850 had made it plain before his sudden death that he would use force, if necessary, to crush the secessionists tendencies which that year became so dangerous. A similar display of principle and resolution seven years later might well have left the disunionist chieftains of the Deep South so weakened in prestige that Yancey and his fellow plotters would have been helpless. The lessons of this failure in statesmanship, so plain to Douglas, ought not to be forgotten. The greatest mistake a nation can make is to put at its helm a man so pliable and unprincipled that he will palter with a clean-cut and momentous issue.

Allan Nevins, professor of history at Columbia University, is serving as general editor of the AMERICAN HERITAGE series on ''Times of Trial in American Statecraft,'' of which his own article in No. 4.

Hayfoot, Strawfoot!

Bruce Catton

The volunteer soldier in the American Civil War used a clumsy muzzle-loading rifle, lived chiefly on salt pork and hardtack, and retained to the very end a loose-jointed, informal attitude toward the army with which he had cast his lot. But despite all of the surface differences, he was at bottom blood brother to the G.I. Joe of modern days.

Which is to say that he was basically, and incurably, a civilian in arms. A volunteer, he was still a soldier because he had to be one, and he lived for the day when he could leave the army forever. His attitude toward discipline, toward his officers, and toward the whole spit-and-polish concept of military existence was essentially one of careless tolerance. He refused to hate his enemies—indeed, he often got along with them much better than with some of his own comrades—and his indoctrination was often so imperfect that what was sometimes despairingly said of the American soldier in World War II would apply equally to him: he seemed to be fighting chiefly so that he could some day get back to Mom's cooking.

What really set the Civil War soldier apart was the fact that he came from a less sophisticated society. He was no starry-eyed innocent, to be sure—or, if he was, the army quickly took care of that—but the America of the 1860's was less highly developed than modern America. It lacked the ineffable advantages of radio, television, and moving pictures. It was still essentially a rural nation; it had growing cities, but they were smaller and somehow less urban than today's cities; a much greater percentage of the population lived on farms or in country towns and villages than is the case now, and there was more of a backwoods, hay-seed-in-the-hair flavor to the people who came from them.

For example: every war finds some ardent youngsters who want to enlist despite the fact that they are under the military age limit of eighteen. Such a lad today simply goes to the recruiting station, swears that he is eighteen, and signs up. The lad of the 1860's saw it a little differently. He could not swear that he was eighteen when he was only sixteen; in his innocent way, he felt that to lie to his own government was just plain wrong. But he worked out a little dodge that got him into the army anyway. He would take a bit of paper, scribble the number *18* on it, and put it in the sole of his shoe. Then, when the recruiting officer asked him how old he was, he could truthfully say: "I am *over* eighteen." That was a common happening, early in the Civil War; one cannot possibly imagine it being tried today.

Similarly, the drill sergeants repeatedly found that among the raw recruits there were men so abysmally untaught that they did not know left from right, and hence could not step off on the left foot as all soldiers should. To teach these lads how to march, the sergeants would tie a wisp of hay to the left foot and a wisp of straw to the right; then, setting the men to march, they would chant, "Hay-foot, straw-foot, hay-foot, straw-foot"—and so on, until everybody had caught on. A common name for a green recruit in those days was "strawfoot."

On the drill field, when a squad was getting basic training, the men were as likely as not to intone a little rhythmic chant as they tramped across the sod—thus:

> *March! March! March old soldier march!*
> *Hayfoot, strawfoot,*
> *Belly-full of bean soup—*
> *March old soldier march!*

Because of his unsophistication, the ordinary soldier in the Civil War, North and South alike, usually joined up with very romantic ideas about soldiering. Army life rubbed the romance off just as rapidly then as it does now, but at the start every volunteer went into the army thinking that he was heading off to high adventure. Under everything else, he enlisted because he thought army life was going to be fun, and usually it took quite a few weeks in camp to disabuse him of this strange notion. Right at the start, soldiering had an almost idyllic quality; if this quality faded rapidly, the memory of it remained through all the rest of life.

Early days in camp simply cemented the idea. An Illinois recruit, writing home from training camp, confessed: "It is fun to lie around, face unwashed, hair uncombed, shirt unbuttoned and everything un-everythinged. It sure beats clerking." Another Illinois boy confessed: "I don't see why people will stay at home when they can get to soldiering. A year of it is worth getting shot for to any man." And a Massachusetts boy, recalling the early days of army life, wrote that "Our drill, as I remember it, consisted largely of running around the Old Westbury town hall, yelling like Devils and firing at an imaginary foe." One of the commonest discoveries that comes from a reading of Civil War diaries is that the chief worry, in training camp, was a fear that the war would be over before the ardent young recruits could get into it. It is only fair to say that most of the diaries looked back on this innocent worry, a year or so afterward, with rueful amusement.

There was a regiment recruited in northern Pennsylvania in 1861—13th Pennsylvania Reserves officially, known to the rest of the Union Army as the Bucktails because the rookies decorated their caps with strips of fur from the carcass of a deer that was hanging in front of a butcher shop near their camp—and in mid-spring these youthful soldiers were ordered to rendezvous at Harrisburg. So they marched crosscountry (along a road known today as the Bucktail Trail) to the north branch of the Susquehanna, where they built rafts. One raft, for the colonel, was made oversized with a stable; the colonel's horse had to ride, too. Then the Bucktails floated down the river, singing and firing their muskets and having a gay old time, camping out along the bank at night, and finally they got to Harrisburg; and they served through the worst of the war, getting badly shot up and losing most of their men to Confederate bullets, but they never forgot the picnic air of those first days of army life, when they drifted down a river through the forests, with a song in the air and the bright light of adventure shining just ahead. Men do not go to war that way nowadays.

Discipline in those early regiments was pretty sketchy. The big catch was that most regiments were recruited locally—in one town, or one county, or in one part of a city—and everybody more or less knew everybody else. Particulary, the privates knew their officers—most of whom were elected to their jobs by the enlisted men—and they never saw any sense in being formal with them. Within reasonable limits, the Civil War private was willing to do what his company commander told him to do, but he saw little point in carrying it to extremes.

So an Indiana soldier wrote: "We had enlisted to put down the Rebellion, and had no patience with the red-tape tomfoolery of the regular service. The boys recognized no superiors, except in the line of legitimate duty. Shoulder straps waived, a private was ready at the drop of a hat to thrash his commander—a thing that occurred more than once." A New York regiment, drilling on a hot parade ground, heard a private address his company commander thus: "Say, Tom, let's quit this darn foolin' around and go over to the sutler's and get a drink." There was very little of the "Captain, sir" business in those armies. If a company or regimental officer got anything especial in the way of obedience, he got it because the enlisted men recognize him as a natural leader and superior and not just because he had a commission signed by Abraham Lincoln.

Odd rivalries developed between regiments. (It should be noted that the Civil War soldiers' first loyalty went usually to his regiment, just as a navy man's loyalty goes to his ship; he liked to believe that his regiment was better than all others, and he would fight for it, any time and anywhere.) The army legends of those days tell of a Manhattan regiment, camped near Washington, whose nearest neighbor was a regiment from Brooklyn, with which the Manhattanites nursed a deep rivalry. Neither regiment had a chaplain; and there came to the Manhattan colonel one day a minister, who volunteered to hold religious services for the men in the ranks.

The colonel doubted that this would be a good idea. His men, he said, were rather irreligious, not to say godless, and he feared they would not give the reverend gentleman a respectful hearing. But the minister said he would take his chances; after all, he had just held services with the Brooklyn regiment, and the men there had been very quiet and devout. That was enough for the colonel. What the Brooklyn regiment could do, his regiment could do. He ordered the men paraded for divine worship, announcing that any man who talked, laughed, or even coughed would be summarily court-martialed.

So the clergyman held services, and everyone was attentive. At the end of the sermon, the minister asked if any of his hearers would care to step forward and make public profession of faith; in the Brooklyn regiment, he said, fourteen men had done this. Instantly the New York colonel was on his feet.

"Adjutant!" he bellowed. "We're not going to let that damn Brooklyn regiment beat us at anything. Detail twenty men and have them baptized at once!"

Each regiment seemed to have its own mythology, tales which may have been false but which, by their mere existence, reflected faithfully certain aspects of army life. The 48th New York, for instance, was said to have an unusually large number of ministers in its ranks, serving not as chaplains but as combat soldiers. The 48th, fairly early in the war, found itself posted in a swamp along the South Carolina coast, toiling mightily in semitropical heat, amid clouds of mosquitoes, to build fortifications, and it was noted that all hands became excessively profane, including the one-time clergymen. A visiting general, watching the regiment at work one day, recalled the legend and asked the regiment's lieutenant colonel if he himself was a minister in private life.

"Well, no, General," said the officer apologetically. 'I can't say that I was a regularly ordained minister. I was just one of these ______ ______ local preachers."

Another story was hung on this same 48th New York. A Confederate ironclad gunboat was supposed to be ready to steam through channels in the swamp and attack the 48th's outposts, and elaborate plans were made to trap it with obstructions in the channel, a tangle of ropes to snarl the propellers, and so on. But it occurred to the colonel that even if the gunboat was trapped the soldiers could not get into it; it was sheathed in iron, all its ports would be closed, and men with axes could never chop their way into it. Then the colonel had an inspiration. Remembering that many of his men had been recruited from the less savory districts of New York City, he paraded the regiment and (according to legend) announced:

"Now men, you've been in this cursed swamp for two weeks—up to your ears in mud, no fun, no glory and blessed poor pay. Here's a chance. Let every man who has had experience as a cracksman or a safeblower step to the front." To the last man, the regiment marched forward four paces and came expectantly to attention.

Not unlike this was the reputation of the 6th New York, which contained so many Bowery toughs that the rest of the army said a man had to be able to show that he had done time in prison in order to get into the regiment. It was about to leave for the South, and the colonel gave his men an inspirational talk. They were going, he said, to a land of wealthy plantation owners, where each Southerner had riches of which he could be despoiled; and he took out his own gold watch and held it up for all to see, remarking that any deserving soldier could easily get one like it, once they got down to plantation-land. Half an hour later, wishing to see what time it was, he felt for his watch . . . and it was gone.

If the Civil War army spun queer tales about itself, it had to face a reality which, in all of its aspects, was singularly unpleasant. One of the worst aspects had to do with food.

From first to last, the Civil War armies enlisted no men as cooks, and there were no cooks' and bakers' schools to help matters. Often enough, when in camp, a company would simply be issued a quantity of provisions—flour, pork, beans, potatoes, and so on—and invited to prepare the stuff as best it could. Half a dozen men would form a mess, members would take turns with the cooking, and everybody had to eat what these amateurs prepared or go hungry. Later in the war, each company commander would usually detail two men to act as cooks for the company, and if either of the two happened to know anything about cooking the company was in luck. One army legend held that company officers usually detailed the least valuable soldiers to this job, on the theory that they would do less harm in the cook shack than anywhere else. One soldier, writing after the war, asserted flatly: "A company cook is a most peculiar being: he generally knows less about cooking than any other man in the company. Not being able to learn the drill, and too dirty to appear on inspection, he is sent to the cook house to get him out of the ranks."

When an army was on the march, the ration issue usually consisted of salt pork, hardtack, and coffee, (In the Confederate Army the coffee was often missing, and the hardtack was frequently replaced by corn bread; often enough the meal was not sifted, and stray bits of cob would appear in it.) The hardtack was good enough, if fresh, which was not always the case; with age it usually got infested with weevils, and veterans remarked that it was better to eat it in the dark.

In the Union Army, most of the time, the soldier could supplement his rations (if he had money) by buying extras from the sutler—the latter being a civilian merchant licensed to accompany the army, functioning somewhat as the regular post exchange functions nowadays. The sutler charged high prices and specialized in indigestibles like pies, canned lobster salad, and so on; and it was noted that men who patronized him regularly came down with stomach upsets. The Confederate Army had few sutlers, which helps to explain why the hungry Confederates were so delighted when they could capture a Yankee camp: to seize a sutler's tent meant high living for the captors, and the men in Lee's army were furious when, in the 1864 campaign, they learned that General Grant had ordered the Union Army to move without sutlers. Johnny Reb felt that Grant was really taking an unfair advantage by cutting off this possible source of supply.

If Civil War cooking arrangements were impromptu and imperfect, the same applied to its hospital system. The surgeons, usually, were good men by the standards of that day—which were low since no one on earth knew anything about germs or about how wounds became infected, and antisepsis in the operating room was a concept that had not yet come into existence; it is common to read of a surgeon whetting his scalpel on the sole of his shoe just before operating. But the hospital attendants, stretcher-bearers, and the like were chosen just as the company cooks were chosen; that is, they were detailed from the ranks, and the average officer selected the most worthless men he had simply because he wanted to get rid of men who could not be counted on in combat. As a result, sick or wounded men often got atrocious care.

A result of all of this—coupled with the fact that many men enlisted without being given any medical examinations—was that every Civil War regiment suffered a constant wastage from sickness. On paper, a regiment was supposed to have a strength ranging between 960 and 1,040 men; actually, no regiment ever got to the battlefield with anything like that strength, and since there was no established system for sending in replacements a veteran regiment that could muster 350 enlisted men present for duty was considered pretty solid. From first to last, approximately twice as many Civil War soldiers died of disease—typhoid, dysentery, and pneumonia were the great killers—as died in action; and in addition to those who died a great many more got medical discharges.

In its wisdom, the Northern government set up a number of base hospitals in Northern states, far from the battle fronts, on the theory that a man recovering from wounds or sickness would recuperate better back home. Unfortunately, the hospitals thus established were under local control, and the men in them were no longer under the orders of their own regiments or armies. As a result, thousands of men who were sent north for convalescence never returned to the army. Many were detailed for light work at the hospitals, and in these details they stayed because nobody had the authority to extract them and send them back to duty. Others, recovering their health, simply went home and stayed there. They were answerable to the hospital authorities, not to the army command, and the hospital authorities rarely cared very much whether they returned to duty or not. The whole system was ideally designed to make desertion easy.

On top of all of this, many men had very little understanding of the requirements of military discipline. A homesick boy often saw nothing wrong in leaving the army and going home to see the folks for a time. A man from a farm might slip off to go home and put in a crop. In neither case would the man look on himself as a deserter; he meant to return, he figured he would get back in time for any fighting that would take place, and in his own mind he was innocent of any wrongdoing. But in many cases the date of return would be postponed from week to week; the man might end as a deserter, even though he had not intended to be one when he left.

This merely reflected the loose discipline that prevailed in Civil War armies, which in turn reflected the underlying civilian-mindedness tha pervaded the rank and file. The behaving of Northern armies on the march in Southern territory reflected the same thing—and, in the end, had a profound effect on the institution of chattel slavery.

Armies of occupation always tend to bear down hard on civilian property in enemy territory. Union armies in the Civil War, being imperfectly disciplined to begin with—and suffering, furthermore, from a highly defective rationing system—bore down with especial fervor. Chickens, hams, cornfields, anything edible that might be found on a Southern plantation, looked life fair game, and the loose finger of stragglers that always trailed around the edges of a moving Union army looted with a fine disregard for civilian property rights.

This was made all the more pointed by the fact that the average Northern soldier, poorly indoctrinated though he was, had strong feelings about the evils of secession. To his mind, the Southerners who sought to set up a nation of their own were in rebellion against the best government mankind had ever known. Being rebels, they had forfeited their rights; if evil things happened to them, that (as the average Northern soldier saw it) was no more than just retribution. This meant that even when the army command tried earnestly to prevent looting and individual foraging, the officers at company and regimental levels seldom tried very hard to carry out the high command's orders.

William Tecumseh Sherman has come down in history as the very archetype of the Northern soldier who believed in pillage and looting; yet during the first years of the war Sherman resorted to all manner of ferocious punishments to keep his men from despoiling Southern property. He had looters tied up by the thumbs, ordered courts-martial, issued any number of stern orders—and all to very little effect. Long before he adopted the practice of commandeering or destroying Southern property as a war measure, his soldiers were practicing it against his will, partly because discipline was poor and partly because they saw nothing wrong with it.

It was common for a Union colonel, as his regiment made camp in a Southern state, to address his men, pointing to a nearby farm, and say: "now, boys, that barn is full of nice fat pigs and chickens. I don't want to see any of you take any of them"—whereupon he would fold his arms and look sternly in the opposite direction. It was also common for a regimental commander to read, on parade, some ukase from higher authority forbidding foraging, and then to wink solemnly—a clear hint that he did not expect anyone to take the order seriously. One colonel, punishing some men who had robbed a chicken house, said angrily: "Boys, I want you to understand that I am not punishing you for stealing but for getting caught at it."

It is nearly a century since that war was fought, and things look a little different now than they looked at the time. At this distance, it may be possible to look indulgently on the wholesale foraging in which Union armies indulged; to the Southern farmers who bore the brunt of it, the business looked very ugly indeed. Many a Southern family saw the foodstuffs needed for the winter swept away in an hour by grinning hoodlums who did not need and could not use a quarter or what they took. Among the foragers there were many lawless characters who took watches, jewels, and any other valuables they could find; it is recorded that a squad would now and then carry a piano out to the lawn, take it apart, and use the wires to hang pots and pans over the campfire. . . . The Civil War was really romantic only at a considerable distance.

Underneath his feeling that it was good to add chickens and hams to the army ration, and his belief that civilians in a state of secession could expect no better fate, the Union soldier also came to believe that to destroy Southern property was to help win the war. Under orders, he tore up railroads and burned warehouses; it was not long before he realized that anything that damaged the Confederate economy weakened the Confederate war effort, so he rationalized his looting and foraging by arguing that it was a step in breaking the Southern will to resist. It is at this point tha the institution of human slavery enters the picture.

Most Northern soldiers had very little feeling against slavery as such, and very little sympathy for the Negro himself. They thought they were fighting to save the Union, not to end slavery, and except for New England troops most Union regiments contained very little abolition sentiment. Nevertheless, the soldiers moved energetically and effectively to destroy slavery, not because they especially intended to but simply because they were out to do all the damage they could do. They were operating against Southern property—and the most obvious, important, and easily removable property of all was the slave. To help the slaves get away from the plantation was, clearly, to weaken Southern productive capacity, which in turn weakened Confederate armies. Hence the Union soldier, wherever he went, took the peculiar institution apart, chattel by chattel.

As a result, slavery had been fatally weakened long before the war itself came to an end. The mere act of fighting the war killed it. Of all institutions on earth, the institution of human slavery was the one least adapted to survive a war. It could not survive the presence of loose-jointed, heavy-handed armies of occupation. It may hardly be too much to say that the mere act of taking up arms in slavery's defense doomed slavery.

Above and beyond everything else, of course, the business of the Civil War soldier was to fight. He fought with weapons that look very crude to modern eyes, and he moved by an outmoded system of tactics, but the price he paid when he got into action was just as high as the price modern soldiers pay despite the almost infinite development of firepower since the 1860's.

Standard infantry weapon in the Civil War was the rifled Springfield—a muzzle-loader firing a conical lead bullet, usually of .54 caliber.

To load was rather laborious, and it took a good man to get off more than two shots a minute. The weapon had a range of nearly a mile, and its "effective range"— that is, the range at which it would hit often enough to make infantry fire truly effective—was figured at about 250 yards. Compared with a modern Garand, the old muzzle-loader is no better than a museum piece; but compared with all previous weapons—the weapons on which infantry tactics in the 1860's were still based—it was a fearfully destructive and efficient piece.

For the infantry of that day still moved and fought in formations dictated in the old days of smoothbore muskets, whose effective range was no more than 100 yards and which were wildly inaccurate at any distance. Armies using those weapons attacked in solid mass formations, the men standing, literally, elbow to elbow. They could get from effective range to hand-to-hand fighting in a very short time, and if they had a proper numerical advantage over the defensive line they could come to grips without losing too many men along the way. But in the Civil War the conditions had changed radically; men would be hit while the rival lines were still half a mile apart, and to advance in mass was simply to invite wholesale destruction. Tactics had not yet been adjusted to the new rifles; as a result, Civil War attacks could be fearfully costly, and when the defenders dug entrenchments and got some protection—as the men learned to do, very quickly—a direct frontal assault could be little better than a form of mass suicide.

It took the high command a long time to revise tactics to meet this changed situation, and Civil War battles ran up dreadful casualty lists. For an army to lose 25 per cent of its numbers in a major battle was by no means uncommon, and in some fights— the Confederate army at Gettysburg is an outstanding example—the percentage of loss ran close to one-third of the total number engaged. Individual units were sometimes nearly wiped out. Some of the Union and Confederate regiments that fought at Gettysburg lost up to 80 per cent of their numbers: a regiment with such losses was usually wrecked, as an effective fighting force, for the rest of the war.

The point of all of which is that the discipline which took the Civil War soldier into action, while it may have been very sketchy by modern standards, was nevertheless highly effective on the field of battle. Any armies that could go through such battles as Antietam, Stone's River, Franklin or Chickamauga and come back for more had very little to learn about the business of fighting.

Perhaps the Confederate General D. H. Hill said it, once and for all. The battle of Malvern Hill, fought on the Virginia peninsula early in the summer of 1862, finished the famous Seven Days campaign, in which George B. McClellan's Army of the Potomac was driven back from in front of Richmond by Robert E. Lee's Army of Northern Virginia. At Malvern Hill, McClellan's men fought a rear-guard action—a bitter, confused fight which came at the end of a solid week of wearing, costly battles and forced marches. Federal artillery wrecked the Confederate assault columns, and at the end of the day Hill looked out over the battlefield, strewn with dead and wounded boys. Shaking his head, and reflecting on the valor in attack and in defense which the two armies had displayed, Hill never forgot about this. Looking back on it, long after the war was over, he declared, in substance:

"Give me Confederate infantry and Yankee artillery and I'll whip the world!"

The Slaves Freed

Stephen B. Oates

When the cold, fastidious Mississippian rose to speak, a hush fell over the crowded Senate chamber. It was January 21, 1861, and Jefferson Davis and four other senators from the Deep South were here this day to announce their resignations. Over the winter, five Southern states had seceded from the Union, contending that Abraham Lincoln's election as President doomed the white man's South, that Lincoln and his fellow Republicans were abolitionist fanatics out to eradicate slavery and plunge Dixie into racial chaos. Though the Republicans had pledged to leave the peculiar institution alone where it already existed, Deep Southerners refused to believe them and left the Union to save their slave-based society from Republican aggression.

For his part, Jefferson Davis regretted that Mississippi had been obliged to secede, and he had spent a sleepless night, distressed about the breakup of the Union and fearful of the future. To be sure, he loved the idea of a Southern confederacy; and he had warned Republicans that if the South could not depart in peace, a war would begin, the likes of which man had never seen before. But today, as he gave his valedictory in the Senate, Davis was sad and forlorn, his voice quavering. He bore his Republican adversaries no hostility, he said, and wished them and their people well. He apologized if in the heat of debate he had offended anybody—and he forgave those who had insulted him. "Mr. President and Senators," he said with great difficulty, "having made the announcement which the occasion seemed to me to require, it only remains for me to bid you a final adieu."

Several senators were visibly moved, and there were audible sobs in the galleries. As Davis made his exit, with Southern ladies waving handkerchiefs and crying out in favor of secession, Republicans stared grimly after him, realizing perhaps for the first time that the South was in earnest, the Union was disintegrating.

As Lincoln's inauguration approached and more Southern congressmen resigned to join the Confederacy, Republicans gained control of both houses and voted to expel the secessionists as traitors. Senator Lyman Trumbull of Illinois pronounced them all mad, and Charles Sumner of Massachusetts exhorted the free states to stand firm in the crisis.

Michigan's Zachariah Chandler vowed to whip the South back into the Union and preserve the integrity of the government. And Ben Wade of Ohio predicted that secession would bring about the destruction of slavery, the very thing Southerners dreaded most. "The first blast of civil war," he had thundered at them, "is the death warrant of your institution."

After the events at Fort Sumter, Wade, Chandler, and Sumner called repeatedly at the White House and spoke with Lincoln about slavery and the rebellion. Sumner was a tall, elegant bachelor, with rich brown hair, a massive forehead, blue eyes, and a rather sad smile. He had traveled widely in England, where his friends included some of the most eminent political and literary figures. A humorless, erudite Bostonian, educated at Harvard, Sumner even looked English, with his tailored coats, checkered trousers, and English gaiters. He was so conscious of manners "that he never allowed himself, even in the privacy of his own chamber, to fall into a position which he would not take in his chair in the Senate. 'Habit,' he said, "is everything.' " Sumner spoke out with great courage against racial injustice and was one of the few Republicans who advocated complete Negro equality. Back in 1856 Representative Preston Brooks of South Carolina had beaten him almost to death in the Senate Chamber for his "Crime Against Kansas" speech, and Sumner still carried physical and psychological scars from that attack. The senator now served as Lincoln's chief foreign policy adviser, often accompanied him on his carriage rides, and became the President's warm personal friend.

Zachariah Chandler was a Detroit businessman who had amassed a fortune in real estate and dry goods. Profane, hard-drinking, and eternally grim, Chandler had been one of the founders of the national Republican Party and had served on the Republican National Committee in 1856 and 1860. Elected to the Senate in 1857, he had plunged into the acrimonious debates over slavery in the West, exhorting his colleagues not to surrender another inch of territory to slaveholders. When Southerners threatened to murder Republicans, brandishing pistols and bowie knives in the Senate itself, Chandler took up calisthenics and improved his marksmanship in case he had to fight. Once civil war commenced, he demanded that the government suppress the "armed traitors" of the South with all-out warfare.

Now serving his second term in the Senate, Benjamin Franklin Wade was short and thick chested, with iron-gray hair, sunken black eyes, and a square and beardless face. He was blunt and irascible, known as "Bluff Ben" for his readiness to duel with slaveowners, and he told more ribald jokes than any other man in the Senate, but he also had a charitable side: once when he spotted a destitute neighbor robbing his corncrib, Wade moved out of sight in order not to humiliate the man. Once the war began, he was determined that Congress should have equal voice with Lincoln in shaping Union war policies. According to diplomat Rudolf Schleiden, Wade was "perhaps the most energetic personality in the entire Congress." "That queer, rough, but intelligent-looking man," said one Washington observer, "is old Senator Wade of Ohio, who doesn't care a pinch of snuff whether people like what he says or not." Wade hated slavery as Sumner and Chandler did. But like most whites of his generation, he was prejudiced against blacks: he complained about their "odor," growled about all the "Nigger" cooks in Washington, and insisted that he had eaten food "cooked by Niggers until I can smell and taste the Nigger . . . all over." Like many Republicans, he thought the best solution to America's race problem was to ship all Negroes back to Africa.

As far as the Republican party was concerned, the three senators belonged to a loose faction inaccurately categorized as "radicals," a misnomer that has persisted through the years. These "more advanced Republicans," as the Detroit *Post* and *Tribune* referred to them, were really progressive, nineteenth-century liberals who felt a powerful kinship with English liberals like John Bright and Richard Cobden. What advanced Republicans wanted was to reform the American system—to bring their nation into line with the Declaration's premise—by ridding it of slavery and the South's ruling planter class. But while the advanced Republicans supported other social reforms, spoke out forthrightly against the crime and anachronism of slavery, and refused to compromise with the "Slave Power," they desired no radical break from basic American ideals and liberal institutions. Moreover, they were often at odds with one another on such issues as currency, the tariff, and precisely what rights black people should exercise in American white society.

Before secession, the advanced Republicans had endorsed the party's hands-off policy about slavery in the South: they all agreed that Congress had no constitutional authority to menace slavery as a state institution; all agreed, too, that the federal government could only abolish slavery in the national capital and outlaw it in the national territories, thus containing the institution in the South where they hoped it would ultimately perish. But civil war had removed their constitutional scruples about slavery in the Southern states, thereby bringing about the first significant difference between them and the more "moderate" and "conservative" members of the party. While the latter insisted that the Union must be restored with slavery intact, the advanced Republicans argued that the national government could now remove the peculiar institution by the war powers, and they wanted the President to do it in his capacity as Commander-in-Chief. This was what Sumner, Wade, and Chandler came to talk about with Lincoln. They respected the President, had applauded his nomination, campaigned indefatigably in his behalf, and cheered his firm stand at Fort Sumter. Now they urged him to destroy slavery as a war measure, pointing out that this would maim and cripple the Confederacy and hasten an end to the rebellion. Sumner flatly asserted that slavery and the rebellion were "mated" and would stand or fall together.

Lincoln seemed sympathetic. He detested human bondage as much as they did, and he wanted to stay on good terms with advanced Republicans on Capitol Hill, for he needed their support in prosecuting the war. Moreover, he respected the senators and referred to men like Sumner as the conscience of the party.

Yet to the senators' dismay, he would not free the slaves, could not free them. For one thing, he had no intention of alienating moderate and conservative Republicans—the majority of the party—by issuing an emancipation decree. For another, emancipation would almost surely send the loyal slave states—Delaware, Maryland, Kentucky, and Missouri—spiraling into the Confederacy, something that would be calamitous to the Union. Then, too, Lincoln was waging a bipartisan war with Northern Democrats and Republicans alike enlisting in his armies. An abolition policy, Lincoln feared, would splinter that coalition, perhaps even cause a new civil war behind Union lines.

Though deeply disappointed, the three senators at first acquiesced in Lincoln's policy because they wanted to maintain Republican unity in combating the rebellion. Sumner told himself that at bottom Lincoln was "a deeply convinced and faithful anti-slavery man" and that the sheer pressure of war would force him to strike at Negro bondage eventually.

On July 4, 1861, the Thirty-seventh Congress convened with a rebel army entrenched less than thirty miles away. Republicans controlled both houses, and the advanced Republicans quickly gained positions of leadership out of proportion to their numbers. Many had been in Congress for years, and their uncompromising stand against slavery expansion and concessions to secessionists had won them accolades from all manner of Republicans. Like Chandler, several advanced Republicans had helped establish the national party; all were prominent in their state parties. Their prestige, skill, and energy—Chandler, for example, routinely put in eighteen-hour workdays—had helped bring them to positions of power on Capitol Hill.

In the Senate, advanced Republicans chaired nearly all the crucial committees. Sumner ran the committee on foreign relations, Chandler the committee on commerce, and Wade the committee on territories. In addition, Lyman Trumbull of Illinois, a dry, logical speaker with sandy hair and gold-rimmed spectacles, headed the judiciary committee. Henry Wilson, Sumner's Massachusetts colleague, a stout, beardless, red-faced businessman who had once been a shoemaker's apprentice, held Jefferson Davis's old job as chairman of the committee on military affairs. William Pitt Fessenden of Maine, impeccably dressed in his black jackets and black silk ties, famous for his forensic duels with Stephen A. Douglas before the war, chaired the finance committee and cooperated closely with Salmon Chase, Lincoln's Secretary of the Treasury. Fessenden had been born out of wedlock—a terrible stigma in that time—and the awful, unspoken shame of his illegitimacy had made him proud and quick to take offense, intolerant of human failings in others as well as himself. He and Sumner had once been friends, had called one another "my dear Sumner" and "my dear Fessenden," and often entered the Senate arm in arm. But Fessenden had taken umbrage at what he thought were Sumner's haughty airs, and their friendship had changed to bristling animosity. Fessenden remained "old friends" with Wade and Chandler, though, and also hobnobbed with Jacob Collamer of Vermont, a Republican conservative.

Advanced Republicans were equally prominent in the House. There was James Ashley of Ohio, an emotional, dramatic man with a curly brown mane, who chaired the committee on territories. There was George Washington Julian from Indiana, protégé of Joshua "Old War Horse" Giddings and a contentious, frowning individual who proved himself a formidable antislavery legislator. There was portly, unkempt Owen Lovejoy of

Illinois, brother of Elijah, the abolitionist martyr; an eloquent antislavery orator, he headed the committee on agriculture. Like Sumner, Lovejoy was a close friend of Lincoln's—"the *best* friend I had in Congress," the President once remarked—and strove to sustain administration policies while simultaneously pushing the main cause of emancipation.

Finally there was sixty-nine-year-old Thaddeus Stevens of Pennsylvania, who controlled the nation's purse strings as chairman of the powerful committee on ways and means. Afflicted with a clubfoot, Stevens was a grim, sardonic bachelor with a cutting wit ("I now yield to Mr. B," he once said, "who will make a few feeble remarks") and a fondness for gambling that took him almost nightly to Washington's casinos. To the delight of his colleagues, he indulged in witticisms so off color that they had to be deleted from the *Congressional Globe*. A wealthy ironmaster with a Jekyll-and-Hyde personality, he had contributed generously to charities and causes, crusaded for public schools in Pennsylvania, and defended fugitive slaves there. Crippled, as Fawn Brodie has noted, Stevens spoke of bondage "in terms of shackled limbs and a longing for freedom to dance." He lived with his mulatto housekeeper, Lydia Smith, and there is strong evidence that they were lovers. Antimiscegenation laws made marriage impossible, and their liaison not only generated malicious gossip but probably kept Stevens from becoming what he most wanted to be—a United States senator. He liked to quote the Bible that "He hath made of one blood all nations of men," yet he never championed complete equality for blacks—"not equality in all things," he once asserted, "simply before the laws, nothing else." Serving a fourth term as congressman, this bitter, intimidating, high-minded man was to rule the Civil War House and become '"the master-spirit," said Alexander McClure, "of every aggressive movement in Congress to overthrow the rebellion and slavery."

As the session progressed that summer, congressional Republicans demonstrated remarkable harmony. They all wanted to preserve the Union and help the President fight the war through to a swift and successful conclusion. In agreement with Lincoln's slave policy, congressional Republicans also voted for the so-called Crittenden-Johnson resolutions, which declared that the sole purpose of the war was to restore the Union. For the sake of party unity, most advanced Republicans reluctantly supported the resolutions, too. But they agreed with Congressman Albert Riddle of Ohio that slavery ought to be destroyed. "You all believe that it is to go out, when it does, through convulsion, fire and blood," Riddle stormed on the House floor. "That convulsion is upon us. The man is a delirious ass who does not see it and realize this. For me, I mean to make a conquest of it; to beat it to extinction under the iron hoofs of our war horses."

For the advanced Republicans, the first chance to strike at slavery came late in July, after the Union rout at Bull Run. Observing that rebel forces used slaves to carry weapons and perform other military tasks, the advanced Republicans vigorously championed a confiscation bill, which authorized the seizure of any slave employed in the Confederate war effort, and they mustered almost unanimous Republican support in pushing the measure through Congress. Border-state Democrats like John J. Crittenden of Kentucky complained that the bill was unconstitutional, but most Republicans agreed with Henry Wilson that "if traitors use bondmen to destroy this country, my doctrine is that the Government shall at once convert those bondmen into men that cannot be used to destroy our country." In war, Republicans contended, the government had every right to confiscate enemy property—including slave property—as legitimate contraband. Though the bill was hardly a general emancipation act advanced Republicans hailed its passage as an important first step. They were glad indeed when Lincoln signed the bill into law and commanded his armies to enforce it. At last the President appeared to be coming around to their views.

But they had misunderstood him. When General John Charles Frémont, commander of the Western Department, ordered that the slaves of all rebels in Missouri be "declared freemen," Lincoln pronounced this a dangerous and unauthorized political act that would alienate the loyal border and commanded Frémont to modify his order so that it accorded strictly with the congressional confiscation act. Tough border Unionists applauded Lincoln, advanced Republicans were dismayed that he had overruled Frémont's emancipation decree. Sumner declared that Lincoln "is now a dictator." Wade charged that Lincoln's opinions on slavery "could only come of one, born of 'poor white trash' and educated in a slave State." And Fessenden denounced the President for his "weak and unjustifiable concession to the Union men of the border States."

Still, the Frémont episode did not cause an irreparable split between Lincoln and the advanced Republicans, as some writers have claimed. In fact, when Lincoln subsequently removed the general from command, Trumbull, Chandler, and Lovejoy sustained the President, conceding that the celebrated Pathfinder and first standardbearer of their party was a maladroit administrator. But in the fall and winter of 1861, advanced Republicans did mount an all-out campaign to make the obliteration of slavery a Union war objective. One after another they came to the White House—Wade, Chandler, and Trumbull, Sumner, Julian, and Lovejoy—and implored and badgered the President to issue an emancipation proclamation on military grounds. With the war dragging on, they insisted that slavery must be attacked in order to weaken the Confederate ability to fight.

Moreover, they argued, slavery had caused the conflict and was now the cornerstone of the Confederacy. It was absurd to fight a war without removing the thing that had brought it about. Should Lincoln restore the Union with slavery preserved, Southerners would just start another war whenever they thought the institution threatened, so that the present struggle would have been in vain. If Lincoln really wanted to salvage the Union, he must hurl his armies at the heart of the rebellion. He must tear slavery out root and branch and smash the South's arrogant planters—those mischievous men the advanced Republicans believed had masterminded secession and fomented war. The annihilation of slavery, Julian asserted, was "not a debatable and distant alternative, but a pressing and absolute necessity." So what if most of the country opposed emancipation lest it result in an exodus of Southern blacks into the

North? "It was the duty of the President," he said "to lead, not follow public opinion."

Sumner, as Lincoln's foreign policy adviser, also linked emancipation to opinion overseas. There was a strong possibility that Britain would recognize the Confederacy as an independent nation—potentially disastrous for the Union since the Confederacy could then form alliances and seek mediation, perhaps even armed intervention. But, Sumner argued, if Lincoln made the destruction of slavery a Union war aim, Britain would balk at recognition and intervention because of her own antislavery tradition. And whatever powerful Britain did, the rest of Europe was sure to follow.

Also, as Sumner kept saying, emancipation would break the chains of several million oppressed human beings and right America at last with her own ideals. Lincoln and the Republican party could no longer wait to remove slavery. The President must do it by the war powers. The rebellion, monstrous and terrible though it was, had given him the opportunity.

But Lincoln still did not agree. "I think Sumner and the rest of you would upset our applecart altogether if you had your way," he told some advanced Republicans one day. "We didn't go into the war to put down slavery, but to put the flag back; and to act differently at this moment would, I have no doubt, not only weaken our cause, but smack of bad faith. . . . this thunderbolt will keep." And in his message to Congress in December of 1861, the President declared that he did not want the war degenerating into "a violent and remorseless revolutionary struggle." He was striving, he said, "to keep the integrity of the Union prominent as the primary object of the contest."

Advanced Republicans were deeply aggrieved. Fessenden thought the President had lost all hold on Congress, and Wade complained that not even a galvanic battery could inspire Lincoln to "courage, decision and enterprise." "He means well," wrote Trumbull, "and in ordinary times would have made one of the best of Presidents, but he lacks confidence in himself and the *will* necessary in this great emergency."

By year's end, though, Lincoln's mind had begun to change. He spoke with Sumner about emancipation and assured the senator that "the only difference between you and me on this subject is a difference of a month or six weeks in time." And he now felt, he said, that the war "was a great movement by God to end Slavery and that the man would be a fool who should stand in the way." But out of deference to the loyal border states, Lincoln still shied away from a sweeping executive decree and searched about for an alternative. On March 6, 1862, he proposed a plan to Congress he thought would make federal emancipation unnecessary—a gradual, compensated abolition program to begin along the loyal border and then be extended into the rebel states as they were conquered. According to Lincoln's plan, the border states would gradually remove slavery over the next thirty years, and the national government would compensate slaveholders for their loss. The whole program was to be voluntary; the states would adopt their own emancipation laws without federal coercion. At the same time (as he had earlier told Congress), Lincoln favored a voluntary colonization program, to be sponsored by the federal government, that would resettle liberated blacks outside the country.

On Capitol Hill Stevens derided Lincoln's scheme as "diluted milk-and-water-gruel." But other advanced Republicans, noting that Lincoln's was the first emancipation proposal ever offered by an American President, acclaimed it as an excellent step. On April 10 the Republican-controlled congress endorsed Lincoln's emancipation plan. But the border-state representatives, for whom it was intended, rejected the scheme emphatically. "I utterly spit at it and despise it," said one Kentucky congressman. "Emancipation in the cotton States is simply an absurdity. . . . There is not enough power in the world to compel it to be done."

As Lincoln promoted his gradual, compensated scheme, advanced Republican on Capitol Hill launched a furious antislavery attack of their own. They sponsored a tough new confiscation bill, championed legislation that weakened the fugitive-slave law and assailed human bondage in the national capital as well as the territories. What was more, they won over many Republican moderates to forge a new congressional majority so far as slavery was concerned. As the war ground into its second year, moderate Republicans came to agree with their advanced colleagues that it was senseless to pretend the Union could be restored without removing the cause of the rebellion.

So, over strong Democratic opposition, the Republican Congress approved a bill that forbade the return of fugitive slaves to the rebels, and on March 13, 1862, Lincoln signed it into law. Congress also adopted legislation which abolished slavery in Washington, D.C., compensated owners for their loss, and set aside funds for the voluntary colonization of blacks in Haiti and Liberia, and Lincoln signed this as well. Democrats howled. One castigated the bill as an entering wedge for wholesale abolition, another predicted that liberated Negroes would crowd white ladies out of congressional galleries. Washingtonians accused the "abolitionists" in Congress of converting the capital into " a hell on earth for the white man." Republicans brushed aside all such criticism "if there be a place upon the face of the earth," asserted a Minnesota Republican, "where human slavery should be prohibited, and where every man should be protected in the rights which God and Nature have given him, that place is the capital of this great Republic."

In June the Republican Congress lashed at slavery again: it passed a bill that outlawed human bondage in all federal territories, thus overriding the Dred Scott decision, and Lincoln signed the measure into law. Congress and the President also joined together in recognizing the black republics of Haiti and Liberia, a move that would facilitate colonization efforts in those lands. Meanwhile, a fierce debate raged over the second confiscation bill, which authorized the seizure and liberation of all slaves held by those in rebellion. Advanced Republicans not only pushed the bill with uninhibited zeal but also advocated that emancipated blacks be enlisted in the army. But even some Republicans thought full-scale confiscation too drastic, and "conservatives" like Jacob Collamer of Vermont, Orville Browning of Illinois, and Edgar Cowan of Pennsylvania sided with the Democrats in denouncing the bill as uncivilized and unconstitutional.

"Pass these acts," cried one opponent, "confiscate under the bills the property of these men, emancipate their negroes, place arms in the hands of these human gorillas to murder their masters and violate their wives and daughters, and you will have a war such as was never witnessed in the worst days of the French Revolution, and horrors never exceeded in San Domingo."

On July 4, in the midst of the debate, Sumner hurried back to the White House and admonished Lincoln to attack slavery himself. Sumner was extremely disappointed in the President, for he did not seem a month or six weeks behind the senator at all. In fact, Lincoln recently had overruled another general, David Hunter, who liberated the slaves inside his lines, and again the advanced Republicans had groaned in despair. Now, on July 4, Sumner urged "the reconsecration of the day by a decree of emancipation." The senator pointed out that the union was suffering from troop shortages on every front and that the slaves were an untapped reservoir of manpower. "You need more men," Sumner argued, "not only at the North, but at the South, in the rear of the Rebels; you need the slaves." But Lincoln insisted that an emancipation edict was still "too big a lick." And, in a White House interview, he warned border-state Legislators that his gradual, state-guided plan was the only alternative to federal emancipation and that they must commend it to their people. Once again they refused.

On July 17, five days after Lincoln spoke with the border men, Congress finally passed the second confiscation bill. If the rebellion did not end in sixty days, the measure warned, the executive branch would seize the property of all those who supported, aided, or participated in the rebellion. Federal courts were to determine guilt. Those convicted would forfeit their estates and their slaves to the federal government, and their slaves would be set free. Section nine liberated other categories of slaves without court action: slaves of rebels who escaped to Union lines, who were captured by federal forces or were abandoned by their owners, "shall be deemed captives of war, and shall be forever free." On the other hand, the bill exempted loyal Unionists in the rebel South, allowing them to retain their slaves and other property. Another section empowered Lincoln to enlist Negroes in the military. Still another, aimed at easing Northern racial fears and keeping Republican unity, provided for the voluntary resettlement of confiscated blacks in "some tropical country." A few days later Congress appropriated $500,000 for colonization.

Controversial though it was, the second confiscation act still fell far short of genuine emancipation. Most slaves were to be freed only after protracted case-by-case litigation in the courts. And of course, the slaves of loyal masters were not affected. Yet the bill was about as far as congress could go in attacking slavery, for most Republicans still acknowledged that Congress had no constitutional authority to eradicate bondage as a state institution. Only the President with his war powers—or a constitutional amendment—could do that. Nevertheless, the measure seemed a clear invitation for the President to exercise his constitutional powers and annihilate slavery in the rebellious states. And Stevens, Sumner, and Wilson repeatedly told him that most congressional Republicans now favored this. On the other hand, conservatives like Orville Browning beseeched Lincoln to veto the confiscation bill and restore the old Union as it was. "I said to him that he had reached the culminating point in his administration," Browning recorded in his diary, "and his course upon this bill was to determine whether he was to control the abolitionist and radicals, or whether they were to control him."

For several days, Lincoln gave few hints as to what he would do, and Congress awaited his response in a state of high tension. Finally, on July 17, he informed Capitol Hill that he agreed entirely with the spirit of the confiscation bill remarking that "the traitor against the general government" deserved to have his slaves and other property forfeited as just punishment for rebellion. While he thought some of the wording unfortunately vague, he nevertheless raised no objection to the sections on slave liberation. He did, however, disagree with other portions on technical grounds, especially those which permanently divested a rebel of the title to his land, and Lincoln hinted that he would veto the bill as a consequence. To avoid that, congressional Republicans attached an explanatory resolution removing most of Lincoln's complaints. Satisfied, the President signed the bill and commanded the army to start enforcing it after sixty days.

Even so, several advanced Republicans were angered by Lincoln's threatened veto and peeved by what they perceived as his legalistic quibbling when the Union was struggling for its life against a mutinous aristocracy founded on slavery. Julian, for his part, thought Lincoln's behavior "inexpressibly provoking," and when Congress adjourned, he called at the White House to find out once and for all where the President stood on emancipation and all-out war against the rebels. Julian said he was going home to Indiana and wanted to assure his constituents that the President would "co-operate with Congress in vigorously carrying out the measures we had inaugurated for the purpose of crushing the rebellion, and that now the quickest and hardest blows were to be dealt." Complaining that advanced Republicans had unfairly criticized him, Lincoln said he had on objection at all to what Julian wished to tell his constituents. In Indiana that summer, Julian announced that Lincoln had now decided on a radical change in his policy toward slavery.

In August Sumner learned that Lincoln had at last decided to issue an emancipation proclamation. Convinced that the peculiar institution could be destroyed only through executive action, Lincoln actually had drawn up a draft of the proclamation and read it to his Cabinet. But couldn't Sumner have predicted it? Lincoln had let Secretary of State William H. Seward dissuade him from issuing the edict until after a Union military victory. At the White House, Sumner demanded that the decree "be put forth— the sooner the better—without any reference to our military condition." But the President refused, and Sumner stalked out, dismayed again at what he once called Lincoln's "immense *vis inertia.*" The senator feared that only the confiscation act would ever free any slaves.

But in September Lincoln came through. After the Confederate reversal at Antietam, he issued his preliminary emancipation proclamation, a clear warning that if the rebellion did not cease in one hundred days, the executive branch would use the military to free *all* the slaves in the rebel states—those belonging to secessionists and loyalists alike. Thus the President would go beyond the second confiscation act—he would handle emancipation himself, avoid tangled litigation over slavery in the courts, and vanquish it as an institution in the South. He believed he could do this by the war powers, and he deemed it "a fit and necessary military measure" to preserve the Union.

The advanced Republicans, of course, were delighted. "Hurrah for Old Abe and the proclamation," Wade exulted. Stevens extolled Lincoln for his patriotism and said his proclamation "contained precisely the principles which I had advocated." "Thank God that I live to enjoy this day!" Sumner exclaimed in Boston. "Freedom is practically secured to all who find shelter within our lines, and the glorious flag of the Union, wherever it floats, becomes the flag of Freedom." A few days later, Sumner announced that "the Emancipation Proclamation . . . is now the corner-stone of our national policy."

As it turned out, though, the preliminary proclamation helped lead to a Republican disaster in the fall by-elections of 1862. Northern Democrats already were angered by Lincoln's harsh war measures, especially his use of martial law and military arrests. Now, Negro emancipation was more than they could bear, and they stumped the Northern states beating the drums of Negrophobia and warning of massive influxes of Southern blacks into the North once emancipation came. Sullen, war-weary, and racially antagonistic, Northern voters dealt the Republicans a smashing blow as the North's five most populous states—all of which had gone for Lincoln in 1860—now returned Democratic majorities to Capitol Hill. Republicans narrowly retained control of Congress, but they were steeped in gloom as it convened that December.

Though most Republicans stood resolutely behind emancipation, Browning and other conservatives now begged Lincoln to abandon his "reckless" abolition policy lest he shatter his party and wreck what remained of his country. At the same time, Sumner and Wade admonished Lincoln to stand firm, and he promised that he would. On January 1, 1863, the President officially signed the final proclamation in the White House. In it Lincoln temporarily exempted all of Tennessee and certain occupied places in Louisiana and Virginia (later, in reconstructing those states, he would withdraw the exemptions and make emancipation mandatory). He also excluded the loyal slave states because they were not in rebellion and he lacked the legal authority to uproot slavery there. With these exceptions, the final proclamation declared that all slaves in the rebellious states "from henceforth shall be free." The document also asserted that black men—Southern and Northern alike—might now be enlisted in Union military forces.

All in all, the advanced Republicans were pleased. Perhaps the President should not have exempted Tennessee and southern Louisiana, Horace Greeley said, "but let us not cavil." Lincoln had now "played his grand part" in the abolition of slavery, Julian declared, and "brought relief to multitudes of anxious people." "On that day," Sumner wrote of January 1, 1863, "an angel appeared upon the earth."

In truth, Lincoln's proclamation was the most revolutionary measure ever to come from an American President up to that time, and the advanced Republicans took a lot of credit for goading him at last to act. Slavery would now die by degrees with every Union advance, every Northern victory.

Now that Lincoln had adopted emancipation, advanced Republicans watched him with a critical eye, making sure that he enforced his edict and exhorting him to place only those firmly opposed to slavery in command of Union armies. In February rumor had it that if Lincoln wavered even once in his promise of freedom to the slaves, Wade would move for a vote of "no confidence" and try to cut off appropriations. But Lincoln did not waiver. Even though a storm of anti-Negro, anti-Lincoln protest broke over the land, the President refused to retract a single word of his decree. "He is stubborn as a mule when he gets his back up," Chandler said, "& *it is up* now on the Proclamation." "His mind acts slowly," Lovejoy observed, "but when he moves, it is *forward.*"

In the last two years of the war, Lincoln and the advanced Republicans had their differences, but they were scarcely locked in the kind of blood feud depicted in Civil War histories and biographies of an earlier day. Several advanced Republicans did oppose Lincoln's renomination in 1864 because the war was going badly and they thought him an inept administrator. In addition, Sumner, Stevens, and Wade clashed bitterly with Lincoln over whether Congress or the President should oversee reconstruction. Sumner, Julian, Chandler, and a handful of other legislators also insisted that Southern black men be enfranchised. But Lincoln, sympathetic to Negro voting rights, hesitated to force them on the states he reconstructed. Nevertheless, in April, 1865, he publicly endorsed limited Negro suffrage and conceded that the black man deserved the right to vote.

In truth, despite their differences, Lincoln and the advanced Republicans worked together closely. And they stood together on several crucial issues: they all wanted to abolish slavery entirely in the South and to muzzle the rebellious white majority there so that it could not overwhelm Southern Unionists and return the old Southern ruling class to power. They also came to see that colonization was probably an unworkable solution to the problem of racial adjustment. All Lincoln's colonization schemes had foundered, and anyway most blacks adamantly refused to participate in the Republicans' voluntary program. In place of colonization, the Lincoln administration devised a refugee system for blacks in the South, a program that put them to work in military and civilian pursuits there and prepared them for life in a free society. And in 1864 the Republican Congress canceled all funds it had set aside for colonization efforts.

Most important of all, advanced Republicans cooperated closely with Lincoln in pushing a constitutional amendment through Congress that would guarantee the permanent freedom of all slaves, those in the loyal border as well as in the rebel South. Since he had issued the proclamation, Lincoln and his congressional associates had worried that it might be nullified in the courts or thrown out by a later Congress or a subsequent administration. As a consequence, they wanted a constitutional amendment that would safeguard the proclamation and prevent emancipation from ever being overturned. Accordingly,in December, 1863, Iowa senator James F. Wilson introduced an

A Black Citizen's Appraisal
of the President

"An American of the Americans"

The advanced Republicans on Capitol Hill who relentlessly pressured Lincoln toward emancipation were all white, of course. But blacks, too, played their part in influencing the cautious President. Most prominent among them was Frederick Douglass, the eloquent abolitionist speaker and writer, who was himself a former slave.

Douglass liked Lincoln personally. "In all my interviews with Mr. Lincoln," he wrote, "I was impressed with his entire freedom from popular prejudice against the colored race. He was the first great man that I talked with in the United States freely, who in no single instance reminded me of the difference between himself and myself, of the difference of color. . . ."

But when Douglass was invited in 1876 to dedicate the Emancipation Monument, a Washington, D.C., statue of Lincoln freeing a slave, he put personal friendship aside and offered what is still among the shrewdest judgments ever made of the President's role in the struggle against slavery:

". . . [Lincoln] was preeminently the white man's President, entirely devoted to the welfare of white men. He was ready and willing at any time during the first years of his administration to deny, postpone, and sacrifice the rights of humanity in the colored people to promote the welfare of the white people of this country. In all his education and feeling he was an American of the Americans. He came into the Presidential chair upon one principle alone, namely, opposition to the extension of slavery. His arguments in furtherance of this policy had their motive and mainspring in his patriotic devotion to the interests of his own race. . . .

The race to which we belong were not the special objects of his consideration. Knowing this, I concede to you, my white fellow-citizens, a preeminence in this worship at once full and supreme. . . . You are the children of Abraham Lincoln. We are at best only his stepchildren; children by adoption, children by forces of circumstances and necessity. To you it especially belongs to sound his praises. . . . [But] while Abraham Lincoln saved for you a country, he delivered us from a bondage, according to Jefferson, one hour of which was worse than ages of the oppression your fathers rose in rebellion to oppose. . . . His greatest mission was to accomplish two things: first, to save his country from dismemberment and ruin; and, second, to free his country from the great crime of slavery. To do one or the other, or both, he must have the earnest sympathy and the powerful cooperation of his loyal fellow countrymen. . . . Had he put the abolition of slavery before the salvation of the Union, he would have inevitably driven from him a powerful class of the American people and rendered resistance to rebellion impossible. Viewed from the genuine abolition ground, Mr. Lincoln seemed tardy, cold, dull, and indifferent; but measuring him by the sentiment of his country, a sentiment he was bound as a statesmen to consult, he was swift, zealous, radical, and determined . . . taking him for all in all, measuring the tremendous magnitude of the work before him, considering the necessary means to ends, and surveying the end from the beginning, infinite wisdom has seldom sent any man into the world better fitted for his mission than Abraham Lincoln."

emancipation amendment in the Senate, and the following February Trumbull reported it from the judiciary committee, reminding his colleagues that nobody could deny that all the death and destruction of the war stemmed from slavery and that it was their duty to support this amendment. In April the Senate adopted it by a vote of thirty-eight to six, but it failed to muster the required two-thirds majority in the House.

After Lincoln's re-election in 1864, advanced Republicans joined forces with the President to get the amendment passed. In his message that December, Lincoln conceded that this was the same House that earlier had failed to approve the amendment. But since then a national election had taken place which Lincoln insisted was a mandate for permanent emancipation. If the present House refused to pass the amendment, the next one "almost certainly" would. So "at all events," the President said, "may we not agree that the sooner the better?"

As December passed, Republicans who sponsored the amendment plotted with Lincoln to pressure conservative Republicans and recalcitrant Democrats for their support. On January 6, 1865, a heated debate began over the amendment, with James Ashley quoting Lincoln himself that "*if slavery is not wrong, nothing is wrong.*" A week later, Thaddeus Stevens, still tall and imposing at seventy-two, limped down the aisle of the House and closed the debate with a spare and eloquent address, declaring that he had never hesitated, even when threatened with violence, "to stand here and denounce this infamous institution." With the outcome much in doubt, Lincoln and congressional Republicans participated in secret negotiations never made public—negotiations that allegedly involved patronage, a New Jersey railroad monopoly, and the release of rebels kin to congressional Democrats—to bring wavering opponents into line. "The greatest measure of the nineteenth century," Stevens claimed, "was passed by corruption, aided and abetted by the purest man in America." When the amendment did pass, by just three votes, a storm of cheers broke over House Republicans, who danced, embraced one another, waved their hats and canes. "It seemed to me I had been born into a new life," Julian recalled, "and that the world was overflowing with beauty and joy." Lincoln, too, pronounced the amendment a "great moral victory" and "a King's cure" for the evils of slavery. When ratified by the states, the amendment would end human bondage in America.

See, Julian rejoiced, "the world *does* move." He could have added that he and his advanced Republican colleagues, in collaboration with their President, had made it move, had done all they could in the smoke and steel of civil war to right their troubled land with its own noblest ideas.

Stephen B. Oates, a frequent contributor to our pages, is the author of biographies of Nat Turner, John Brown, and Abraham Lincoln.

Why They Impeached Andrew Johnson

David Donald

Reconstruction after the Civil War posed some of the most discouraging problem ever faced by American statesmen. The South was prostrate. Its defeated armies straggled homeward through a countryside desolated by war. Southern soil was untilled and exhausted; southern factories and railroads were worn out. The four billion dollars of southern capital invested in Negro slaves was wiped out by advancing Union armies, ''the most stupendous act of sequestration in the history of Anglo-American jurisprudence.'' The white inhabitants of eleven states had somehow to be reclaimed from rebellion and restored to a firm loyalty to the United States. Their four million former slaves had simultaneously to be guided into a proper use of their new-found freedom.

For the victorious Union government there was no time for reflection. Immediate decisions had to be made. Thousands of destitute whites and Negroes had to be fed before long-range plans of rebuilding the southern economy could be drafted. Some kind of government had to be established in these former Confederate states, to preserve order and to direct the work of restoration.

A score of intricate questions must be answered: Should the defeated southerners be punished or pardoned? How should genuinely loyal southern Unionists be rewarded? What was to be the social, economic, and political status of the now free Negroes? What civil rights did they have? Ought they to have the ballot? Should they be given a freehold of property? Was Reconstruction to be controlled by the national government, or should the southern states work out their own salvation? If the federal government supervised the process, should the President or the congress be in control?

Intricate as were the problems, in early April, 1865, they did not seem insuperable. President Abraham Lincoln was winning the peace as he had already won the war. He was careful to keep every detail of Reconstruction in his own hands; unwilling to be committed to any ''exclusive, and inflexible plan,'' he was working out a pragmatic program of restoration not, perhaps, entirely satisfactory to any group, but reasonably acceptable to all sections. With his enormous prestige as commander of the victorious North and as victor in the 1864 election, he was able to promise freedom to the Negro, charity to the southern white, security to the North.

The blighting of these auspicious beginnings is one of the saddest stories in American history. The reconciliation of the sections, which seemed so imminent in 1865, was delayed for more than ten years. Northern magnanimity toward a fallen foe curdled into bitter distrust. Southern whites rejected moderate leaders, and inveterate racists spoke for the new South. The Negro, after serving as a political pawn for a decade, was relegated to a second-class citizenship, from which he is yet struggling to emerge. Rarely has democratic government so completely failed as during the Reconstruction decade.

The responsibility for this collapse of American statesmanship is, of course, complex. History is not a tale of deep-dyed villains or pure-as-snow heroes. Part of the blame must fall upon ex-Confederates who refused to recognize that the war was over; part upon freedmen who confused liberty with license and the ballot box with the lunch pail; part upon northern antislavery extremists who identified patriotism with loyalty to the Republican party; part upon the land speculators, treasury grafters, and railroad promoters who were unwilling to have a genuine peace lest it end their looting of the public till.

Yet these divisive forces were not bound to triumph. Their success was due to the failure of constructive statesmanship that could channel the magnanimous feelings shared by most Americans into a positive program of reconstruction. President Andrew Johnson was called upon for positive leadership, and he did not meet the challenge.

Andrew Johnson's greatest weakness was his insensitivity to public opinion. In contrast to Lincoln, who said, "Public opinion in this country is everything," Johnson made a career of battling the popular will. A poor white, a runaway tailor's apprentice, a self-educated Tennessee politician, Johnson was a living defiance to the dominant southern belief that leadership belonged to the plantation aristocracy.

As senator from Tennessee, he defied the sentiment of his section in 1861 and refused to join the secessionist movement. When Lincoln later appointed him military governor of occupied Tennessee, Johnson found Nashville "a furnace of treason," but he braved social ostracism and threats of assassination and discharged his duties with boldness and efficiency.

Such a man was temperamentally unable to understand the northern mood in 1865, much less to yield to it. For four years the northern people had been whipped into wartime frenzy by propaganda tales of Confederate atrocities. The assassination of Lincoln by a southern sympathizer confirmed their belief in southern brutality and heartlessness. Few northerners felt vindictive toward the South, but most felt that the rebellion they had crushed must never rise again. Johnson ignored this postwar psychosis gripping the North and plunged ahead with his program of rapidly restoring the southern states to the Union. In May, 1865, without any previous preparation of public opinion, he issued a proclamation of amnesty, granting forgiveness to nearly all the millions of former rebels and welcoming them back into peaceful fraternity. Some few Confederate leaders were excluded from his general amnesty, but even they could secure pardon by special petition. For weeks the White House corridors were thronged with ex-Confederate statesmen and former southern generals who daily received presidential forgiveness.

Ignoring public opinion by pardoning the former Confederates, Johnson actually entrusted the formation of new governments in the South to them. The provisional governments established by the President proceeded, with a good deal of reluctance, to rescind their secession ordinances, to abolish slavery, and to repudiate the Confederate debt. Then, with far more enthusiasm, they turned to electing governors, representatives, and senators. By December, 1865, the southern states had their delegations in Washington waiting for admission by Congress. Alexander H. Stephens, once vice president of the Confederacy, was chosen senator from Georgia; not one of the North Carolina delegation could take a loyalty oath; and all of South Carolina's congressmen had "either held office under the Confederate States, or been in the army, or countenanced in some way the Rebellion."

Johnson himself was appalled. "There seems in many of the elections something like defiance, which is all out of place at this time," he protested. Yet on December 5 he strongly urged the Congress to seat these southern representatives "and thereby complete the work of reconstruction." But the southern states were omitted from the roll call.

Such open defiance of northern opinion was dangerous under the best of circumstances, but in Johnson's case it was little more than suicidal. The President seemed not to realize the weakness of his position. He was the representative of no major interest and had no genuine political following. He had been considered for the vice presidency in 1864 because, as a southerner and a former slaveholder, he could lend plausibility to the Republican pretension that the old parties were dead and that Lincoln was the nominee of a new, nonsectional National Union party.

A political accident, the new Vice President did little to endear himself to his countrymen. At Lincoln's second inauguration Johnson appeared before the Senate in an obviously inebriated state and made a long, intemperate harangue about his plebeian origins and his hard-won success. President, Cabinet, and senators were humiliated by the shameful display, and Charles Sumner felt that "the Senate should call upon him to resign." Historians now know that Andrew Johnson was not a heavy drinker. At the time of his inaugural display, he was just recovering from a severe attack of typhoid fever. Feeling ill just before he entered the Senate chamber, he asked for some liquor to steady his nerves, and either his weakened condition or abnormal sensitivity to alcohol betrayed him.

Lincoln reassured Republicans who were worried over the affair: "I have known Andy for many years; he made a bad slip the other day, but you need not be scared. Andy ain't a drunkard." Never again was Andrew Johnson seen under the influence of alcohol, but his reformation came too late. His performance on March 4, 1865, seriously undermined his political usefulness and permitted his opponents to discredit him as a pothouse politician. Johnson was catapulted into the presidency by John Wilkes Booth's bullet. From the outset his position was weak, but it was not necessarily untenable. The President's chronic lack of discretion made it so. Where common sense dictated that a chief executive in so disadvantageous a position should act with great caution, Johnson proceeded to imitate Old Hickory, Andrew Jackson, his political idol. If Congress crossed his will, he did not hesitate to defy it. Was he not "the Tribune of the People"?

Sure of his rectitude, Johnson was indifferent to prudence. He never learned that the President of the United States cannot afford to be a quarreler. Apprenticed in the rough-and-tumble politics of frontier Tennessee, where orators exchanged violent personalities, crude humor, and bitter denunciations, Johnson continued to make stump speeches from the White House. All to often he spoke extemporaneously, and he permitted hecklers in his audience to draw from him angry charges against his critics.

On Washington's birthday in 1866, against the advice of his more sober advisers, the President made an impromptu address to justify his Reconstruction policy. "I fought traitors and treason in the South," he told the crowd; "now when I turn around, and at the other end of the line find men—I care not by what name you call them—who will stand opposed to the restoration of the Union of these states, I am free to say to you that I am still in the field."

During the "great applause" which followed, a nameless voice shouted, "Give us the names at the other end. . . . Who are they?"

"You ask me who they are," Johnson retorted. "I say Thaddeus Stevens of Pennsylvania is one; I say Mr. Sumner is another; and Wendell Phillips is another." Increasing applause urged him to continue. "Are those who want to destroy our institutions . . . not satisfied with the blood that has been shed? . . . Does not the blood of Lincoln appease the vengeance and wrath of the opponents of this government?"

The President's remarks were untrue as they were impolitic. Not only was it manifestly false to assert that the leading Republican in the House and the most conspicuous Republican in the Senate were opposed to "the fundamental principles of this government" or that they had been responsible for Lincoln's assassination; it was incredible political folly to impute such actions to men with whom the President had to work daily. But Andrew Johnson never learned that the President of the United Stats must function as a party leader.

There was a temperamental coldness about this plain-featured, grave man that kept him from easy, intimate relations with even his political supporters. His massive head, dark, luxuriant hair, deep-set and piercing eyes, and cleft square chin seemed to Charles Dickens to indicate "courage, watchfulness, and certainly strength of purpose," but this was a grim face, with "no genial sunlight in it." The coldness and reserve that marked Johnson's public associations doubtless stemmed from a deep-seated feeling of insecurity; this self-educated tailor whose wife had taught him how to write could never expose himself by letting down his guard and relaxing.

Johnson knew none of the arts of managing men, and he seemed unaware that face-saving is important for a politician. When he became President, Johnson was besieged by advisers of all political complexions. To each he listened gravely and noncommitally, raising no questions and by his silence seeming to give consent. With Radical Senator Sumner, already intent upon giving the freedmen both homesteads and the ballot, he had repeated interviews during the first month of his presidency. "His manner has been excellent, & even sympathetic." Sumner reported triumphantly. With Chief Justice Salmon P. Chase, Sumner urged Johnson to support immediate Negro suffrage and found the President was "well-disposed, & sees the rights & necessities of the case." In the middle of May, 1865, Sumner reassured a Republican caucus that the President was a true Radical; he had listened repeatedly to the Senator and had told him "there is no difference between us." Before the end of the month the rug was pulled from under Sumner's feet. Johnson issued his proclamation for the reconstruction of North Carolina, making no provisions for Negro suffrage. Sumner first learned about it through the newspapers.

While he was making up his mind, Johnson appeared silently receptive to all ideas; when he had made a decision, his mind was immovably closed, and he defended his course with all the obstinacy of a weak man. In December, alarmed by Johnson's Reconstruction proclamations, Sumner again sought an interview with the President. "No longer sympathetic, or even kindly," Sumner found, "he was harsh, petulant, and unreasonable." The senator was depressed by Johnson's "prejudice, ignorance, and perversity" on the Negro suffrage issue. Far from listening amiably to Sumner's argument that the South was still torn by violence and not yet ready for readmission, Johnson attacked him with cheap analogies. "Are there no murders in Massachusetts?" the President asked.

"Unhappily yes," Sumner replied, "sometimes."

"Are there no assaults in boston? Do not men there sometimes knock each other down, so that the police is obliged to interfere?"

"Unhappily yes."

"Would you consent that Massachusetts, on this account, should be excluded from Congress?" Johnson triumphantly queried. In the excitement of the argument, the President unconsciously used Sumner's hat, which the Senator had placed on the floor beside his chair, as a spittoon!

Had Johnson been as resolute in action as he was in argument, he might conceivably have carried much of his party with him on his Reconstruction program. Promptness, publicity, and persuasion could have created a presidential following. Instead Johnson boggled. Though he talked boastfully of "kicking out" officers who failed to support his plan, he was slow to act. His own Cabinet, from the very beginning, contained members who disagreed with him, and his secretary of war, Edwin M. Stanton, was openly in league with the Republican elements most hostile to the President. For more than two years he impotently hoped that Stanton would resign; then in 1867, after Congress had passed the Tenure of Office act, he tried to oust the Secretary. This belated firmness, against the letter of the law, led directly to Johnson's impeachment trial.

Instead of working with his party leaders and building up political support among Republicans, Johnson in 1866 undertook to organize his friends into a new party. In August a convention of white southerners, northern Democrats, moderate Republicans, and presidential appointees assembled in Philadelphia to endorse Johnson's policy. Union General Darius Couch of Massachusetts marched arm in arm down the convention aisle with Governor James L. Orr of South Carolina, to symbolize the states reunited under Johnson's rule. The convention produced fervid oratory, a dignified statement of principles—but not much else. Like most third-party reformist movements it lacked local support and grass-roots organization.

Johnson himself was unable to breathe life into his stillborn third party. Deciding to take his case to the people, he accepted an invitation to speak at a great Chicago memorial honoring Stephen A. Douglas. When his special train left Washington on August 28 for a "swing around the circle," the President was accompanied by a few Cabinet members who shared his views and by the war heroes Grant and Farragut.

At first all went well. There were some calculated political snubs to the President, but he managed at Philadelphia, New York, and Albany to present his ideas soberly and cogently to the people. But Johnson's friends were worried lest his tongue again get out of control. "In all frankness," a senator wrote him, do not "allow the excitement of the moment to draw from you any *extemporaneous speeches.*"

At St. Louis, when a Radical voice shouted that Johnson was a "Judas," the President flamed up in rage. "There was a Judas and he was one of the twelve apostles," he retorted. ". . . The twelve apostles had a Christ. . . . If I have played the Judas, who has been my Christ that I have played the Judas with? Was it Thad Stevens? Was it Wendell PHillips? Was it Charles Sumner?" Over mingled hisses and applause, he shouted, "These are the men that stop and compare themselves with the Saviour; and everybody that differs with them . . . is to be denounced as a Judas."

Johnson had played into his enemies' hands. His Radical foes denounced him as a "trickster," a "culprit," a man "touched with insanity, corrupted with lust, stimulated with drink." More serious in consequence was the reaction of northern moderates, such as James Russell Lowell, who wrote, "What an anti-Johnson lecturer we have in Johnson! Sumner has been right about the *cuss* from the first. . . ." The fall elections were an overwhelming repudiation of the President and his Reconstruction policy.

Johnson's want of political sagacity strengthened the very elements in the Republican party which he most feared. In 1865 the Republicans had no clearly defined attitude toward Reconstruction. Moderates like Gideon Welles and Orville Browning wanted to see the southern states restored with a minimum of restrictions; Radicals like Sumner and Stevens demanded that the entire southern social system be revolutionized. Some Republicans were passionately concerned with the plight of the freedmen; others were more interested in maintaining the high tariff and land grant legislation enacted during the war. Many thought mostly of keeping themselves in office, and many genuinely believed, with Sumner, that "the Republican party, in its objects, is identical with country and with mankind." These diverse elements came slowly to adopt the idea of harsh Reconstruction, but Johnson' stubborn persistency in his policy left them no alternative. Every step the President took seemed to provide "a new encouragement to (1) the rebels at the South, (2) the Democrats at the North and (3) the discontented elements everywhere." Not many Republicans would agree with Sumner that Johnson's program was "a defiance to God and Truth," but there was genuine concern that the victory won by the war was being frittered away.

The provisional governments established by the President in the South seemed to be dubiously loyal. They were reluctant to rescind their secession ordinances and to repudiate the Confederate debt, and they chose high-ranking ex-Confederates to represent them in Congress. Northerners were even more alarmed when these southern governments began to legislate upon the Negro's civil rights. Some laws were necessary—in order to give former slaves the right to marry, to hold property, to sue and be sued, and the like—but the Johnson legislatures went far beyond these immediate needs. South Carolina, for example, enacted that no Negro could pursue the trade "of an artisan, mechanic, or shopkeeper, or any other trade or employment besides that of husbandry" without a special license. Alabama provided that "any stubborn or refractory servants" or "servants who loiter away their time" should be fined $50 and, if they could not pay, be hired out for six months' labor. Mississippi ordered that every Negro under eighteen years of age who was an orphan or not supported by his parents must be apprenticed to some white person, preferably the former owner of the slave. Such southern laws indicated a determination to keep the Negro in a state of peonage.

It was impossible to expect a newly emancipated race to be content with such a limping freedom. The thousands of Negroes who had served in the Union armies and had helped conquer their former Confederate masters were not willing to abandon their new-found liberty. In rural areas southern whites kept these Negroes under control through the Ku Klux Klan. But in southern cities white hegemony was less secure, and racial friction erupted in mob violence. In May, 1866, a quarrel between a Memphis Negro and a white teamster led to a riot in which the city police and the poor whites raided the Negro quarters and burned and killed promiscuously. Far more serious was the disturbance in New Orleans two months later. The Republican party in Louisiana was split into pro-Johnson conservatives and Negro suffrage advocates. The latter group determined to hold a constitutional convention, of dubious legality, in New Orleans, in order to secure the ballot for the freedmen and the offices for themselves. Through imbecility in the War department, the Federal troops occupying the city were left without orders, and the mayor of New Orleans, strongly opposed to Negro equality, had the responsibility of preserving order. There were acts of provocation on both sides, and finally, on July 30, a procession of Negroes marching toward the convention hall was attacked.

"A shot was fired . . . by a policeman, or some colored man in the procession," General Philip Sheridan reported. "This led to other shots, and a rush after the procession. On arrival at the front of the Institute [where the convention met], there was some throwing of brick-bats by both sides. The police . . . were vigorously marched to the scene of disorder. The procession entered the Institute with the flag, about six or eight remaining outside. A row occurred between a policeman and one of these colored men, and a shot was again fired by one of the parties, which led to an indiscriminate firing on the building, through the windows, by the policemen.

"This had been going on for a short time, when a white flag was displayed from the windows of the Institute, whereupon the firing ceased and the police rushed into the building. . . . The policemen opened an indiscriminate fire upon the audience until they had emptied their revolvers, when they retired, and those inside barricaded the doors. The door was broken in, and the firing again commenced when many of the colored and white people either escaped out of the door, or were passed out by the policemen inside, but as they came out, the policemen who formed the circle nearest the building fired upon them, and they were again fired upon by the citizens that formed the outer circle."

Thirty-seven Negroes and three of their white friends were killed; 119 Negroes and seventeen of their white sympathizers were wounded. Of their assailants, ten were wounded and but one killed. President Johnson was, of course, horrified by these outbreaks, but the Memphis and New Orleans riots, together with the Black Codes, afforded a devastating illustration of how the President's policy actually operated. The southern states, it was clear, were not going to protect the Negroes' basic rights. They were only grudgingly going to accept the results of the war. Yet, with Johnson's blessing, these same states were expecting a stronger voice in Congress than ever. Before 1860, southern representation in Congress had been based upon the white population plus three fifths of the slaves; now the Negroes, though not permitted to vote, were to be counted like all other citizens, and southern states would be entitled to at least nine additional congressmen. Joining with the northern Copperheads, the southerners could easily regain at the next presidential election all that had been lost on the Civil War battlefield.

It was this political exigency, not misguided sentimentality nor vindictiveness, which united Republicans in opposition to the President.

Johnson's defenders have pictured Radical Reconstruction as the work of a fanatical minority, led by Sumner and Stevens, who drove their reluctant colleagues into adopting coercive measures against the South. In fact, every major piece of Radical legislation was adopted by the nearly unanimous vote of the entire Republican membership of Congress. Andrew Johnson had left them no other choice. Because he insisted upon rushing Confederate-dominated states back into the Union, Republicans moved to disqualify Confederate leaders under the Fourteenth Amendment. When, through Johnson's urging, the southern states rejected that amendment, the Republicans in Congress unwillingly came to see Negro suffrage as the only counterweight against Democratic majorities in the South. With the Reconstruction Acts of 1867 the way was open for a true Radical program toward the South, harsh and thorough.

Andrew Johnson became a cipher in the white House, futilely disapproving bills which were promptly passed over his veto. Through his failure to reckon with public opinion, his unwillingness to recognize his weak position, his inability to function as a party leader, he had sacrificed all influence with the party which had elected him and had turned over its control to Radicals vindictively opposed to his policies. In March, 1868, Andrew Johnson was summoned before the Senate of the Untied States to be tried on eleven accusations of high crimes and misdemeanors. By a narrow margin the Senate failed to convict him, and historians have dismissed the charges as flimsy and false. Yet perhaps before the bar of history itself Andrew Johnson must be impeached with an even graver charge—that through political ineptitude he threw away a magnificent opportunity.

A Mississippian by birth, David Donald teaches history at Columbia University. He is the author of Lincoln Reconsidered *and other books on the Civil War, and is now at work on a biography of Senator Charles Sumner.*